Suicide Prevention Contracting

Suicide Prevention Contracting

The Pitfalls, Perils, and Seven Safer Alternatives

STEPHEN J. EDWARDS

With Christopher Goj

JASON ARONSON
Lanham • Boulder • New York • Toronto • Plymouth, UK

Tables 5.2, 5.3, 5.4, 5.5, 6.1, and 7.1 originally appeared in "No-Suicide Contracts, No-Suicide Agreements, and No-Suicide Assurances: A Study of Their Nature, Utilization, Perceived Effectiveness, and Potential to Cause Harm" by Stephen J. Edwards and Mark D. Sachman, published in Crisis 2010, Vol. 31 (6) on pp. 290–302.

Published by Jason Aronson
A wholly owned subsidiary of Rowman & Littlefield
4501 Forbes Boulevard, Suite 200, Lanham, Maryland 20706
www.rowman.com

10 Thornbury Road, Plymouth PL6 7PP, United Kingdom

British Library Cataloguing in Publication Information Available

Library of Congress Cataloging-in-Publication Data Available

ISBN 978-0-7657-0996-7 (cloth : alk. paper)
ISBN 978-0-7657-0997-4 (electronic)

∞™ The paper used in this publication meets the minimum requirements of American National Standard for Information Sciences—Permanence of Paper for Printed Library Materials, ANSI/NISO Z39.48-1992.

Printed in the United States of America

Contents

Preface

Suicide Prevention Contracting (SPC)—also known as a No Suicide Contract—is an intervention which invites patients to either sign a written 'contract' or make a verbal 'agreement' not to commit suicide. Usually a specified 'no suicide' time period is set, and often the 'contract' or 'agreement' is reviewed at the next contact with the patient or before they're discharged from hospital.

According to Marcia Goin, MD, past president of the American Psychiatric Association—in professional jargon—'to contract' has become unashamedly commonplace despite more than a decade of controversy and debate about its effectiveness and place in modern-day health care and human services (Goin, 2003). Clearly, clinicians in the United States, in Canada, and in Australia think well of SPC. I suspect that some clinicians think equally well of SPC in villages, towns and cities across the United Kingdom, although it's yet to be proven empirically. I also suspect it's used often in many parts of Europe, South America, New Zealand, and in places across the Asian continent.

Multi-site U.S. and international studies report large variations from 30 percent to 100 percent of study participants' (psychiatrists, psychologists, mental health nurses, occupational therapists, social workers, crisis center para-professionals and volunteers) use of an SPC procedure. (See chapter 5 for a summary of these studies.) These are remarkable numbers when you consider that there are no studies confirming the procedures' ability to prevent suicidal behavior or cause no harm. Until now surprisingly little was known about the true nature of SPC, and even less about its capacity to cause harm.

The aim of this book is to show that a very widely practiced but far less widely discussed clinical intervention, namely SPC, is all-too-easily counterproductive and therefore potentially harmful for both patients and the clinicians aiming to help them. The book will also explain how this suicide intervention modality that actually creates hazards has become so widespread, in spite of the field of mental health care and social services being defined by the drive for evidence-based practice and quality improvement standards.

In the pages that follow I hope to fully justify what may seem like an alarming pronouncement. Inevitably there will be those who do not share my conclusions. However, I hope to show that they are based on the best available research, and through integrating all the available data, I also hope to provide a convincing, yet practical and pragmatic, text for clinicians, educators and others. To this end I will make clear the reasons why SPC is potentially hazardous, some of which may implicate current users, and in the main will leave aside SPC's apparent benefits. I will also recommend alternatives to SPC procedures, of which there are many, rather than mere modifications to current practice. I trust it will be a pocketbook of new knowledge and an important page in the manual for our own professional development and, critically, the better care of our clients and patients.

Stephen J. (Ed) Edwards, PhD
29 June, 2013

Acknowledgments

No piece of work of any significance is ever done in isolation: so then, I must thank Chris Goj for his dedication to this project. Next is U.S. publishing professional Scott Edelstein. Scott did one big thing to see this book onto the book shelves of clinics, universities and such: he did what he initially said he would do; thanks, Scott. To Amy King, Acquisition Editor at Rowman & Littlefield Publishers—thank you, Amy. I'd also like to extend a sincere thanks to all my colleagues who had input into the study, or who read, commented on, and provided feedback on the many versions of the final manuscript, and in no particular order: Karen Dickinson, Aaron Groves, MD (Australia), James (Jim) Penhale, MSc (Australia), Professor Mark Sachmann, PhD (Australia), Professor Maria Harries, AM PhD (Australia), Ranjit Kuma, PhD (Australia/India), Stephen Fenner, MD (Australia), Brian McArdle, DPhil (New Zealand), Tony White, MSc (Australia), Jonathon Mahrer, PhD (United States), Alastair Hope, State Coroner (Retired) (Perth, Western Australia), Peter Semmler, QC (Sydney, Australia), Bob Johnstone, MA (Australia/Canada), Stephen Hale, JP (Australia); to Megsi and Triste (New Zealand/Australia) who traversed, in one way or another, this piece of work—a warm thank you. To the some 420 mental health clinicians who opened up and told us what SPC truly was for them, thank you. To the patients like Kelly who I work alongside in clinical practice, it is a privilege to share some of the worst and best of times. I need to acknowledge especially my former Aotearoa-New

Zealand Maori cultural advisor George Hill, BA, and his Rōōpū (suicide prevention reference group), who gave me a new understanding of what working together truly can mean—Kia ora whanau. Finally, I am deeply thankful for my good fortune to be married to Natalie J. Edwards, PhD. Natalie spent many hours considering numerous versions of the manuscript. Not only is she my most helpful critic, but she is also my deepest and most enduring support.

Symbols and Abbreviations

ANOVA	Analysis of Variance
CAMHS	Child and Adolescent Mental Health Service
CBT	Cognitive Behavioral Therapy
CPR	Crisis Plan Response
CTS	Commitment to Treatment Statement
DBT	Dialectical Behavior Therapy
DMS	(SPC) Decision-Making Schema
DSH	Deliberate Self-Harm
EBM	Evidence-Based Medicine
MANOVA	Multivariate Analysis of Variance
NSAg	No Suicide Agreements
NSAs	No Suicide Assurances
NSC	No Suicide Contracts
RT	Redecision Therapy
SOP	Standard Operating Procedure
SPC	Suicide Prevention Contracting
TA	Transactional Analysis
WHO	World Health Authority

Introduction

Evidence Base behind This Book

Evidence-based practice is the integration of the best research evidence with clinical expertise and patient values (Sackett, Straus, Richardson, Rosenberg & Haynes, 2000).

At the heart of this book is the contention that an unreflective use of SPC procedures has the potential to create adverse clinical situations, quite contrary to the intentions of clinicians who use them. There are in fact *many* ways in which patient contracting in clinical practice can compromise treatment, contrary to the widespread perception that patient contracting is risk neutral. Suicide prevention contracting, as I will underscore in the chapters that follow, is riven by a false perception of its legal status and by its perceived risk-free expedient use in clinical practice. It is sometimes misguidedly perceived as a duty of care requirement and valued largely for its capacity to secure the commitment of patients to it. These are but some of the reasons for the growing controversy over SPC's place in clinical practice.

The unintended consequences of actions are a fact of modern-day life. We face the pressing dilemma of climate change, mainly because we enjoy a technologically advanced life. As I write this piece, Australia, North America and the rest of the world barely avoided sliding headfirst into an economic depression. An unintended threat was created in part because we have a highly geared economic system with financial services employees encouraged to take excessive risks with largely untried and complex products. The vast majority of dilemmas humans face are never consciously created, precisely because they are the unforeseen and unexpected outcomes of considered decisions. This point also applies to clinician's use of SPC, I now realise. Those clinicians using SPC procedures unreflectively, indeed naively, are very likely to be creating adverse clinical situations quite contrary to their intentions.

SCOPE OF PATIENT CONTRACTING IN CLINICAL PRACTICE

Written and verbal agreements branded "contracts," created by clinicians and signed by patients, are in common use throughout clinical practice (Volk, Lieber, Kim, Ubel & Schneider, 2012). They include behavioral contracts for managing difficult patients (Harris, Duermeyer, Ehly, Hartig-Toth, Hayes, Holsapple et al., 1999), opioid contracts used in the management of chronic pain (Hariharan, Lamb & Neuner, 2007), suicide prevention contracts (Garvey, Penn, Campbell, Esposito-Smythers & Spirito, 2009) and healthy living contracts (Bosch-Capblanch, Abba, Prictor & Garner, 2007; 2009). As well, Volk and colleagues (2012) cite some practices use a 'no defamatory contract' where patients promise in writing not to litigate or post defamatory comments on the Internet (Sacopulos & Segal, 2009). Today, despite the worldwide use of contracting with patients, little is known about the benefits of these types of patient interventions, and even less about these contracts' capacity to compromise treatment.

Up until relatively recently, the practice of patient contracting had been subject to little detailed critical analysis. Terms like patient 'contracts', 'agreements', 'promises', 'pledges' and so forth, while in widespread use, told us little about the true nature of patient contracting. The current understanding of patient contracting is that its use is largely uni-dimensional. In large part, it was perceived by clinicians to offer a *process* reason for use (e.g., increasing short-term adherence to a treatment regime) and as well, it was used as a facilitator to achieve a pre-designed target such as weight loss or reduction in blood pressure. Here, patient contracting is viewed *behaviorally* as a way of eliciting enough *therapeutic* advantage by "specifying a set of rules regarding some behavior of interest and formalising a commitment to adhere to them" (Dunbar, Marshall & Hovell, 1979, p. 175). Contemporaneously to clinicians' understanding of SPC, this largely functional understanding effectively hides from view not only the other dimensions of patient contracting, but also the aspects of patient contracting potentially associated with compromising treatment.

The desired corrective mechanisms at play when using a patient contract vary depending on the type of presenting complaint and reason for use. Volk and colleagues (2012), for example, understand the objectives of patient contracting include seeking *administrative* goals, such as deterring patients from mistreating clinical personnel or diverting narcotics. Others are *educational*; contracting as a means to facilitate attention and information transfer. Still another goal of patient contracting aims to underscore and *communicate* expectations. For example, a potential organ recipient contracts to substance-abuse rules. And similar, suicide prevention contracting is perceived to *communicate* the clinicians' care and concern for their suicidal patient.

THE HUMANISTIC CASE IN CONTRACTING FOR CHANGE

The stark lack of a clinical understanding of SPC includes its associated philosophical and ethical underpinnings. In chapters 4 and 7, I detail the critical ethical aspects as they related to clinical practice. For now, to quickly grasp the idealistic promise for some in patient contracting, SPC in particular, let's consider the humanistic case with its sharp focus on the value and agency of human beings. Patient contracting began to appear in the literature around the 1970s. In my own profession of social work, scholars such as Columbia University professor Florence Hollis increasingly advocated a more specific and goal-orientated casework practice approach through the use of practitioner-client contracts (Hollis, 1970). Establishing treatment contracts with clients was seen as the endpoint of a process that involved gaining an assurance from the client to commence an agreed course of action; the contract was viewed as tangible evidence of a working relationship, engaging the client in agreed treatments.

The use of *explicit* treatment contracts was one aspect of brief treatments within a social work casework practice approach. In 1974, social work professors Anthony Maluccio & Wilma Marlow detailed the benefits and limitations of treatment contracts. Of note, they alluded to the then burgeoning notion of the client as consumer, offering the concept of "maximum feasible participation" as an explicit element within the practice of treatment contracting with clients (Ibid., 1974, p. 28). To sum up, seen as a clear benefit to casework, patient contracting symbolized the client as an active participant in a professional process, rather than as a passive recipient of aid. Anthony Maluccio & Wilma Marlow (1974) described four features of a treatment contract. These comprised:

1. *Mutual agreement* between client and worker—a sense of mutuality regarding role, goals and task, thereby better supporting communication surrounding the quality, content and direction of the relationship.
2. *Differential participation*—a treatment contract better articulates individual responsibilities, providing client opportunities for choice, self-determination and self-mastery.
3. *Reciprocal accountability*—attention is given to client responsibilities in treatment, supporting the worker/client working relations through the contractual alliance.
4. *Explicitness*—articulating explicit and specific goals, thereby minimizing attention given to covert agendas of either party (pp. 30–33).

Maluccio & Marlow also offered a cautionary note—contraindications—to the use of treatment contracts, specifically regarding the client's social, physical and psychological characteristics that may limit their ability to formulate an explicit treatment contract (p. 34).

I realize these opinions are forty-plus years old. But in a sense, they underscore a basic universal point. As humans, it is in our DNA to expect that a potent relationship with a particular individual can influence them to consider a new course of action; an alternative less detrimental to their well-being.

Let's briefly consider another point of view.

U.K. social work professors John Corden & Michael Preston-Shoot (1987) understood that patient contracting was particularly useful at avoiding double agendas—offering clarity between practitioner/client tasks—and provided an opportunity to discuss and resolve clashes in perspectives by giving consumers a chance to negotiate rules for the intervention, presenting an element of choice in decision-making processes (p. 542). Seen as 'functional contracting', this view of patient contracting emerged out of a task-centered approach with aspects of behavior modification; a superb exemplar of their critique related to institutional dependency. John Corden & Michael Preston-Shoot came to the conclusion that within an increasingly consumer-focused environment, clients as consumers demand/deserve a greater active role in treatment decision-making and that treatment contracts operationalized the principle of client involvement in the practice of casework, balancing up the inherent power differential between client and worker (pp. 536–539). So, then, from the humanistic view patient contracting was seen as a means whereby active client participation could determine the quality of the relationship. As you'll discover in later chapters, these and other early humanistic perspectives of patient contracting set the foundations for positively perceiving its benefits, so positive that a generalization of application took hold in clinical practice.

A NEW UNDERSTANDING OF PATIENT CONTRACTING

In our SPC study we found a very distinct pattern in the data. It led us to launch into developing an emerging nomenclature for SPC and, as it turned out, for patient contracting generally. Before I detail this, perhaps an analogy may clarify the significance of a categorizing system. In 1948, Edwin A. Chapin, curator of insects at the U.S. National Museum, published a meticulous four-page article in the *The Coleopterists Bulletin* detailing genus *Palorus* (of the Tenebrionidae family), a flightless, black beetle no more than a quarter inch in length. This genus of beetle was believed to seriously invade grain stores. Chapin described how since 1869 scientists had sought to describe (provide an *anatomy* of) and classify (provide a *taxonomy* for) these organisms. Part and parcel of this process was to propose a standard set of names and terms relating to the phenomenon (provide a *nomenclature*). Back and forth the scientific debate went, as the lines of demarcation between genus, species and sub-species and the names used to label them were thrashed out amid changing discoveries among entomologists.

Then, at the first post-war meeting of the U.S. Commission of Zoological Nomenclature, attending scientists endorsed the taxonomy and its associated nomenclature for these little creatures. A landmark study conducted across the U.S. National Museum and U.S. Department of Agriculture had revealed the truth. The sole grain-eating species of Tenebrionidae was, in fact, living under dark conditions in the forests of Europe, not lurking about in grain silos in the United States.

The exercise was of more than merely academic interest. For without a clear and common understanding of their anatomy, and an agreed-upon taxonomy, the wrong insects may have been targeted and needlessly eliminated. Millions of wasted dollars and countless wasted days would have been spent on pointless eradication programmes.

OK, you might be wondering, what's the relevance of bugs to patient contracting?

It's a silly analogy, granted. But I'm using it to highlight an important point. According to U.S. suicidologist Ronald W. Maris, PhD, one of the biggest difficulties facing the reliable diagnosis, assessment, treatment, management and prevention of suicides worldwide is the lack of a common descriptive and classificatory system—a common vocabulary—for the field of suicidology.

A common vocabulary, the basis for mutual understanding and cooperation, is critical to the proper functioning of a professional or scientific community. Imagine a community of entomologists who didn't have common names for the many species of beetle they study, or an agreed-upon set of labels for the various parts of beetle anatomy. Without it, such a community is simply not possible. You too probably have a nomenclature, however informal—i.e., a system of terms, concepts and categories—particular to your own profession. Bring to mind the terms common in your professional arena. Try to imagine going to work and not being able to use them. Your ability to share ideas, be understood, communicate directives, make recommendations, or report coherently on activities would be severely compromised, if not downright impossible.

You may well be wondering what nomenclature has to do with SPC and other forms of patient contracting. Isn't SPC used simply to prevent suicidal behavior? Aren't the motivations, purposes, intentions, and reasons for using one kind of patient contract the same for all types of patient contracting procedures?

The answer, perhaps surprisingly, to all of these questions is: No. Not because the label "patient contracting or suicide prevention contracting" doesn't indicate the *overall* goal of its employment; it does. While the overall goal of intervention/prevention is clearly captured, the sheer complexity of the patient contracting phenomenon remains covered up by this superficial description. And, it is clarification of complexity an adequate nomenclature aims to do: reveal reality, and make possible communication about it. If you had the opportunity to sit down and go through all the four-hundred-plus data sets from this SPC study, you'd be struck by the utter absence of a common language used when participants were asked to describe SPC. Yes, these clinicians did talk about patient self-responsibility, clinician self-protection and care and concern. But they never clearly categorized the stages of suicidal patient contracting and rarely defined common elements in the process.

Analyzing the qualitative data from an opened-ended question that we inserted in the study's questionaire was the first point in our research effort that we began to see a series of recurring patterns in the data. These data in fact confirmed results from an earlier report. In 1994, a small team of U.S.-based psychiatrists initially proposed that there were three distinct reasons why clinicians deploy SPC (Stanford, Goetz & Bloom, 1994). Edward J. Stanford, MD, and his review team from the Oregon Health Sciences University conducted a morbidity and mortality case review implicating the inappropriate use of SPC. In reviewing the case at hand, as well as the albeit scant literature, the team concluded SPC was being used for clinico-legal, diagnostic and therapeutic reasons. In order to determine whether these three main motivations were present in our study's clinician data, we undertook two related analyses: a quantitative analysis of the study's Likert scaled questions; and, a content analysis of responses to an open-ended question asking why *other* practitioners use SPC. We found that all of the substantive themes that emerged from the 176 participants' responses to the open-ended question could be allocated to one of these three kinds of deployment: *i)* for perceived clinico-legal protection, *ii)* for perceived diagnostic clarification, and *iii)* for perceived therapeutic advantage.

Later, while working on this introduction to the book, I made a habit of asking my clinic colleagues to take a copy of the patient contracting Decision-Making Schema (DMS) (see figure I.1) and run general patient contracting

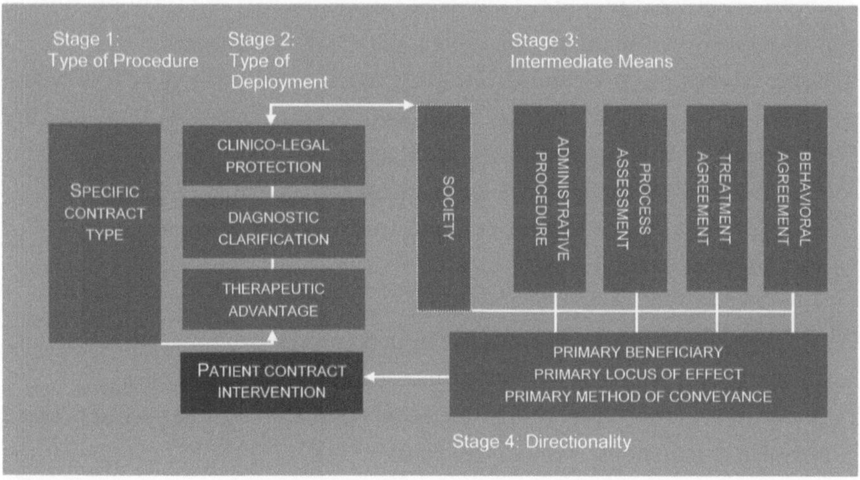

FIGURE I.1
Patient contracting decision-making schema (DMS)

scenarios through it. (The SPC-DMS was developed largely from an iterative process of looping back and forth, developing ideas and testing them against the SPC study data. What finally hung together was a coherent framework which I detail in the first part of chapter 6.) After a few months of sifting and sorting, considering possibilities and tossing some out, we finally came to see that the component parts in patient contracting weren't just a random sample idea.

Based on the findings from the SPC study, we were able to develop what I am calling *The New Vocabulary of SPC.* Essentially, this is a synthesis of our research findings. It comprises an anatomy of SPC, a taxonomy of SPC, and through its emerging nomenclature, a common language that provides the foundation for an understanding of this clinical practice that is clear, simple, and I trust useful. In chapter 6, I detail the complete workings of this emerging nomenclature specific to SPC. For now, to better appreciate the inner workings of patient contracting generally, I'll offer a cut-down version of *The New Vocabulary of SPC.*

The Inner Working of Patient Contracting

Having sketched the early history of patient contracting with a rather broad brush, I want now to take you through each of its dimensions and their components more thoroughly. I will try to keep the technical terminology to a minimum in what will inevitably be a rather dry part of this book, but I'll also try to 'leaven' the discussion with some real-life examples.

Table 1 presents a range of common patient contract types. While the perceived therapeutic advantages of patient contracting is well known, what is less discussed are the other *Types of Deployments,* specifically using patient contracting for diagnostic clarification and perceived clinico-legal protection.

To begin with, a word about nomenclature: in general a formal system of terminology has three features:

1. A base name referring to both the dimensions of patient contracting and all significant components found in that dimension's structure.
2. A rule or sub-rule designating functional relationships that may be present between dimensions.
3. Names of similar relationships, other than the base name, that complete the dimension's structure. (NB. These rules, sub-rules, relationships between

Table I.1. Common types of patient contracts

Contract Type	Setting	Aim	Therapeutic Intent	Diagnostic Intent	Clinico-legal Intent
Addiction treatment contracts	• Treatment of addiction	• Engage in relapse prevention • Assess motivation	High	Low	-
Psychological treatment contracts	• Treatment of mental ill health	• Increase adherence to treatment • Assess support for proposed treatment • Documents good practice	High	Moderate	Low
No suicide agreements No suicide contracts	• Inpatient/ outpatient (mental health) • Community (e.g., crisis centers, schools)	• Prevent suicide • Assess risk • Perceived clinico-legal protection (i.e., professionals)	High	High	Moderate
Transplant substance abuse contracts	• Organ transplantation	• Communicate substance abuse criteria for receipt of organ transplant • Assess compliance pre-transplant	Low	High	Low
Opioid contracts	• Chronic narcotic prescription user	• Educate re: medication side effects • Assess compliance • Prevent misuse and trafficking in narcotics	Low	Moderate	High
Safe treatment contracts/ drug monitoring	• High risk medication (e.g.immunosuppressants)	• Educate on medication side effects • Increase adherence to laboratory monitoring	Moderate	Unclear	Unclear
Healthy-living contracts	• Lifestyle modification (diet, exercise)	• Engage patient in goal of lifestyle modification • Clarification of motivation/ potential barriers	High	Moderate	-
Difficult patient contracts	• Disruptive patients	• Engage patient in goal of decreasing disruptive behavior • Clarify motivation to change • Clarify clinic rules/civil law	Moderate	Moderate	Moderate

Adapted from: Volk, M. L., Lieber, S. R., Kim, S. Y., Ubel, P. A., & Schneider, C. E. (2012). Patients contracts in clinical practice. *Lancet*, 379, (9810), 7–9.

dimensions and any additional names are located in the notes section on page 159.)

You will notice that in my discussion of each of the four dimensions, I will cover each of these three features where they become relevant. In general, the schema relies upon the concept of outcomes—the apparent goals of clinicians when employing a patient contract.

Stage 1) Type of Procedure

Based on the intervention type offered by a Cochrane Collaboration Review (2009), the following defines *Type of Procedure:* Patient contracts concern treatment, prevention and health promotion activities aimed at improving patients' adherence. Patient contracts include any verbal or written statement specifying at least one treatment, prevention or health promotion activity to be observed, and a commitment of adherence to it.

Patient contracts are undertaken by health care practitioners or services and patients or their carers, between patients and their carers, or by the patient themselves (self-commitment). Patient contracts can relate to any diagnostic procedure, therapeutic regimen, rehabilitation measure, general health advice, referral instruction, or any other activity or combination of activities involved in the management of patients (Bosch-Capblanch, Abba, Prictor & Garner, 2009, p. 5).[1]

Stage 2) Type of Deployment (Reasons for Use)[2,3]

(i) A *diagnostic* deployment entails using patient contracting to gain diagnostic clarification—albeit subjective—of a patient's support for a proposed intervention; motivation pre-treatment; compliance; potential barriers to treatment. For example, the nature and quality of a patient's response to a clinician's offer to contract might indicate adjustment to a treatment plan, or no care in the case of transplant substance abuse contracts.

(ii) A *therapeutic* deployment entails using patient contracting to effect a pre-defined outcome.

(iii) A *clinico-legal deployment* entails using patient contracting as a means of increasing a clinician's clinico-legal protection in the event of an adverse clinical outcome; to reinforce clinic rules and civil law requirements to specific individuals.

Stage 3) Intermediate Means

The *Intermediate Means* dimension has four components: process assessment, suicide treatment agreement, suicide behavioral agreement, and administrative procedure:

(i) *Process assessment:* using patient contracting to assess patient permission and assurance for a course of action—attunement (i.e., the clinician's) to the patient and their thoughts, relational impasse checking; an empathic procedure towards alliance building.

(ii) *Treatment agreement*: perceived as a procedure establishing options for treatment/clarifying what precipitating/maintaining factors need to be addressed.

(iii) *Behavioral agreement:* perceived to effect a course of action; reinforcing new behavior, controlling symptoms—offering the patient a sense of mastery over targeted behavior.

(iv) *Administrative procedure*: a documentation procedure enacted to make plain specific instructions; to present the clinician as competent at a future time.

Stage 4) Directionality

The *Directionality* dimension of patient contracting reflects a general pattern. In every one of the 176 SPC study cases, the three sub-structures (primary beneficiary, primary locus of effect, primary method of conveyance) were located in the data. They were discovered by asking these questions: How is patient contracting primarily conveyed to a patient? Who is the primary beneficiary of patient contracting? When is the primary effect of patient contracting expected to take place?

Indeed, it was hardly ever that these questions could be answered independently of each other; rather, the answers in many instances depended on having answered other questions first. In other words, it was not always immediately obvious, for example, what the mode of conveyance would be until the primary beneficiary had been identified. In short, these three sub-dimensions of directionality are deeply intertwined, one with another.

The first sub-structure is the primary beneficiary, also titled the Orientation of a particular patient contract. To establish the primary beneficiary; first, locate and establish *Type of Deployment* and assign an *Intermediate*

Means structure. Then ascertain the primary beneficiary of the *Intermediate Means*. Consider the example of using NSC to *'provide legal protection'*. In this case, the *Type of Deployment* is for clinico-legal; *Intermediate Means* is an administrative procedure, so the primary beneficiary is clinician orientated.

Primary locus of effect

Once a substantive *Type of Deployment* is identified, established and assigned to the related *Intermediate Means* and primary beneficiary sub-structures, it is then possible to ascertain the primary locus of effect. Locus of effect refers to the chronology of the *Intermediate Means* as it takes effect, such as using SPC for 'clinician self-protection'. In this case the *Type of Deployment* would comprise clinico-legal protection; the *Intermediate Means* is an administrative procedure; the beneficiary is the clinician; with the locus of effect being the *future* as opposed to *present*. Essentially, the clinician is perceived to have employed SPC to minimize future recriminations should there be an adverse clinical outcome.

Primary mode of conveyance

The final sub-structure of *Directionality* is the mode of conveyance, a fundamental element in the anatomy of patient contracting. The mode of conveyance refers to how the *Intermediate Means* is offered to a patient. It represents a salient measure of the ability of patients to be explicitly involved and fully informed—that is, of their capacity to give informed consent to being exposed to the risks and benefits when participating in patient contracting generally and SPC specifically (*cf.* The Six Core Concepts of SPC and the Four Fatal Flaws of SPC). Essentially there are only two modes of conveyance, explicit and implicit.

Consider again the sub-structure we discussed earlier, 'provides legal protection', where the *Intermediate Means* was an administrative procedure. In this case the method of conveyance would constitute an implicit offer. The patient is unaware that the primary motivation (i.e., intermediate means being an administrative procedure) is self-protection.

Consider the case of using patient contracting as an 'opportunity for self-control'. The *Type of Deployment* would be therapeutic advantage; the *Intermediate Means* would be either treatment agreement or behavioral agreement; and in *Directionality* the primary beneficiary is the patient; and the locus of effect is primarily the future. The mode of conveyance here is primarily *explicit.* In this instance, the 'opportunity for self-control' indicates that a clinician has likely revealed the agenda and negotiated openly with the patient.

As you can hopefully see from these simple examples, this anatomy of patient contracting helps us describe in quite some subtlety the particular utilization of a contracting procedure. My hope is that it will become a useful tool for illuminating any and every utilization of SPC, and thus serve to raise speedy alarms. Indeed, I believe that by accurately reflecting contemporary SPC clinical practices, the anatomy of SPC will enable clinicians, managers, supervisors and such like to *fully* examine or justify utilizing (or not) an SPC procedure, and to encourage clinicians to question the use of SPC altogether. And, for teaching purposes, it will provide measures for assessing whether a procedure is being used prudently.

THE CASE AGAINST CONTRACTS BETWEEN PATIENTS AND HEALTH CARE PRACTITIONERS FOR IMPROVING PATIENTS' ADHERENCE TO RECOMMENDED HEALTH CARE ACTIVITIES

In essence, those who do use patient contracting do so with some sense that it does one, perhaps two, or maybe even all of the following three things: it helps *therapeutically* to achieve pre-defined outcomes, it helps *diagnostically* to assess motivation, compliance or potential barriers to treatment, and it helps *clinico-legally* to increase clinician protection in case of an adverse clinical outcome or to make sure that clinic policies are made crystal clear.

Which among these uses could possibly compromise treatment, let alone be a threat, you may ask? The short answer, paradoxically, is *all of them.* As I shall explain in upcoming chapters, SPC use can undermine the therapeutic alliance and therefore increase risk; it can also generate an entirely illusory assessment of suicide risk; and lastly, it can not only fail to provide clinico-legal protection but actually increase the clinico-legal risk. In fact, there are five paradoxes of SPC which between them lay bare the dangers—*the manufactured hazards*—inherent in its use.

As you'll see in later chapters, the case against general patient contracts reflects a similar pattern to that of SPC. Not only do patient contracts have multiple perceived *Type of Deployments* (benefits), the evidence base is just not there. A Cochrane review analyzed thirty mainly North American RCTs (randomised control trials) comprising 4,691 participants, involving several types of patient contracting procedures (Bosch-Capblanch, Abba, Prictor & Garner, 2009). The main health problems targeted were substance addictions, hypertension and being overweight.

In fifteen of the RCTs at least one outcome showed statistically significant differences in favor of the contracts group, albeit some of the improvements in adherence did not last suggestive of short-term adherence only. In six RCTs at least one outcome favored standard care, and twenty-six RCTs showed no difference. The authors concluded the lack of enough reliable evidence precludes any recommendation for the routine use of contracts in health services to improve patients' adherence to health care activities or other outcomes (p. 2).

In other cases, patient contracting offers relatively weak evidence. A recent systematic review by Starrels, Becker, Alford, Kapoor, Williams & Turner (2010) reported limited evidence supporting the effectiveness of opioid treatment agreements and urine drug testing in reducing opioid misuse by patients with chronic pain. Other patient contract types such as SPC have not been empirically studied for effectiveness, due in part to the ethical questions in conducting an RCT on a perceived life-saving intervention with suicidal patients.

In 2012, when questioning the place of patient contracting generally in clinical practice, Sarah Lieber, MD, Michael Volk, MD, and colleagues came to a practical set of conclusions:

- The term 'contract' is quazi-legally ladened and misleading.
- Ethical considerations arise when the term 'contract' is used, implying a breach of contract may compromise access to ongoing care.
- The potential of implied consequences, if breached, to fundamentally skew the patient-physician relationship—a relationship traditionally founded on unconditional loyalty—is significant.
- Patient contracting negatively impacts communication between the parties due to fear of consequences following nonadherence.
- Proforma implementation of contracts fuels feelings of being threatened, coerced; a precursor to feelings of abandonment for some patients.
- An existing power relationship exists between clinician and patient, making negotiation of the terms of a contract implausible at best, especially when most patient contracts in clinical practice are proforma, pre-printed types.

- The use of formal patient contracting moves from an opportunity to persuade a patient to change, for example, unhealthy habits, to a reduced opportunity for negotiation. Persuasion moves into control and coercion (Lieber, Kim & Volk, 2011; Volk, Lieber, Kim, Ubel & Schneider, 2012).

THE SPC STUDY

The current evidence base in relation to SPC is limited to eighteen descriptive, primarily clinician surveys. As such it is insufficient to provide SPC with anything like the status of an evidence-based practice. What this also means is that there is insufficient evidence to justify either *definitive* assessments of its dangerousness or *categorical* recommendations about the most effective alternatives. However, as I shall show throughout this book, the existing research provides sufficient reason to strongly recommend replacing SPCs with alternative clinical protocols.

The current paucity of data on SPC can be understood as having arisen for two main reasons. Firstly, until relatively recently SPC was not reported as a potentially detrimental or hazardous procedure (American Psychiatric Association Practice *Guidelines for the Assessment and Treatment of Patients with Suicidal Behavior*, 2003; Australian and New Zealand College of Psychiatry's *Clinical Practice Guidelines for the Management of Adult Deliberate Self-Harm*, 2004).

Secondly, gold standard RCT (randomised control trial) methods for determining the effectiveness of any intervention measure face severe, and perhaps insuperable, difficulties in the area of suicide prevention. The methodological rigor required today to establish evidence-based best practice would create ethical and methodological issues that are daunting. It would require randomly assigning some suicidal folk to a hypothesised best treatment and others to a placebo or standard practice (Goldney, 2010) and assessing the relative merits of the treatments on the basis of the quantity of suicidal behavior of the respective cohorts. No ethics committee today would approve such a study. The theoretical and methodological purity of RCTs is therefore a standard that may never be fully met in the field of suicide research. Therefore, a pragmatic, relativistic approach to such research is necessary (Goldney, 2005).

In particular, descriptive and correlational studies have been fundamental to the acquisition of new knowledge in the field. In many ways, descriptive research techniques and the clinical evaluation of a child, youth or adult patient are not too dissimilar. The evaluator gathers as much information as possible from a variety of sources: clinical and developmental assessments, standardized testing, past clinical experience, and the available research literature as well as other descriptive information, and out of all these data formulates a hypothesis about the presenting problem, known precipitating and perpetuating factors, and the available evidence-based treatments that might be effective.

For the Western Australian SPC study—henceforth known as 'the SPC study'—on which this book is primarily based, such a descriptive approach proved to be well suited (Edwards, Harries & Kumar, 2006; Edwards & Harries, 2007; Edwards, 2008; Edwards & Sachmann, 2010). The findings of this study—to date, the largest survey of clinicians who use SPC—have been integrated with the best available, largely descriptive research data to develop the full evidence base for this work.

FATAL FLAWS AND COMPROMISING PARADOXES OF SPC

To bring this section to a close, I would like to introduce you to the remainder of this book. In the next chapter, I introduce *The Confluence Effect* in order to explain how the contemporary practice of SPC developed historically in a manner which detached it from its original theoretical underpinnings.

I found that contemporary SPC procedures evolved largely out of four significant streams—how for the most part, related historical events flowed into a series of watershed moments, leading to the quiet proliferation of SPC and its unintended consequences experienced today. In Part II of the book, I detail *The Anatomy of SPC* as it arose from our findings. And, at the same time, I give instruction on how to recognize it and also how to teach it.

In Part III, we lay bare *The Four Fatal Flaws of SPC*, essentially how clinicians can offer SPC in the absence of hard data attesting to its validity, efficacy *AND*, at the same time, are largely unaware of its potential to cause harm. In these chapters, I also present and explain *The Five Paradoxes of SPC*. These five paradoxes were named after the clinician(s) who initially raised them as possibilities. Though we expected that contemporary SPC would consist at least of some contradictions, we found instead that it's littered with potentially harmful paradoxical situations with the ability to compromise treatment for both patient and clinician. Briefly:

Mahrer's Paradox (The Use by Experience Curve). We theorized that as clinicians become more experienced and consequently exposed to more suicidality, their practice behavior is likely directed less by their initial training, and more by a developing set of beliefs regarding what is effective practice (which interventions work . . . and which don't). Here, our findings told us that the old adage 'When you're on to a good thing stick to it' seemed not to apply here. We found instead that it was likely not the more experienced clinicians who were using more SPC procedures, but the less experienced.

McArdle's Paradox (The Use by Risk Curve). What came somewhat as a surprise were the data showing that the relatively high-risk patients were likely being offered a specific type of SPC procedure—the written NSC—despite its complete lack of evidence base (McArdle's Paradox). And, at the same time, we revealed a related ethical dilemma we came to call *Farrow's Paradox.*

Miller's Paradox (The 3 Cs). Regardless of whether we're speaking about the SPC procedures of the 1970s or those used today, a key reason for use is: communication. We found that fully 80 percent of clinicians agreed that communication was a central plank of SPC. Astonishing to us were the findings that revealed an apparent lack of appreciation of the potential for a breakdown in such communication. In particular, a patient can perceive a clinician's reasons for offering an SPC procedure as mere clinician self-protection. This perception thereby likely increases the risk to the therapeutic alliance and potentially leads, in turn, to increased risk for suicidal behavior.

The One in Four Concept (Determining quadrant four patients). We came to a stark theoretical conclusion that clinicians have merely a 'one in four chance' of offering NSAg or NSC to possibly 'the right patient'. Just because you have never had a patient seriously attempt or complete suicide whilst 'contracted' and may therefore think well of SPC typically, that doesn't necessarily mean you can confidently use SPC with all suicidal patients. We learned instead that the perfunctory deployment of SPC must a fortiori be replaced by a new approach, the One in Four Concept, which reflects both a deep understanding of the real nature of SPC procedures, and, critically, a new way of thinking about our patients' beliefs about SPC.

Simon's Paradox. We were surprised, stunned really, to discover the number of clinicians who used SPC procedures for the reason of perceived clinico-legal self-protection. Paradoxically, we found that clinicians are, in fact, potentially increasing their risk for a professional and legal debacle, not reducing it. We learned that not only does SPC offer no legal protection, but that a reliance on SPC can, in fact, constitute a clinician's failure in their duty of care.

One of the senior clinicians whom we initially interviewed had expected a very particular result from our study: that one form of 'SPC type procedure' represents a universal intervention, where the others are for quite specific purposes—this being the single most obviously beneficial aspect of No Suicide Assurances (NSAs): *Fenner's Rule.*

In the context of forty years or more, and operating within a dramatically changing society, the practice of SPC has been influenced less by real understanding and more by a fanatical attention to risk, and the unrelenting need to control it. In chapter 7, we also explore how this and other factors have generated for some an underlying assumption that SPC use is somehow certified best practice, exposing the fundamental legal and ethical flaws in the practice of SPC, and then present in Part IV the simplest of responses to avoiding them.

In Part IV, we also detail—based on our findings and a survey of four decades of the SPC literature—the *Primary and Secondary Contra indications for SPC* and the *Seven Alternatives to SPC*. In the *Teaching Tools* Appendix, I return to the key findings of the study and link them to the Seven Alternatives to SPC.

As you may now appreciate, our four-year study produced an array of insights, several of which challenge popular belief and may even be confronting for some. Yet one finding stands out above all others. We believe that by learning and embracing the core concepts we have discovered about SPC, any clinician can retain any perceived benefits of SPC procedures when using alternative techniques while greatly reducing their own and their patient's exposure to unnecessary risk. It is in fact very easy to avoid the unintended consequences of SPC that can potentially lead to increasing a patient's suicidality, clinician litigation and other professional recriminations.

Here, then, until consensus is reached on the determination of contemporary SPC's nature and character, and the aforementioned ethical and other methodological barriers to RCTs in suicide prevention surmounted, is today's best evidence to describe and explain the hazards of SPC. So, I ask you to come with me on an intriguing adventure, where Suicide Prevention Contracting is explained. I offer the findings from our study, their interpretations, and recommendations for your careful consideration.

I

CURRENT UNDERSTANDING OF SUICIDE PREVENTION CONTRACTING

A middle-aged man suffering mental ill health developed a liking for repeatedly crossing a busy road at a particular crosswalk. Some drivers reluctantly stopped, others would stop and overtly acknowledge the man; while others stopped in a matter-of-fact manner and would wait to be thanked.

And what of the man?

Sometimes he would treat the cars as enemies, with contempt. Other times he'd cross seeking minimal disruption. When asked why, the man simply said that he enjoyed the moment when the cars stopped for him—that he experienced a feeling of importance at that point (Hage, 2000, pp. 29–31).

The man crossing the road at a crosswalk attains existential status by being recognized as a human being. Australian anthropologist professor Ghassan Hage understands the crosswalk moment is at the heart of the ethical compulsions that define the notion of mutual social obligation (i.e., the social contract), and it is linked with the social conditions of its prevalence (Ibid). "Generally then, contemporary society is merely replicating itself as an ethical society only by continuing to offer individuals the very ethical conditions it wants them to be obligated to reproduce (Ibid., p. 32)."

1

A Personal Journey with Suicide Prevention Contracting

> The tools of the mind become burdens when the environment which made them necessary no longer exists. —Henri Bergson (in Harris, T., 1969, p. 97)

TWENTY YEARS OF REFLECTION

Why would someone undertake a four-year study and dedicate another two years to writing a book about SPC? It's a valid question. The answer is: because I have an extensive list of long-standing unanswered questions about it, and a high index of suspicion.

Let me explain.

In more than twenty years of practicing, researching and teaching in the area of suicidology, I've had the pleasure of working with all of the health care and human service disciplines involved in the prevention of suicide: clinicians from the fields of addictions, emergency medicine, primary care, occupational therapy, nursing, psychiatry, psychology, social work and youth work. Along the way I gained from these clinicians a clear awareness of the philosophical, theoretical and practical questions they wrestle with every day working with suicidal patients.

On occasion I functioned as an informal and sometimes formal consultant to these clinicians regarding their experiences with suicidal patients. Younger nurses, social workers and especially physicians new to clinical practice spoke of their anxieties about suicide. In addition, usually when prompted, they spoke about a lack of clarity in the use of SPC. Others presented with more self-assurance. Some would even boast of their 100 percent record in 'not losing a patient' when contracting. Others felt it was simply a certified standard of care. Still other clinicians spoke about never being completely sure SPC makes any difference to suicidal behavior, whereas some felt SPC makes it clear that suicidal possibilities are to be overtly included in therapy.

Put simply, throughout these years, the flame of my curiosity has remained strong because of my high index of suspicion. I continually questioned what I thought I knew about SPC. Why do clinicians continue to use it, I wondered, despite sporadic but documented case reports of life-ending consequences (Stanford, Goetz & Bloom, 1994; Potter, Vitale-Nolen & Dawson, 2005)?

In these twenty years of teaching, researching and practicing with professionals and para-professionals in health care and human services whose responsibility it is to prevent suicidal behavior, I have come into contact with dozens of individuals who have struggled with the use of SPC; struggled particularly with concerns that their reliance on the intervention (by and large, to any degree) may, in fact, be misguided. I suspect that some of the doubts and questions these clinicians have shared with me may also be familiar to you:

> After 20 years as a mental health nurse, I still don't know if they actually assist a situation. —Mary, a mental health nurse with twenty years' experience

> We've tried to slow the pace of seeing patients in our clinic, but we just don't seem to be able to spend much quality time with them. It sometimes feels like a production line. I'm not even sure I truly know if we help and what's really important . . . contracting then, I believe, can be used to absolve workers from responsibilities and used to blame patients. —Carol, a social worker with twenty years' experience

> I sometimes ask for reassurance that the patient will be able to ask for help or notify someone if they're feeling suicidal. Why do I do this when I know situations change rapidly and often for the worst? —Jerry, a psychiatrist with ten years' experience

> Starting at my first psychology position after my undergraduate training was as much exciting as it was frightening. There is a great degree of difference

between largely observing your supervisor's practice and you having full responsibility for your own cases. When faced with my first suicidal patient, my new supervisor told me to contract with the patient and document it. I wasn't sure how to contract for living. —Jim, a psychologist with five years' experience

I'm busy pretty much most of the time. Contracts give me a feeling of predictability in an unpredictable and stressful situation. Still, I wonder just how useful they really are? —Patricia, a social worker with thirty years' experience

I think they cause more harm than good. I would hate to see them become routine. —Caroline, a psychiatrist with seventeen years' experience

I use agreements to structure problem solving and distress tolerance to help patients find ways to manage intense distress without acting . . . client empowerment. Assessing suicide risk is important as well as non-coercion on the part of myself. I see no value in a contract that, to me, implies a lack of trust in the client and a cynical attempt by a worker to be seen to have done their job. A contract also implies that the client or myself has the power to stop these urges, that, I think, is an added burden. —Jack, a clinical psychologist with five years' experience

I enjoy teaching new graduates . . . it's very important new graduates don't assume contracting is the only treatment or clinical response to suicidal behaviour. I'm sure though, some will see it this way. —Dallas, a clinical psychologist with fifteen years' experience

I don't use written contracts, as I've been concerned that if a client did attempt after signing a contract, how this would cause further distress to them. —Tony, a social worker with ten years' experience

I can see a use for assurances as an informal tool for nurses or other professionals, but the other forms [agreements and contracts] are vain absurdities of intellectually pretentious delinquents. —Jim, a mental health nurse with five years' experience

For clinicians responsible for ensuring the safety of their patients as best they can, these representative comments indicate significant problems, problems that until now have remained largely unrecognized.

Several years ago I, too, was struggling with this kind of concern. Back then, the practice of SPC reminded me of the superstition that one should walk around an open ladder rather than take the shorter route under it. Some will do that, reasonably enough, to avoid the threat of something falling on them. Others, in unreflective acceptance of the superstition, wouldn't consider any other alternative. Others still, however, even though fully aware that it's superstitious to do so will avoid passing under the ladder, despite there being nothing overhead. In other words, they do so *just in case.*

Analogously, the practice of SPC is seen variously from widely dissimilar positions today. On the one hand, some clinicians view SPC as compellingly and obviously beneficial, so that not to use it would seem quite counterintuitive. This leaves many, who are either skeptical of or prefer not to use SPC, at risk of seeming negligent—perhaps even irrational—not to go along with the prevailing superstition.

The fact is, we have remarkably little scientific understanding of either the practice of SPC or its effectiveness and suitability. Does SPC reduce the risk of suicide? Many have blithely assumed that it does, even though we've had no data to categorically answer this question in the affirmative. The research data we do have, however, only tells us that SPC is a widespread, almost mandatory practice among some clinicians, in some settings.

Widespread use of an intervention procedure without the support of evidence? There is a clear history of such practice in psychiatry and psychology, where, in the absence of conclusive empirical data, beliefs are based on mere speculation or supposition. Consider the idea widespread throughout the last century that it was simply 'bad mothering' that led to schizophrenia. Or the widespread, almost mandatory, use in the 1980s and 1990s of single-session post-traumatic incident debriefing. Even in an information rich environment, it is common that complex phenomena receive simplistic explanations, and even give rise to myths, especially when people have a limited understanding of the true and complex nature of things.

IN THE FIRST FIVE YEARS

Early in my career, my use of and opinion toward SPC seemed, for the most part, pretty uncomplicated. Yet when I look back with the wisdom of hindsight, there was clearly more going on than I was aware of at the time. Consider, for example, how I used a written no-suicide contract just once, early in my career (in the first five years), with a young man (I'll call him Kelly), and then never again. Why was that? I think now because as I gained more clinical practice skills I saw less of a need to use 'a contract'.

Kelly was at high risk for suicide (moderate depressive symptomatology, alcohol and drug abuse and prior attempts). So why did I opt to use a written no-suicide contract with him? I evaluated him to be sufficiently competent (despite being at high risk) to be able to work with me. I also wanted to avoid hospitalizing him. I felt that contracting was an alternative to hospital. (In later supervision sessions it became patently clear to me that I fundamentally liked Kelly, and my countertransference response included contracting to avoid what I believed would have been a negative experience to hospitalize him.)

Furthermore, I believed our long-standing therapeutic relationship meant he'd truly appreciate why I had asked him to contract with me. And, at the same time, I believed a written no-suicide contract would communicate my care and concern for Kelly—that he would understand this and, I suppose, step up to the plate and honor the therapeutic relationship. Principally, I believed he would uphold a promise not to engage in suicidal behavior and simply comply with what I had asked of him.

And Kelly's response to SPC?

Later that evening, whilst drunk, stoned and ambivalent about life, he attempted suicide. He cut one wrist, gouged at it really, with a knife. Thankfully, he woke the next day and dressed his wounds. Seven years on from that fateful day, we met by chance. Free from depression and suicidal ideation, he thanked me for my time back then. When I asked him about the written contract, he said in a firm voice, "Talking with you was really helpful. Just being there was what helped me the most."

It is clear to me now that my use of SPC as a response to Kelly's situation set up a raft of potentially dangerous clinical paradoxes.

Stop and think about it for a minute. I was a novice clinician offering an untested intervention. I was offering a written no-suicide contract to a high-risk patient. I hoped Kelly would realise I was using a written no-suicide contract because I truly cared. And, therefore, I assumed he knew what SPC was, and that he was able to give his informed consent to the intervention.

AS A MIDDLE-CAREER CLINICIAN

Later, some of the problems with 'contracting' became clearer to me when I was asked by the Australian federal government to study both the presentation of youth suicidal behavior in Australian primary care physician practices and the effectiveness of a training program I had devised for physicians. During a break while working with a test group of physicians, one well-experienced physician (I'll call him Lou) leaned over with a smile and confided, "You know, Stephen, I think the study will be great. Unfortunately, the training program will be pointless."

Curious, and somewhat bemused, I asked him to explain.

"The main issue for us doctors," he answered, "and for any clinician needing to evaluate and respond to a suicidal patient, is protecting yourself." Lou went on to give an analogy to underline his point. "It's like holding on to the tail of a tiger. Most clinicians won't choose to hold on to a tiger's tail. For those that have to, they're never quite completely sure where the tiger will lead them. And, the vast majority would do just about anything within reason to avoid being bitten."

Sometime after that conversation, I realized what Lou had meant and that he was at least partly correct. Yes, for the most part, clinicians would likely choose not to have to 'predict' if a patient will engage in suicidal behavior. Indeed, few would freely volunteer to provide ongoing treatment to and management of a suicidal patient. (The evaluation, treatment and management of suicidality is Lou's "holding on to the tail of the tiger.") Yet for those who are required to do so, they can be justifiably concerned about not recognizing the signs of suicidal intent or falsely assessing the risk as negative—hence evaluating a patient as low risk only for that patient to seriously attempt or complete suicide. I suspect, then, that whether they're fearful or fearless, most clinicians are equally concerned about the potential for negative legal and professional consequences. (That's the point where Lou's tiger turns round and bites you.)

Lou's exaggerated "pointless" comment about my suicide prevention training program was more an observation than a fact. Even the most cursory investigation reveals that clinicians, for the most part, are prudent yet pragmatic folk. To be sure, some walk a fine line between being proactive with patient care, on the one hand, and being pre-emptive or even defensive as a means of self-protection on the other. Indeed, many clinicians feel squeezed by the increasing demands on service delivery: on the one side, increasing and often more complex patient presentations; and, on the other side, government and other regulatory bodies impinging on the consultation room. This is why—sometimes obviously, sometimes less obviously, always potentially—one of the pressures impinging on professional practices since the 1980s is the threat (irrespective of whether it's perceived or real) of legal action following claims of malpractice.

Our study's findings led us to believe that no other intervention better underscores the pressures faced by clinicians, pressures also felt by patients, than the use of SPC. In this book, I use the term 'clinician' to describe health and welfare professionals, para-professionals and others responsible for preventing suicidal behavior. For me, any individual working in a professional setting to identify, manage and prevent the suicidal behavior of another is practicing the virtues of sincerity and right-mindedness and as such aptly fits the term.

A decade on from that fortunate conversation with Lou, I can now say with little doubt that SPC is not helpful (and may actually compromise treatment) for both patients and clinicians. Indeed, we now understand the factors that can cause this harm to occur. To be clear, if we've learned nothing else from over four years of studying the international SPC literature of the past four decades or more, it's this: SPC constitutes unjustifiable 'gambling' with the first dictum of care—to cause no harm—when, for example, clinical interventions are employed in the absence of a truly mutually understood transaction. (In chapter 4 you will learn that some clinicians and patients can have monumentally different understandings of SPC.)

Yet in mental health care—in any type of professional intervention really—to say something is absolutely ineffective, without proof, would be incorrect. Indeed, without conclusive empirical evidence, we cannot say for sure that in some cases SPC may not have some beneficial effect for some patients, and offer some advantage to some clinicians. Yet it was this very last point that fuelled my curiosity and heightened my 'index of suspicion' about clinicians' use of SPC. Can any uncertain benefit to some patients from SPC outweigh the risks to others? One thing, though, was piercingly clear. If we were going to address this and other questions, we first needed to uncover and explain the practical, ethical, legal and other problems with SPC that may actually compromise treatment.

Our findings led to the conclusion that the study's clinicians saw multiple benefits in SPC, not *just* the perceived reduction of legal liability. For example, on average 70 percent of participants felt that NSAg and NSC were unlikely to weaken a therapeutic relationship. For us, this explicit, above-the-water line understanding of SPC was widespread, albeit not widely discussed. Yes, we also understood that every disciplinary paradigm employs concepts that are less conscious and explicit in the thinking of its clinicians. Yet, one of the key tasks then was to make clearer the key elements of the below-the-water line portion of the use of SPC.

GETTING BELOW THE SPC WATERLINE

One particular point in developing the key concepts for the book stands out in my mind as I complete this first chapter. For one year, while finishing the research and working on the book, I stared thousands of times at a collection of diagrams graphically depicting some of our key findings and the peer-reviewed evidence I had stuck on a pin board hanging next to my computer screen. Late in the piece, trying to best understand why so many clinicians had an apparent *blind spot* about the practical, ethical, legal and other problems with SPC, I began assembling these pieces of evidence—literally sitting

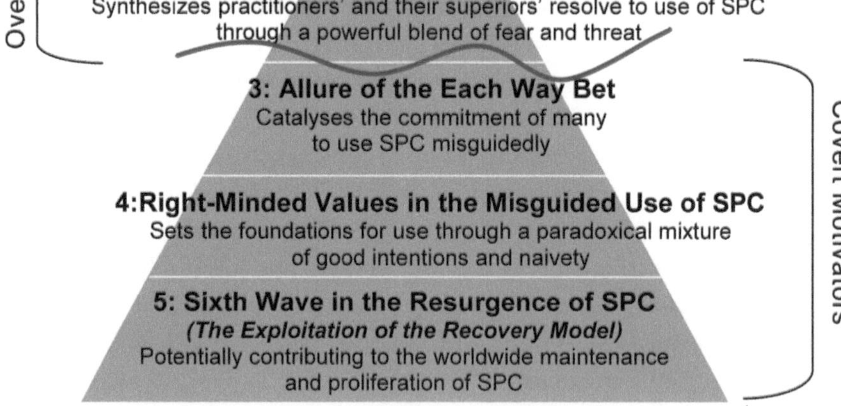

FIGURE 1.1
Motivating factors ranking in the misguided use of SPC

on the floor, cutting and pasting onto a piece of card. I soon realised that what I had been staring at were five pieces of a hierarchy ultimately leading to some of the answers to the question: Why do some clinicians use SPC as a perfunctory certified part of clinical practice, and others don't?

Figure 1.1 depicts what I finally came to call the *SPC iceberg heirarchy*. It's not presented here as the definitive account of why clinicians misguidedly use SPC for patient care/clinician self-protection. At this point in history, this contention is fully open to debate and criticism. Even so, the *SPC iceberg hierarchy* provides a largely data-driven vehicle for organizing some of the SPC study findings in a logical manner.

The *iceberg* consists of five discrete layers, each of which precipitate either a positive or a negative appraisal of SPC. The first four of these levels are *data-driven*, with level 5 based primarily upon clinical observation and concern. For me, the transition from level 2 to level 3 represents a waterline. Note the spatial nature of each of the levels. As I worked down from level 1 through 4 beyond the waterline, my hypothesis based upon our descriptive evidence is that more clinicians misguidedly use SPC as a *values-driven* good practice intervention. Level 5 is included more as a pre-emptive indication of how the use of SPC has the intrinsic potential for being seen as a good practice intervention in a distorted understanding of the recovery model philosophy as it applies to mental health services.

The five layers are divided between *overt and covert motivating factors* (factors above and below the waterline) for using SPC. In the chapters that follow I describe SPCs quasi-legal status (chapters 4 and 7), value-driven motivations for use (chapters 4 and 7) and the potential for a resurgence of SPC due to an exploitation of the mental health recovery philosophy (Conclusion). For now, let me provide a brief description of levels 2 and 3, competing factors maintaining a clinical blind spot in understanding the potential for SPC to compromise treatment, rendering it an unhelpful tactic.

Four Clinico-Legal Sides to SPC

Whilst the related SPC study findings were not significant in statistical terms, they did, however, confirm multiple factors driving clinician's use of SPC for self-protection, which I came to call the *Four Clinico-Legal Sides to SPC*. Clinicians were asked three questions relating to their use of NSAg and NSC to improve their clinico-legal status in the event of an adverse clinical outcome (see tables 5.2–5.5 in chapter 5). The majority of clinicians (n = 173/312; 55.5 percent) 'often to always' used NSAg for clinico-legal protection, less so for NSC (n = 74/154; 48 percent), and to abide by a superior's request to use NSAg (n = 60/308; 19.5 percent). However, participants used NSC more when lacking suitable resources for responding to suicide risk (n = 47/154; 30.5 percent; NSAg n = 89/311; 28.6 percent).

More precisely, the *four clinico-legal sides to SPC* emerged out of a subsequent analysis about the intersection of the following components in the clinico-legal matrix of SPC:

- *Four sides* (reasons why clinicians use SPC for perceived self-protection): *(i)* Reduce legal liability, *(ii)* Abide by a superior's request, *(iii)* Reduce professional recriminations, and *(iv)* Due to reduced access to resources. (Now, consider how these four dimensions and the associated fear/threat motivator are intrinsically linked not only to the attending clinician *BUT*, at the same time, to the supervisor, superior, manager or service requesting the clinician use SPC.)
- *Fear/threat motivator: (i)* Perceived fearful situation (suicidal crisis), generating countertransference reactions, *(ii)* Perceived threatening consequence of an adverse clinical outcome (completed suicide or serious attempted suicide). Both factors establishing a fear/threat balance motivating a response.
- *Fear/threat balance* mediates an assessment of the need for self protection. (This relates directly to *The ABC-SPC Stress Defence Model* [how SPC is activated] detailed in chapter 6.)

To quickly grasp the multiple effects of the four sides, consider the following. Suppose you were a busy crisis nurse and felt that your assessment alone would not be sufficient in the event of an adverse outcome. ("If they suicide and my assessment is reviewed, I'm sure they will blame me.") *AND, at the same time,* you frequently lack resources to do your job (including limited access to inpatient care). ("What can I do with them, if I can't get them admitted?") Reluctantly or otherwise, SPC had become a routine procedure in your clinical practice, frustrating circumstances and motivating you to routinely secure a NSC with a majority of the patients seen. With mounting factors, you quickly find yourself vulnerable to not adequately assessing the appropriateness of SPC (i.e., use when contraindicated, see chapter 9 for a list of these); you likely increase the chances of compromising treatment by activating two of the fatal flaws of SPC (*cf. The Curse of the False Positive, All Things to Some People* in chapter 7). Indeed, this common scenario makes clear a central point of this entire book that much of the SPC is at best a waste of energy. If we organize the majority of our work time around applying the *Critical Elements in the Management of Suicidal Behavior* (Alternative #7 in chapter 10) and pretty much ignored SPC, our clinical practice with suicidality is clinico-legally sound.

The Allure of the Each Way Bet

Level three of the iceberg is the point where a clinician's reasons for using SPC can become less obvious—below the waterline. One of the dominant themes from the SPC study is that SPC is seen by some clinicians as a diligently executed decision, potentially producing multiple advantages (*the three faces SPC*—clinico-legal, therapeutic, diagnostic advantage—leading to the notion of SPC as *All Things to Some People*).

In 2006 the foundations of this point became patently clear for me when I was supervising a Bhutanese intern counselor. Sonam Tsung is a leader in his community, a schoolteacher by profession, and was studying counseling in Australia. Close to the end of his placement and our time together, I suggested we have lunch at a nearby bar.

It was the first Tuesday in November, a landmark day for any Australian. We had arrived at the bar ten minutes before the racing of the most watched thoroughbred horse race in the southern hemisphere—the Melbourne Cup. Prior to the race, I explained the fundamentals of local betting: how some people will put money 'on the nose' (a win only) every time, whilst others will try to improve their chances of winning by placing a single bet each way (a win and a place). Depending on how much *risk* you're willing to take, this effectively places two bets on the same horse: half your stake on the win, half on the place. Generally, I explained, the bigger the starting price—increased risk for losing—the stronger the case for betting each way.

Later, in a respectful Buddhist tone, he asked, "Do many Australians bet on horses to come second or third?" Simply, without being immersed in a culture of risk calculation and insurance, he'd failed to fully appreciate the notion of *the each way bet*.

Sonam returned to Bhutan to train others in the fundamentals of solution-focused counseling. His farewell *gift* to me, I now understand, was a new appreciation of just how much some societies have pinned their future on the allocation of enormous resources on relentless attempts to tame and control *risk*.

Clearly, fear and threat are powerful motivating emotions.

In the fearful presence of uncertainty, for example, we religiously take out insurance to protect our treasured belongings because of what *might* happen. Many people also appear to distrust and dislike individuals or groups they believe *might* turn against them, often giving these unrealized fears a foothold in reality. It seems that much of society worries about the future, relentlessly endeavoring to head off risk by searching for the tools they perceive will provide a level of control and self-protection. This anxiety about risk is one of the key things keeping individuals and today's institutions balanced upon a knife edge.

What does all this talk about general uncertainty, future-anxiety, insurance and gambling have to do with practitioners' use of SPC today?

Absolutely everything!

As the case of betting on a horse race shows, placing a bet on two different outcomes is an attempt to minimize the risk of losing and maximize the probability of winning. The same kind of risk calculation, I now understand, occurs in the deployment of SPC: on the one hand, clinicians use it in the sincere hope of a positive outcome (i.e., therapeutic advantage, diagnostic clarification), but also to minimize the losses should a negative outcome occur instead (i.e., clinico-legal protection).

The first *bet* is largely a perceived *values-based* expression of a clinician's care and concern for the patient (recall from the Introduction *Miller's Paradox-The 3Cs*), which I describe in chapter 7. The second *bet* is an expression of the clinician's anxiety in the face of the risk of losing, which makes SPC deployment motivated (in part) by self-protection. As such, the use of SPC to place an each way bet demonstrates its fundamental duality, a misguided duality whose problematic nature you will witness in coming chapters over and over in examples where the reasons for using SPC are precisely the reasons why it manufactures hazards.

Despite its vital importance (or, rather, because of its perceived vital importance), when you look over the book's key findings, you'll understand two things: perceived clinico-legal protection is implicated in many of the book's key findings. Yet defensive or even pre-emptive practices are just one of three significant areas for advocating an end to the use of SPC. Critically, though, such self-protective tactics directly oppose the fundamental reasons why so many of us entered the healing professions. Rather than reinforcing or reawakening the passion for practice, such defensive and pre-emptive practices merely erode the empathy and compassion we offer our patients. Without doubt, we are practicing the art of healing in a remarkably challenging moment—clinico-legally and sociologically—in history.

2

Historical Review

We should not look back unless it is to derive useful lessons from past errors, and for the purpose of profiting by dearly bought experience.
—George Washington

KEY POINTS

- SPC has been documented in the psychiatric literature since the mid-twentieth century.
- Research is yet to provide evidence for the validity or effectiveness of SPC.
- The 'no-suicide decision' portrayed in Transactional Analysis is theoretically and clinically different from the contemporary SPC procedures.

INTRODUCTION

The use of SPC has moved away from the therapeutic setting originally associated with no suicide decisions described in Transactional Analysis, essentially reducing the procedure from being an integral part of an extended therapeutic process to operating in part within brief crisis relationships. The combined emergence of brief therapies, volunteer suicide crisis centers, significant social change with SPC contemporaneously having failed to establish a standard definition and a theoretical or conceptual model led to the procedure being widely used and often adapted without evidence of effectiveness. SPC has taken on an array of hybrid forms around the world. Indeed, even a cursory survey of the place of SPC in contemporary practice would conclude with the observer asking, "How has SPC taken on a life of its own?" In this chapter the reasons for this situation will be explained.

INITIAL ENGLISH REPORTS

The idea of contracting for living (or similar) with suicidal patients is likely found nowhere in early-twentieth-century scholarship. One of the earliest reports on communicating clinically with suicidal patients date back to the 1950s. It was then that the founding fathers of modern-day suicidology, Edwin Shneidman, PhD, and Norman Farberow, MD, first discussed in some detail the process of 'negotiating with suicidal patients' (Shneidman & Farberow, 1957). However, their clear and rigorous account contained no recommendation to elicit anything resembling SPC.

In the following decade, U.S. psychiatrist J. R. Ewart, MD, referred to a notion somewhat resembling SPC (Ewart, 1967, pp. 1179–1187). In the *Comprehensive Textbook of Psychiatry*, Ewart cautioned clinicians against procuring a 'patient promise' not to suicide, recommending instead to acknowledge a patient's destructive thoughts and to fully explore their origins. He argued that the primary exploration phase of such consultations would be threatened if a premature promise not to commit suicide was extracted (ibid., p. 1183). By short-circuiting the patient's opportunity to ventilate and express psychological pain, Ewart understood that the securing of a no suicide promise can adversely affect the nature and quality of the therapeutic relationship.

Between the late 1960s and early 1970s, Transactional Analysis (TA) took hold in clinical practice, placing a significant emphasis given to patient contracting. At the time, TA appears to have had a theoretical blind spot regarding endings (death) (Mothersole, 1996), and no mention of a SPC type was documented in the early writing of its founder, Eric Berne. By the mid to late 1970s, however, the founders of Redecision Therapy (RT), an offshoot of Berne's TA, wrote extensively about a modality they titled a no suicide decision (Drye, Goulding & Goulding, 1973; Goulding & Goulding, 1978; Goulding & Goulding, 1979). When considering the place of SPC in clinical practice today, these writings are significant, and as such, RT will be discussed in detail later in the chapter.

By the 1980s and early 1990s, psychiatry, psychology and nursing had all contributed in different ways to the historical development of SPC. Substantial attention from nursing included widespread commentary and support for the no suicide decision and other hybrid forms of SPC developed within the profession (Twiname, 1981; Hatton, Valente & Rink, 1984; MacEnany & Teschler, 1985; Loomis, 1985; Neville & Barnes, 1985; Assey, 1985; Bradley & Shawler, 1993; Duffy, 1993; Badger, 1995). Psychiatry and psychology's contribution during this period can be gauged in various publications that questioned the clinico-legal and therapeutic efficacy of SPC (Hipple & Cimbolic, 1979; Stone, 1980; Maltsberger, 1988; Jacobs, 1989; Hillard, 1990; Bongar, 1991; Simon, 1991; Jacobs, 1992a, b; Busch, Clark, Fawcett & Kravitz, 1993; Mahrer, 1993; Stanford, Goetz & Bloom, 1994). This approach to questioning the place of SPC was not evident in any other professional discipline until the beginning of the twenty-first century.

THEORETICAL INFLUENCES PERPETUATING USE OF SPC

There are a number of clinical approaches that maintained and extended SPC's use in health and social care settings.

Crisis Theory and Casework

During the mid-twentieth century, brief treatments involving patient contracting were extensively explored: goal-oriented practice approaches (Rapoport, 1970; Hollis, 1972; Butcher and Maudal, 1976); contracting as the endpoint of a process; gaining an assurance from the client to continue contact; and establishing a working relationship and engaging the client in treatment (Maluccio and Marlow, 1974, pp. 32–34) were all associated with time-limited brief treatments using clinician-client contracts (Hollis, 1970, p. 45). Such pre-existing terminology likely facilitated the notion of contracting for living.

Transactional Analysis

Mid-twentieth century U.S. West Coast humanistic theorists such as Eric Berne (TA) and Mary and Robert Goulding (Redecision Therapy) emerged out of dissatisfaction with the psychoanalytic tradition and created their own therapeutic modalities (Mothersole, 1996, p. 155). Transactional Analysis authors emphasized the importance of patient contracting and positioned this clinical maneuver as one of the therapy's basic treatment principles (Mothersole, 1996). By the 1980s Transactional Analysis as a therapeutic approach had become well established in the mental health field (Stewart & Joines, 1987).

Gudrun Stummer (2002, pp. 121–123) describes three different types of TA patient contracting, each with its own function:

- Treatment contracts—either an explicit or implicit contract to ascertain and focus the course of treatment;
- Process contracts—an implicit contract used to seek a patient's permission to proceed with treatment; also aiding attunement to the patient; and,
- Behavioral contracts—an explicit contract to control or extinguish a symptom.

Redecision Therapy

In the *American Journal of Psychiatry* (Drye, Goulding & Goulding, 1973), the authors of the article titled "No Suicide Decisions: Patient Monitoring of Suicidal Risk" opened with the following promise:

> In this paper we describe a method to be used by anyone evaluating a patient as a suicidal risk; the method enables the evaluator to make the following judgements: Is suicide a risk at all for this patient? If it is a risk, to what degree and for how long can the patient be trusted not to kill himself? (p. 171)

Their method, Redecision Therapy (RT), is an early example of a brief, focused psychotherapy that relies on the patient's desire to change, a desire which is harnessed and structured into a *redecision.* In essence, a suicide redecision is a TA therapeutic contract made by the patient and witnessed by the therapist. Redecision Therapy focuses on identifying and undoing the *injunctions* perpetuating dysfunctional adult behavior. Such injunctions are viewed as responses to early childhood messages that, internalized by the child, may result in chronic life problems (McNeel, 1999, p. 104). The theory also asserts that underlying self-destructive behaviors are *lethal injunctions* which the patient decided to believe as a child when they felt unwanted, unloved, and a hindrance or an obstacle to the parent (Goulding & Goulding, 1979, p. 35).

In a therapeutic setting, the therapist using RT undertakes a process of 'tracking back' to where early destructive decisions were made. As a result, the patient experiences the early scene, including the accompanying feeling state, and 'completes' it by expressing what was left unexpressed by the child. With the support of their adult experience and knowledge, the patient then makes a redecision and expresses this new decision in the imagined original scene, reinforcing the redecision by stating it to the therapist (or encounter group members), who in turn occasionally restate (i.e., randomly reinforce) the redecision to the patient (Goulding & Goulding, 1979, pp. 172–173).

Using RT to reduce suicidality, a therapist will guide the patient to the point of the early decision (the lethal injunction). The patient is then asked to recite their redecision—a *no suicide decision*—by saying, without qualification, the following script: "No matter what, I will not kill myself, accidentally or on purpose, at any time" (ibid., p. 173).

Following this pronouncement, the patient reports on their inner responses to the statement. Throughout the process the therapist assesses for incongruence, listening for *objections* (i.e., the patient's refusal or inability to make the scripted statement), and *qualifications* (the patient's changing the wording to include 'escape clauses', such as 'I'll try not to', 'unless I get drunk', etc.). Qualifications are deemed to allow the patient to retain their suicidal fantasies and avoid having to relinquish suicide as an available form of problem solving (ibid., p. 172). The research data on the efficacy of a no suicide decision as a prevention modality is presented later in this chapter.

PROBLEM-SOLVING BRIEF THERAPY AND BEHAVIORAL THERAPY

Problem-Solving Brief Therapy

As a casework process, 1970s problem-solving therapy placed contracts at the center of the casework transaction. The aims of patient contracting here were to increase client self-determination by not treating the client as merely a recipient of social aid (Rapoport, 1970) and, through establishing mutually agreed-upon actions, to support the client to be an active participant rather than a passive recipient of treatment (Perlman, 1970, pp. 134–136).

Behavioral Therapy

Early reports devoted solely to SPC as a means of behavior modification are sparse (O'Farrell, Goodenough and Cutter, 1981; Liberman & Eckman,

1981). Learning theory was for a time the dominant paradigm for capturing the primary dimensions of suicidal behavior (Cautlea, 1973), learning being central to shaping and modifying behavior. Behavioral approaches to suicide intervention increasingly involved mutually contracted treatment goals with particular emphasis given to contingencies (i.e., pre-defined safety strategies) to increase the client's level of self-control.

Learning theory, with its focus on operant conditioning, emphasized that behavior is a function of environmental precursors, and it stressed that people learn best when they are aware of the rules governing the consequences of their actions. Practically speaking, this led to tailoring treatment to specific problems for specific people (Thomas, 1970). The contingency contract used incentives (i.e., reinforcement) for achieving treatment goals (Janz & Hartman, 1988, p. 169); for example, positive reinforcement in the form of feedback from the clinician regarding achieved goals. Conversely, a contingency contract can comprise negative or aversive consequences in the form of negative or neutral feedback from the clinician. For example, a patient's awareness of not meeting the goals contained in a contingency contract effectively represents a 'breach of contract'. Consequently, both modes of reinforcement are aimed at decreasing or positively shaping certain behaviors (ibid., p. 165).

SOCIETAL INFLUENCES PERPETUATING USE OF SPC

It is plausible that several social factors generated an increasing interest in and use of SPC procedures.

Crisis Centers

The scientific literature makes clear that community crisis centers provided fertile soil for the widespread adaptation and deployment of SPC. In the decade preceding the 1973 *American Journal of Psychiatry* report on the no suicide decision, Crisis Theory emerged as a brief treatment modality that emphasized *contracting* with individuals (Rapoport, 1970). During the same decade, the United States witnessed the rise of the 'Free Clinic' movement (Smith, 1974). The movement fostered community crisis-focused clinics, staffed by professionals and para-professionals catering to at-risk, marginalized populations—significantly ex-servicepersons (Butcher & Maudal, 1976). In the late 1950s, Norman Farberow and Edwin Shneidman established the first community suicide crisis center in the United States (Goldney, 1998).

These centers multiplied rapidly, and in 1974 (just one year after the publication of the *American Journal of Psychiatry* article), a review of twelve suicide prevention centers in the United States reported volunteers had engaged 20 percent of callers in a version of SPC (MacGee, 1974), with training and supervision routinely provided by psychiatrists and registered mental health nurses (Hirsch, 1981, p. 407). At the largest of these centers, the Los Angeles Suicide Prevention Center, volunteers used an approach termed *relationship maintenance* (Weiss, 2001), where a volunteer would call a person at least once a week to 'befriend' them—a fertile context for a form of SPC to be instigated, reviewed and adapted.

The Rise of Consumerism

There were significant changes in public attitudes to mental health in the last three decades of the twentieth century. One such change was the re-emergence of the mental health consumer movement during the 1970s (McLean, 1995). Within an increasingly consumer-focused economic environment, a logic emerged where *patients* were seen as *consumers* who deserved/demanded a greater role in treatment decision-making.

In response to this shift in the client-clinician relationship, social work practically portrayed client contracting as one institutional apparatus. Treatment contracting with clients, for example, was seen as embodying the principle of client involvement in the clinical practice of case management, thereby counterbalancing the inherent power differential between client and worker (Corden & Preston-Shoot, 1987a, b). Corden and Preston-Shoot (1988) stated that treatment contracts embodied the principle of client involvement in the practice of casework (pp. 536–539). Maluccio and Marlow (1974) detailed both the benefits and limitations of treatment contracts with regards to social work practice, including the then burgeoning notion of the client as consumer and offering the concept of "maximum feasible participation" as an explicit element within the practice of treatment contracting with clients (ibid., p. 28).

These change-fuelled decades, briefly chronicled here, were fertile ground for the search for an apparatus with the potential to transform the unpredictable into the predictable. Many forms of patient contracting as well as SPC were offered as precisely this kind of apparatus, notwithstanding the inherent unpredictability of suicide.

TWENTIETH-CENTURY SPC RESEARCH

All but one of the twentieth-century SPC studies are North American–based, and none meet RCT requirements. The failure to meet RCT standards is in part due to the low base rate of suicide, the already mentioned ethical problem of assigning suicidal folk to controls, and the sheer impossibility of recruiting enough participants to gain statistical power.

No Suicide Decisions

The earliest of these studies was conducted by Drye, Goulding & Goulding (1973). The study followed up on thirty-one therapists postattendance at a no suicide decision training workshop conducted by the authors. The completed questionnaires reported on 609 patients placed on a no suicide decision, with 266 of these assessed as severe suicide risk. No completed suicides were recorded for those having entered into a no suicide decision, with twenty completed or serious suicide attempts by patients where they had not entered into a no suicide decision.

However, the study was subject to significant methodological flaws, including not accounting for the low base rate for completed suicide, providing insufficient patient or clinician details and thus preventing replication of the study, and inadequate statistical analysis methods used to support claims of technique efficacy (Rudd, Mandrusiak & Joiner, 2006, p. 244; Stanford, Goetz & Bloom, 1994).

Case File Reviews and Nursing Interventions

Jones and O'Brien (1990) surveyed the attitudes of thirty-nine youth patients towards specific nursing interventions. They found that patient contracting (not limited to contracting for the reduction of suicidal behavior) was a routine intervention within this child and adolescent inpatient setting. In a later pre- and postretrospective study of 360 hospitalized children and adolescents, Jones, O'Brien and McMahon (1993) found 16 percent were involved in some sort of disruptive or risk-related behavior. Following the implementation of a contracting system to reduce such occurrences, of a total of 570 children and adolescents treated, only 1.4 percent of the participants were involved in a future incident, suggesting the participants found SPC to be beneficial. However, the lack of a randomized allocation of participants and control groups, along with its retrospective design, meant that the research was unable to account for incorrect medical file entries, preventing any correlations being made between SPC-specific procedures and their therapeutic efficacy.

In a descriptive analysis of fourteen medical case files of adult inpatients who completed suicide, Busch, Clark, Fawcett & Kravitz (1993) reported that a form of no suicide agreement was in place with 50 percent of these cases prior to death. Green and Grindel (1996), surveying a random sample of staff (n = 105) at North American adult inpatient psychiatric units, reported a high prevalence (75 percent) of SPC use in these settings. Egan (1997), undertaking a concept analysis to extend and clarify the criteria of SPC within the North American mental health nursing field, concluded that as a dispersal method, SPC was widespread.

Psychologists, Psychiatrists and College Students

A questionnaire survey of a randomly selected group of 252 American psychologists (Mahrer, 1993) (response rate 56 percent) found 69 percent of participants had used no suicide contracts/agreements. Two hypotheses were tested. Firstly, it was found that these psychologists enacted a no suicide contract/agreement 'automatically and indiscriminately' with patients rather than following an individual evaluation for the appropriateness of such a procedure. Secondly, the data supported the hypothesis that the use of a no suicide contract/agreement was as much for clinician-oriented reasons as for patient evaluation and to support a patient's therapeutic goals.

Davidson, Wagner & Range (1995) surveyed forty-six psychologists (response rate of 35 percent) and reported that participants felt optimistic that no suicide agreements communicated an expression of care and concern with adult patients and slightly less optimistic about this function with younger patients. Miller, Jacobs and Gutheil (1998) studied a group of 112 psychiatrists and psychologists attending a Harvard University training event. They found that 61 percent and 83 percent, respectively, employed a suicide prevention contract at least half of the time with suicidal patients. In addition, 75 percent of these clinicians indicated that the use of SPC was recommended in their workplace. However, fifty-four (61 percent) of psychiatrists and seventeen (71 percent) of the psychologists surveyed reported that they had not received formal training in the use of SPC.

Decant and Range (1997) reported on 145 university students' perceptions of SPC. All participants were given a description of a no suicide contract and were asked to comment. Survey participants reported they would be 'highly likely' to sign a no suicide contract because it indicated the clinician cared for a patient, and that SPC would strengthen the therapeutic relationship by giving both parties a sense of control. Moreover, participants who had previously been in some form of psychotherapy (n = 29; 20 percent) were significantly more likely to believe SPC would reduce a therapist's legal liability. The study failed to ask if participants had ever been suicidal. Another limitation included the research being restricted to a student population, diminishing the generalizability of results.

Crisis Centers

MacGee (1974) conducted a review of twelve suicide prevention centers in the United States and reported that 20 percent of callers had been engaged in a suicide prevention contract by center volunteers. Mishara and Daigle's (1997) study of different telephone intervention styles by volunteers based at Canadian crisis telephone centers revealed widespread use of SPC in these settings. The researchers observed 617 calls made by 110 volunteers trained in SPC across two sites, with 68 percent of volunteers able to make a no suicide contract with callers.

Gender

In re-analyzing Mahrer's (1993) data, Quarneri (1997) posed the idea that gender socialization provided an explanation for the findings of gender differences in clinicians' use of no suicide contracts/agreements. Mahrer's findings had indicated females were more prone to an individual evaluation for the appropriateness of SPC than their male colleagues (Mahrer, 1993, pp. 10–12). Quarneri referred to self-in-relation theory, social learning theory, cognitive developmental theory and behavior genetics in her assessment of gender as a factor influencing females' approach to SPC.

CONCLUSION

Although clinicians have used SPC for at least half a century, few appear to understand its origins or appreciate its weak theoretical underpinnings. This has led to a situation where most contemporary SPC modalities have become unhitched from their original foundations and are vulnerable to the influence of theoretical fashions, not to mention shifting social tides.

3

Definitions

Myths about suicide abound in the therapeutic setting. They often inhibit the ability of clinicians (and families) to assess the severity and magnitude of a patient's suicide risk. —Thomas Joiner, 2011

KEY POINTS

- There are a plethora of terms attempting to capture SPC's various uses.
- There are no agreed-upon definitions of or classification system for SPC procedures.

INTRODUCTION

For well over four decades now the lack of nomenclature for and classification of SPC has represented a significant impediment to its clinical understanding and application. In formulating a case against SPC, Rudd, Mandrusiak & Joiner (2006, p. 245) stated that the present limitations of SPC rest with the lack of standard definition(s) and a theoretical or conceptual model that clearly articulates the procedure(s). Such a failing is not unfamiliar to the field with Maris (2002) and others similarly bemoaning the lack of consistent understanding of terms in the wider field of suicidology (O'Carroll, Berman, Maris, Moscicki, Tanney & Silverman, 1996; Goldney, 2010).

A nomenclature, when it exists, facilitates communication, enabling proponents to better formulate and document their rationale for use of a procedure. The lack of nomenclature in SPC has prevented the development of an operational definition as well a valid and ratified method for measuring the efficacy of its use in clinical practice.

TWENTIETH-CENTURY NOMENCLATURE

Despite the fact or perhaps because there has been no clearly agreed and defining categorizing system and associated language for SPC, a plethora of terms for its various forms has evolved over time. Not surprisingly, in the 1970s and 1980s SPC was understood as a contingency contract. Emerging from the behavior modification tradition, it was used to facilitate learning and to change behavior (Bartlett, 2006, p. 12). Contemporaneously, some described SPC as a clinician's attempt to develop a form of specialized treatment contract (Miller, Jacobs & Gutheil, 1998, p. 79). In an attempt to understand the rationale for its use (Miller et al., 1998, pp. 82–83; Miller, 1999), SPC's capacity as a therapeutic contract involving two rational people operating under a rubric of informed consent was questioned. That negotiation and review of the agreement's content took place within a flexible professional relationship that emphasized patient choice, reciprocal responsibilities and, ultimately, a patient's decision to cease treatment was critically analysed.

As the nursing profession began to integrate SPC into practice, differences in the definition and theoretical foundations of the procedure also developed in the nursing literature (Bartlett, 2006, pp. 12–13). Twiname (1981), whilst retaining the scripted aspect of Drye et al.'s no suicide decision, renamed the procedure a no suicide contract. She defined the no suicide contract as a mechanism for assessing lethality (pp. 11–12). It is at this juncture that no suicide decisions were beginning to be reinterpreted, rather than simply revised. Specifically, the no suicide decision moved from being a decision a patient made themselves in the presence of a clinician within the confines of a therapeutic milieu to a 'contract' made *for* a clinician.

By the 1980s and 1990s, SPC was an integral part of nursing practice (Egan 1997). Nursing scholars presented different expanded definitions and understandings of the procedure. Assey (1985) defined what was titled a suicide prevention contract as a bilateral commitment and contribution toward the avoidance of the client's self-destruction (p. 99). Egan (1997) offered the term 'contracting for safety'; Potter and Dawson (2001) and others later adopted terms including 'no suicide agreements', 'no suicide contracts', 'safety agreements', and 'no self-harm contracts' (Miller, Jacobs & Gutheil, 1998).

Many of the synonyms for SPC signify different yet interconnected concepts. Some refer specifically to the semantics of the therapeutic relationship and others to clinical assessment and lethality. Inevitably, some forms have assumed a pseudo-legal terminology—'contract and agreement' (Miller, 1999, pp. 472–473). For the clinician, what is important is the validity and efficacy of SPC. Unfortunately, some of the terms for SPC have surreptitiously elevated the procedure to one possessing practice validity. Meanwhile its theoretical and methodological vaguenesses have remained intact (Clark and Kerkhof, 1997, p. 2).

A PRAGMATIC APPROACH TO DEFINING CONTEMPORARY SPC

In describing the difficulty of establishing an agreed-upon nomenclature and classification of suicidal behavior, Goldney (2010) advocated for an observational or ethological approach to categorization. Such an approach appears clinically advantageous to better understanding the place of SPC in contemporary practice by way of documenting what actually occurs in clinical settings.

Characteristics of Contemporary SPC Procedures

The essence of contemporary SPC is to elicit through conversation an agreement, or even a signed contract, not to commit suicide on the part of the suicidal person, at least for a specified time period. Evidence of the person's commitment not to suicide consists of adherence to particular strategies aimed at averting or responding to crises. Based on findings from the SPC study (detailed in chapter 5), no suicide agreements and no suicide contracts are distinct procedures. Specifically, there are two clinical categories:

- No suicide agreements (NSAg) are verbal agreements characterized by an extended process of negotiation whereby a patient agrees to refrain from suicidal behavior for a specified time period. Safety strategies are usually established and agreed upon that each party will undertake in the event of a suicidal crisis.
- No suicide contracts (NSC) are written documents usually co-signed and a copy retained by both the patient and the clinician stating that the patient has agreed to refrain from suicidal behavior, often for a nominated time period. Safety strategies are also included.

An example may be helpful:

Example of a no suicide contract

I, ... (insert patient's name), promise I will not attempt to kill myself or try to harm myself in any way. If I am feeling like I want to commit suicide; to harm or injure myself in any way, or that I want to die for the time period from .... to ...., I will ....
.... (insert agreed-upon coping strategies) and immediately contact .... (insert name of crisis contact) on .... (insert telephone number of crisis contact); or .... on ....; or go to the nearest emergency department for help. If .... (insert patient's name) telephones during the agreed hours .... (insert agreed hours), I, ... (insert clinician's name), will do everything possible to take their call. This no suicide contract will be reviewed on the .... (insert review date).

Signature of patient: .... Signature of clinician: ....
Date: ....

No Suicide Assurances (NSAs)

One of the aims of this book is to redefine how clinicians think about and talk about SPC procedures. This redefinition is crucial to discussing and understanding the topic. Currently the category of SPC is seen as a combination of three procedures: NSAs, NSAg, and NSC. This is not the case, because NSAs (largely a strightforword question-and-answer subjective risk assessment process) are qualitatively different. Instead, to discuss the subject wisely and accurately, only two procedures should be considered as SPC procedures. Henceforth in this book, all references to SPC procedures will refer specifically to NSAg and NSC, but not NSAs. The other key aim of this book is to make a case against NSAg/NSC.

In chapter 8, I present a chapter specifically on NSAs. Here, the albeit limited data on NSAs, showing how and why they carry less risk than NSAg/NSC and how and when they can be potentially helpful, is presented. The chapter will explain how and why NSAs are not subject to some of the same paradoxes, drawbacks, and contraindications evident with NSAg and NSC detailed in chapter 7.

Is an SPC Procedure a Crisis Plan Response (CPR)?

Every mental health practice setting will usually have a slightly different method for documenting treatment plans and CPRs. Some may be purely paper-based, while others may be a combination of pro-forma medical file forms with a summarized duplicate entered into a patient database accessible to other clinicians. These differences are likely due not only to geographical and cultural differences and managed care protocols, but also to the dilemma that a clear and universal nomenclature remains elusive in the evaluation and management of suicidal behavior.

I am not going to belabor the issue and detail all the types of CPR templates possible. However, due to the infinite possibilities of types, one important point is critical: a CPR is *not* an SPC procedure (see table 3.1 below). A CPR contains elements similar to contemporary NSCs and NSAgs (i.e., suggestions of contingencies for a patient to follow in times of elevated risk; what a clinician should do at these times, and in some versions, a review date to assess the plan's relevance, etc.). The point of differentiation is that CPRs *do not* explicitly request, either verbally or in writing, a patient to agree not to engage in suicidal behavior for a specified time period, as do NSC and NSAg.

UNFORESEEN RESEARCH FINDING

Analysis of the SPC study data, detailed later in the book, made possible the development of a new vocabulary of SPC, which is presented in chapter 6. It comprises an anatomy of SPC, a taxonomy of SPC, and through its emerging nomenclature, a common language that provides the foundation for an understanding of this clinical practice that is both pragmatic and has clinical and research application.

Table 3.1. Characteristics of CPR & SPC procedures

	Written or verbal?	Contingencies measures included?	Time period not to attempt suicide noted?	Review period stated?
NSAg	Verbal	Usually	Always	Usually
NSC	Written	Usually	Always	Usually
CPR	Usually written	Always	No	Variable

4

Current Causes of Concern

The hallways of coroner's offices are littered with broken no suicide contracts. (attributed to U.S. psychiatrist Robert I. Simon, MD)

KEY POINTS

- There are few clinical case reports and no research findings conclusively confirming the capacity of SPC to cause harm.
- As a clinical phenomenon, SPC presents as an admixture of competing clinician demands for therapeutic, diagnostic and clinic-legal advantage.
- Psychiatric and psychological associations caution against the use of SPC.

INTRODUCTION

The potential problems with SPC were first mentioned in the psychiatric literature by Ewart (1967), and then the lay largely invisible until Simon (1999) expressed the concern that over-reliance on SPC may come at the expense of a thorough psychiatric evaluation and ongoing suicide risk assessment process. For example, inexperienced clinicians may view a patient promise, combined with apparently congruent body language, as some form of guarantee of safety or diagnostic certification (Jacobs, 1992, p. 164).

Since then, several peak professional bodies have cautioned clinicians about the use of SPC, stating that SPC remains untested and its use may be detrimental (Australian Psychological Society, 1999; American Psychiatric Association, 2003; Australian and New Zealand College of Psychiatry, 2004). More recently, criticism of SPC has been directed at the current state that no standard formulations of SPC procedures have been established, nor an adequate theoretical or conceptual model articulated for its procedures and their implementation (Rudd, Mandrusiak & Joiner, 2006). Despite this, and the equivocal nature of the evidence, they continue to be in widespread use (Edwards & Harries, 2007; Lewis, 2007).

REPORTED ADVERSE OUTCOMES—PEER-REVIEWED AND POPULAR PRESS

Peer-reviewed journals are hardly littered with detailed case reports recounting the potentially adverse influence of SPC on clinical outcomes (Stanford, Goetz & Bloom, 1994; Potter, Vitale-Nolen & Dawson, 2005). We found just one:

Case 1: In their morbidity and mortality case review, Edward J. Stanford, MD, and colleagues from the Oregon Health Sciences University reported the case of a nineteen-year-old male brought by police to an emergency department for psychiatric review. It was a complex case: the medical evaluator noted alcohol intoxication, a history of poly-substance abuse, a recent self-inflicted injury, past suicide attempts, past psychiatric hospitalizations for suicidal ideation and depression. The university medical evaluator employed SPC; the patient agreed to attend a detoxification center and return to the hospital if unable to keep to the 'contract'. Neither an evaluation of the patient's competency, nor the evaluator's risk-benefit rationale for not hospitalizing the patient was noted.

Subsequent questions: Such summaries highlight several of the current concerns with SPC. Why was an apparently moderately to severely suicidal patient offered an intervention without evidence of effectiveness? Did this nineteen-year-old understand the contract as a show of care and concern, or as a device used to deny him due care? How did the medical evaluator determine the youth's positive regard for contracting? And did the medical evaluator perceive some clinico-legal advantage in contracting, leading to a decision to use SPC whilst seemingly contraindicated?

In comparison to journal reports, more common are popular press reports where SPC had been present in several completed and one serious suicide attempt. Between March 2010 and April 2011 there were four separate stories, one in Shenzen, China, two in the United States, and another in Sydney, Australia. Each of these cases can be read as a kind of moral tale about the ill-advised use of SPC, or at least an opportunity to offer critical questioning.

Case 2: You may remember reading that the Chinese IT company Foxconn—maker of Apple, Hewlett Packard and Dell hardware, and employer of some one-hundred-thousand-plus workers—experienced a cluster of completed suicides (Mick, 2010). To their credit, Foxconn constructed net-like devices around their building to catch people should they jump from the factory roof. As part of their response, Foxconn's management also devised and requested all employees to sign a no suicide contract. Later, under the media spotlight, and with Steve Jobs (founder of Apple Computers) adding his voice to the situation, Foxconn revoked the signing of a written contract.

Subsequent questions: Was Foxconn's proposed written pledge designed to appeal to the workers' sense of responsibility to the company, and thereby lower the future risk for suicides? Was the tactic of using a written contract mostly a naïve attempt to limit liability or future claims to compensation? Was Foxconn management merely struggling under stressful circumstances and doing what they felt or were advised was right?

Case 3: An eight-year-old American boy was a victim of bullying at school (O'Hare, 2010). He had indicated to school staff that he'd had enough and was having thoughts of death. Staff, no doubt with the best of intentions, asked the young boy to promise not to hurt himself. Shortly after he had made the no suicide promise, he leapt from the school roof.

Subsequent questions: Does such reliance upon SPC (to whatever degree) inhibit taking other preventative steps such as contacting parents, keeping the student under closer supervision, or taking the student to the emergency medical center? Or is seeking a no suicide promise simply an attempt to express care and concern to the student?

Case 4: In 2009, a cyberbullied thirteen-year-old Florida school student hanged herself in her Wimauma bedroom (Ackerman & Scullin, 2010). Some days after her death, the parents found a written no harm contract she had made with the attending school social worker. Allegedly neither parent was informed of the girl's suicide risk or of the deployed contract. Apparently the social worker had not involved mental health services and appears to have relied largely upon the potency of the no suicide contract.

Subsequent questions: Is the use of NSC with students largely endorsed by school officials due to their similarities with more familiar behavior contracts?

Case 5: Finally, there is the case of a popular Australian news presenter who, while suffering from a major depressive illness, jumped from cliffs at Sydney harbour in spite of being under SPC with her psychiatrist (Cummings, 2010).

Subsequent questions: Is placing patients under a no suicide agreement for the patient's benefit secondary to the clinician's fear of possible litigation? Do clinicians use this type of SPC with every suicidal patient to quickly assess the perceived seriousness of their situation, perceiving a rejection of SPC to indicate more severe or imminent risk? Does routine use of SPC produce an over-reliance on the procedure, and does this in turn negatively affect the clinician's judgement regarding other prevention measures such as hospitalization, increasing the patient's level of supervision, and so forth?

WHY SPC ARE USED

At the individual clinician level, most of the motivations for using SPC fall into three categories, three prevailing 'reasons for use' (Stanford, Goetz & Bloom, 1994; Page & King, 2008; Edwards & Sachmann, 2010):

- Clinico-legal protection—SPC used as a perceived means of increasing a clinician's clinico-legal protection in the event of an adverse clinical outcome
- Diagnostic clarification—SPC used to gain diagnostic clarification of the risk of suicide, and
- Therapeutic advantage—SPC used to bring about a decrease in a patient's level of suicide risk

For the remainder of this chapter I would like to touch upon these categories of potential hazard and their related ethical issues. In later chapters I will discuss the three prevailing 'reasons for use' in greater detail and examine the paradoxical nature of SPC in some depth.

HAZARDS OF SPC POTENTIALLY COMPROMISING TREATMENT

Clinico-Legal Problems with SPC

Emeritus U.S. professor of psychiatry Robert I. Simon (Simon, 1999; Simon, 2003; Simon & Hales, 2006) and others, while arguing against SPC affording any legal protection, describe some of the reasons why it has taken on an aura of quasi-legal status in medical and allied health settings. Specifically, four factors appear to have shaped clinician's perceptions of the apparent clinico-legal benefit of utilizing SPC in case of adverse outcomes:

- The untested legal status of SPC (Simon & Hales, 2006, p. 545).
- The tradition amongst supervising clinicians to request that subordinates secure written NSC or document a patient's verbal agreement not to engage in self-destructive behaviors (Simon, 2003, p. 69).
- The pseudo-legal terminology used—'contract and agreement' (Miller, 1999, pp. 472–473).
- The infrequent nature of suicide litigation claims against clinicians—predominantly health care services are the litigant, rather than a named clinician (Cantor & McDermott, 1994, pp. 431–432).

Key clinico-legal cause for concern: That SPC is used for presumed clinician self-protection despite it being contraindicated, thereby effectively *increasing* a patient's risk status. (Refer to page 121 where a full list of primary and secondary contraindications for SPC is provided.)

Therapeutic Problems with SPC

An emerging body of literature suggests that SPC likely has a number of therapeutically disadvantageous effects. The majority of these reports are expert opinion, with three reports based upon findings from direct patient report.

SPC and Psychopathology

Davis, Williams & Hays (2002) surveyed 135 patients admitted to an inpatient setting. Prior to discharge, patients completed a battery of surveys and test scales, including signing a no suicide contract. Results indicated that patients with a history of multiple suicide attempts, on average, scored the therapeutic dimensions of SPC lower than did patients without such a history. This finding is analogous with previous research indicating that patients with greater levels of psychopathology are more likely to view themselves as poorer problem solvers (Linehan, Goodstein, Nielsen & Chiles, 1983; Rudd, Joiner & Rajab, 1996; Scott, House, Yates & Harrington, 1997).

SPC and Therapeutic Alliance

There is no doubt in the literature regarding the importance of a therapeutic alliance as a prerequisite for the use of SPC (Rudd, 1996; Range, Campbell, Kovac, Marion-Jones, Aldridge, Kogos & Crump, 2002; Simon & Hales, 2006; Reid, 2005). The literature also makes clear the use of SPC in settings where such alliances are less assured. For example, in the emergency department and community crisis settings where a therapeutic relationship may not develop or may be attenuated, SPC has little or no utility (Hillard, 1990; Reid, 2005, pp. 54–57).

Use of SPC in Inpatient Settings

Contemporary health care environments, with their over-reliance on psychotropic medications and short-stay inpatient care at the expense of routine and extended psychosocial care, are not conducive to the development of the kind of therapeutic alliance necessary for SPC (Simon, 2003, pp. 61–77; Kroll, 2007). In addition, as the operations of mental health care environments are becoming more centralized in their management (Detre & MacDonald, 1997), Simon (1999) has stated that routine practices are being instituted more for the sake of service-level perceived clinico-legal benefit than for individualized patient reasons (p. 445). A pertinent example is the standardized and automatic use of SPC when admitting a patient onto an inpatient ward (Mahrer, 1993; Clark & Kerkhof, 1997; Egan, 1997; Miller, 1999). This undercuts the necessity for clinicians to individually evaluate the patient's suitability for entering into SPC. Arguably, such perfunctory use merely reinforces to some the procedure as a valid and effective standard measure, one which, nonetheless, as mentioned previously, has no evidence-based justification.

Use of SPC in Crisis Settings

Hillard (1990) stated that the unpredictable nature of suicidality, the emotional state of those affected, and the changing circumstances between appointments should discourage the clinician from relying too heavily on patients' answers to direct questions about their risk of suicide, including when entering into SPC. Supporting this, Clark and Kerkhof (1993, p. 98) deemed SPC to have limited potency to positively impact the often impenetrable and frequently ambivalent life-death dyad presented by those in crisis. As such, the collaborative and shared approach required for and implied by a contract can be quickly withdrawn, leaving in its place clinician decisions, especially in the midst of crisis, that the patient may dislike and even oppose.

SPC as a Facilitator of Therapeutic Goals

When examining the relationship between therapeutic contracts generally and SPC, Miller, Jacobs & Gutheil (1998, p. 79) pointed out inherent difficulties in the process of SPC absent from other kinds of contract, one of which is the allocation of respective roles and obligations and the implied capacity to make a meaningful choice of treatment. Viewed literally, a contract autonomously entered into, SPC presumes the patient's ability to freely decide for no treatment at all during a suicidal crisis. However, when a suicide threat is in full force, often the requisite capacities for therapeutic contract negotiations such as competence and rational decision making are absent, thus contraindicating SPC.

Data from clinician surveys indicate that clinicians perceive NSAg and NSC primarily as a means of communicating their care and concern to a patient (Mahrer, 1993; Davidson, Wagner & Range, 1995; Edwards & Sachmann, 2010). Yet the primary therapeutic role of SPC of communicating empathy to a patient gives rise to a paradox. As Kroll (2007) and Miller (1999, p. 471) have speculated, and Farrow and colleagues (2002, pp. 243–244) have demonstrated, SPC has a high probability of communicating negative messages to a patient. This paradoxical situation is brought about essentially by the different purposes for using SPC (i.e., therapeutic advantage, diagnostic clarification and clinico-legal protection). In short, these give rise to an ambiguity of purpose that a patient may sense and respond to negatively.

Moreover, the potential for misinterpretation is also facilitated by the context in which SPC is employed. A clinical environment is often characterized by characterologically maladapted patient populations, heightened levels of clinician/patient distress, and limited time to establish therapeutically beneficial alliances. Rudd (1996) noted the inherent danger in portraying SPC as an independent treatment approach, outside the broader context of a comprehensive treatment plan. He argues that all treatment planning, embedded within the principle of informed consent, requires a crisis response plan. He argues further, that because patient consent is implicit when a pre-negotiated treatment plan has commenced, that SPC has no place within a comprehensive medical response (Rudd, 1996, p. 215). The implication is clearly that giving meaningful consent and entering into SPC are inconsistent with each other.

Consumer Perceptions of SPC

Farrow, Simpson and Warren (2002) interviewed eight patients with a recent history of suicide crisis who had come into contact with a crisis team and asked: 'What does a no suicide contract meant to you'? A majority of participants found the procedure to be disempowering and expressed the belief that they were solely responsible for their safety once they had agreed to a no suicide contract. Additionally, a majority of participants felt that they were coerced into agreeing to a no suicide contract, and that once contracted they would be unable to express suicidal intent. Furthermore, they reported that their decision to agree had adversely affected their relationship with the crisis team member, who some participants felt was "just doing their job by securing a contract and thereafter were given less attention" (p. 244).

As mentioned earlier, Decant and Range's (1997) study of university students' perceptions of SPC found that those with a previous history of psychotherapy believed SPC would reduce a therapist's legal liability, compared to participants with no prior therapy experience.

Similarly, Miller (1999) understood SPC as serving clinician self-protection, referring to the "multiple hidden messages" evident in SPC (p. 471). As a result, patients may perceive they are being coerced into SPC by a clinician, a clinical position that Miller (1999, p. 472) argues undercuts what's needed for a therapeutic contract. An example of these hidden messages is demonstrated by the 'pro forma' administrative approach taken by inpatient units in securing all suicidal patients to SPC, where patients can conclude that the provision of certain services is dependent on signing or agreeing, and not signing or agreeing to a no suicide contract will preclude certain inpatient privileges (Simon & Hales, 2006).

Key therapeutic cause for concern: When SPC is used for therapeutic advantage for patients *and* instrumental advantage for clinicians, with the overall therapeutic goal of lowering a patient's level of suicide risk, there are potentially insurmountable obstacles to its unambiguous deployment: variables such as patient suicidality history, practice setting requirements, and the potential for misunderstanding in communication or the clinician's intentions for SPC (due to the multifaceted nature of SPC)—all of which can paradoxically increase the risk of suicide.

Indeed, the renowned U.S. psychologist Aaron T. Beck summed it up nicely during an interview at the 2006 American Psychological Association Convention, New Orleans, when describing the questionable effectiveness of NSC. Beck recommended the use of a 'coping card', a sort of cue card summarizing problematic thoughts as they occur and facilitating the use of a successful strategy. Beck noted that although widely employed as a strategy with suicide-oriented patients, no suicide contracts are of little help where someone is seriously intent on suicide (Farley, 2006).

Diagnostic Problems with SPC

Suicide prevention contracting has been advanced as a tool for the assessment of suicide risk (Drye, Goulding & Goulding, 1973; Hipple & Cimbolic, 1979; Twiname, 1981; Neville, 1985; Stanford et al., 1994; Range et al., 2002). Specifically, the diagnostic use aims to assess a patient's responses to a clinician's request to refrain from suicidal behavior. For example, a patient may offer incongruent verbal or body language and/or reasons why a written contract or verbal agreement is not possible (Drye et al., 1973). Mahrer & Bodgar (1996, p. 282) suggest that the ease with which a patient is able to commit to refraining from suicidal behavior may assist in evaluating the immediate threat.

Other diagnostic advantages advanced include offering SPC in order to assess a patient's competency to form an alliance with the professional (Stanford et al., 1994; Range et al., 2002), and the strength of the alliance itself (Brent & Kolko, 1990, p. 387). Early reports cite SPC as useful in determining a family's competence. For example, SPC is seen to provide additional assessment information on how the family are able, or not, to contain the child's suicidal behaviors in the home environment (Brent, 1997, pp. 277–286). Notwithstanding the aforementioned opinion, despite more than a dozen studies on SPC, none has proved that the procedure is an effective risk assessment tool (Rudd, Mandrusiak & Joiner, 2006, p. 246).

Pertinent here are three findings from the SPC study (Edwards & Sachmann, 2010). First, the majority of participants (n = 163/313; 52 percent) *often to always* used NSAg for assessing suicide risk and to evaluate the need for inpatient or outpatient care (n = 168/312; 53.8 percent), while NSC was used more when assessing precipitating risk factors (n = 51/154; 43.1 percent). Second, unsurprisingly, community-based participants were very highly significantly more likely to use NSAg as a dispersal procedure $\chi 2$ (df = 4, n = 310) = 41.00, $p \leq .001$, $p = .000$, $V = .36$) than their inpatient cohort. Third, some (n = 129/292; 44 percent) mental health clinicians experienced a serious attempt or completed suicide when using NSAg. This rate was higher (n = 167/277; 60 percent) when not using NSAg. One-third (n = 49/147; 33 percent) recalled a serious attempt or completed suicide when using NSC, with a higher perceived rate (n = 87/138; 64 percent) when not using NSC (Edwards & Sachmann, 2010, p. 297). These findings were consistent with previous studies where clinicians reported serious attempts and suicides when using SPC procedures (Kroll, 2000; Page & King, 2008).

Yet without empirical evidence for the effectiveness of SPC, current data are suggestive that the greater number of years in practice increases the likelihood of exposure to serious attempts and suicides, regardless of an SPC having been put in place (Kroll, 2000).

Key diagnostic cause for concern: When SPC is used for routine diagnostic clarification, it establishes a situation where clinicians can, over time, come to rely upon SPC's apparent efficacy as a diagnosis tool, potentially reducing compliance to other proven evaluative methods such as a careful and comprehensive initial assessment.

ETHICAL PROBLEMS WITH SPC

Legal and ethical considerations often lag behind procedural advances. The case of the widespread use of SPC is a case in point. It is only relatively recently that psychiatric and psychological associations and teaching institutions have begun to give a warning about the ethical problems with SPC, questioning its place in clinical practice (Farrow & O'Brien, 2003; Gavazzi, 2011). One of the most worrisome findings from a survey of the available literature is the almost total absence of any discussion of the ethics of SPC.

One area that has received some attention is the question of SPC and informed consent. New Zealand nurse practitioner Tony L. Farrow, PhD, and colleagues disputed that the use of SPC is consistent with the legal and ethical doctrine of informed consent (Farrow, 2002; Farrow, Simpson & Warren, 2002; Farrow & O'Brien, 2003; Farrow, 2003). They examined several conditions essential to informed consent, and they asked whether they are or can be present in the practice of SPC:

1. *Competence:* requires a patient's capacity to understand the options and exercise free choice in the selection of their preferred one, which may in fact be none of those on offer. This assumes that the patient has been given full information about the treatment options (see below) and is able to make their selection without fear of punitive consequences.
2. *Full information:* an argument can be made that a patient may be unable to meaningfully decide—give genuine consent—to agree or not to an SPC based on full information about the consequences of his or her decision in the case where deciding against SPC may lead to being committed to an institution involuntarily.
3. *Voluntariness*: when a patient is aware that not agreeing may lead to involuntary admission, then it can be said that they are unable to make a genuinely voluntary decision.
4. *Paternalism:* clinicians are often wedged between wanting to offer the least intrusive, most therapeutic intervention and their perceived duty of care requirements.

Such fundamental ethical concerns are echoed in the data from the SPC study. Some 42 percent ($n = 176/420$) of the clinicians responded to an open-ended survey question asking for the reasons why *other* clinicians use SPC, with Thematic Analysis as described by Boyatzis (1998) employed to analyze the narrative comments. The findings indicated a scattered view of SPC and related ethical considerations.

While 70 percent (n = 126/176) of clinicians placed more emphasis on the *therapeutic* value of SPC than on the *diagnostic* and the *clinico-legal* benefits, and over one half (n = 90/176) regarded SPC use as solely patient oriented, further analysis revealed a more disparate ethical picture. Some 19 percent (n = 32/176) thought SPC was used for clinico-legal protection, 24 percent (n = 42/176) perceived it as a self-protective administrative procedure, 37 percent (n = 66/176) thought SPC was used primarily for the benefit of the clinician, and 47 percent (n = 83/176) thought the key reasons for use of SPC were implicitly rather than explicitly communicated to the patient (all of which render the issue of informed consent deeply problematic).

Key ethical cause for concern: While SPC might be used with the intention to enact a clinician's objective values such as consideration, care, compassion and concern, because of its unclear typology and multiple reasons for use, its actual use has a high propensity to communicate something entirely different. This is what I call *The Central Values Paradox of SPC.*

CONCLUSION

The very complexity of current concerns about SPC illustrates also the breadth and depth of SPC's use and perceived benefit in clinical practice. In light of our historical overview, it is evident that increasingly during the late twentieth century SPC found fertile ground for widespread uptake, leading to its being seen by clinicians as a device for mediating the competing demands placed upon them during suicidal crisis with patients and clients. It is also evident that although NSAg or NSC may provide some therapeutic advantage to influence some clinical outcomes and increase diagnostic clarification to positively affect clinical judgement regarding dispersal decisions, the nature and magnitude of current concerns and their potential clinical consequence for compromising treatment—at this point in time—arguably outweighs any purported benefits of SPCs.

Moreover, it is no exaggeration to state that in the following chapters where the current understanding of SPC—its profile, paradoxes and contra-indications—is extended, these current concerns are significantly magnified, leaving little room for argument in defense of continued use when sound alternatives are readily available.

II

A NEW UNDERSTANDING OF SUICIDE PREVENTION CONTRACTING

The aspects of things that are most important for us are hidden because of their simplicity and familiarity (Wittgenstein, 1953).

Written documents called "contracts" are appearing with increasing frequency in clinical practice and the medical literature (Volk, Lieber, Kim, Ubel & Schneider, 2012, p. 7). While I have not a weight of evidence to prove it, I believe many professionals in non-crisis settings use SPC procedures. For example, they are used in the school setting (Hansen, Heath, Williams, Foxx, Hudnall & Bledsoe, 2012) where other more general 'behavior contracts' are commonplace; anecdotally in primary care physicians' practices, where brief CBT strategies and the average twelve-minute consultation is fertile ground for SPC; at youth-work services where SPC is anecdotally reported to be rigidly enforced before an at-risk young person receives a crisis bed for the night; and likely in many other health, human service and educational settings, those services that are likely less aware of the debate about the problems with SPC are likely to regard SPC as a first-line treatment. As such, it is therefore important to fully describe the current nature and use of SPC, which in some settings may constitute the primary tool for suicide risk assessment and management procedure.

5

Profile of Contemporary Suicide Prevention Contracting

Primum non nocere, "First, do no harm."

—taken from the Hippocratic Oath

KEY POINTS

- SPC is a widely used suicide intervention/prevention procedure.
- North American and Southern Hemisphere SPC studies reveal broad commonalities in SPC's clinical profile.
- Confirmation of the two types of SPC procedures and related categories of purpose is clinically instructive and a stimulus for further research.

An understanding of the perceived effectiveness of contemporary SPC—its nature and use—dates from the study by Mahrer (1993) of 252 U.S. psychologists. Later, other studies reported similar cross-disciplinary utilization of and attitudes towards SPC (Davidson, Wagner & Range, 1995; Miller, Jacobs & Gutheil, 1998; Kroll, 2000; Drew, 2001; Farrow, 2002; Potter, Vitale-Nolen & Dawson, 2005; Sanders, Ting, Power & Jacobson, 2006; Edwards, 2008; Page & King, 2008; Edwards & Sachmann, 2010), yielding a degree of consensus with regards to the profile of SPC in clinical practice. (Refer to table 5.1 for a summary of SPC studies).

Table 5.1. SPC published reports (1973 to 2012)

Study	Sample	Response Rate	Method	Use of SPC	Training in SPC
Drye, et al. (1973)	31 U.S. clinicians	NR	Self report questionnaire	100%	100% (Yes)
MacGee (1974)	12 U.S. crisis centers	NR	Service review	20%	NR
Jones, et al. (1993)	930 U.S. medical case files	NR	Retrospective case review	NR	NR
Busch, et al. (1993)	14 U.S. file records (suicides)	N/A	Descriptive analysis	50%	NR
Mahrer (1993)	252 U.S. psychologists	56%	Self report questionnaire (Random selection)	69%	60% (No)
Davidson, et al. (1995)	46 U.S. psychologists	35%	Self report questionnaire	NR	NR
Decant, et al. (1997)	145 U.S. college students	NR	Self report questionnaire	N/A	N/A
Mishara, et al. (1997)	110 Canadian crisis center volunteers	95%	Observational survey	68%	NR
Miller, et al. (1998)	89 U.S. psychiatrists 23 U.S. psychologists	78%	Self report questionnaire	61% 83%	61% (No) 71% (No)
Kroll (2000)	267 U.S. psychiatrists	52%	Self report questionnaire	57%	NR
Drew (2001)	650 U.S. file records	N/A	Retrospective case review	33%	NR
Davis, et al. (2002)	135 U.S. inpatients	NR	Battery of tests Patient questionnaire	NR	NR
Farrow (2002)	9 New Zealand (NZ) crisis nurses	NR	Semi-structured interview	NR	100% (No)
Farrow, et al. (2003)	8 adult NZ outpatients	NR	Semi-structured interview	N/A	N/A
Potter, et al. (2005)	70 U.S. nurses	55%	Self report questionnaire	NR	NR
Sanders, et al. (2006)	25 U.S. social workers	NR	Semi-structured interview	NR	NR
Page & King (2008)	312 U.S. mental health clinicians	60%	Self report questionnaire	83%	43% (no)
Hiroto, et al. (2008)	298 Japanese clinicians	NR	Self report questionnaire	NR	NR
Edwards & Sachmann (2010)	420 Australian mental health clinicians	31%	Self report questionnaire	NSC 37% NSAg 76%	70% (no)
Colucci, et al. (2011)	32 Japanese mental health professionals	NR	Delphi panel	NR	NR
Colucci, et al. (2010)	30 South East Asian Indian mental health professionals	NR	Delphi panel	NR	NR
Colucci, et al. (2010)	34 Pilipino mental health professionals	NR	Delphi panel	NR	NR
Hansen, et al. (2012)	229 school-based U.S. mental health professionals	74.5 %	Self report questionnaire	50%	NR

Note. 1. NR = Not Reported 2. SPC = Suicide Prevention Contracting 3. NSC = No Suicide Contracts 4. NSAg = No Suicide Agreements 5. N/A = Not applicable

SPC as a clinical phenomenon is characterized by way of referring to the following factors: clinician training; SPC's frequency of use; and the three categories of motivation which determine the intervention's perceived value and purpose. By means of a more detailed descriptive analysis of the two types of SPC procedure, the SPC study has added significantly to the factors which together make up the clinical profile of SPC, which are now as follows:

1. Training in SPC
2. Use of SPC procedures
3. Use and professional discipline
4. Use of SPC procedures and clinical experience
5. Differences in use of SPC procedures
6. Suicidal behavior and exposure to NSAg and NSC
7. Dimensions of NSAg and NSC
8. Differences in dimensions, reasons for use and opinion towards NSAg and NSC
9. Perspectives on SPC's main functions (therapeutic, diagnostic, clinico-legal)

What follows is, in effect, a summary of the studies listed in table 5.1 as they shed light on these factors. This will give us a more closely focused picture of SPC as it is actually employed and thought about in clinical settings.

TRAINING IN SPC

Formal training in SPC procedures appears to approximate 30 percent of clinicians who use it (Mahrer, 1993; Miller et al., 1998; Edwards & Sachmann, 2010), suggesting in vivo learning is the predominant mode for clinicians to gain an understanding of SPC, its indications and contraindications (Miller, 1999). Canadian researchers Page & King (2008) reported a training rate of 57 percent, which may indicate increased attention to SPC training in that setting. Findings from the SPC study (Edwards & Sachmann, 2010) indicate training status was a significant factor in the utilization of SPC:

- non-use of NSAg and no SPC training $\chi 2$ ($df = 1$, $n = 386$) = 9.608, $p \leq .01$, Fisher's exact $p = 0.002$, $V = .15$;

- use of NSC and general suicide prevention training $\chi2$ (df = 1, n = 394) = 9.732, $p \leq .01$, Fisher's exact p = 0.002, V = .15;
- non-use of NSC and no SPC training $\chi2$ (df = 1, n = 386) = 17.629, $p \leq .001$, Fisher's exact p = 0.000, V = .21.

Instructively, Jonathon Mahrer's (1993) U.S. study proved a hypothesis that training was associated with clinicians using SPC judiciously and being more likely to undertake an individual evaluation for the appropriateness of SPC.

USE OF SPC PROCEDURES

Large-scale clinician surveys reported a majority of clinicians had used NSAg (Mahrer, 1993; Miller et al., 1998; Page & King, 2008; Edwards & Sachmann, 2010); clinicians surveyed comprised psychiatrists, physicians, psychologists, mental health nurses, and social workers, though the incidence was lower for mental health–focused occupational therapists (Edwards & Sachmann, 2010). On average, participants preferred verbal NSAg over written NSC (Mahrer, 1993; Kroll, 2000; Page & King, 2008; Edwards & Sachmann, 2010).

USE AND PROFESSIONAL DISCIPLINE

It was apparent in the SPC study (Edwards & Sachmann, 2010) that community-based allied health clinicians were very highly significantly more likely than medical and nurse clinicians to use NSAg: $\chi2$ (df = 1, n = 149) = 14.14, $p \leq 0.001$; Fisher's exact p = 0.000, Cramer's V = .30. These data are consistent with previous findings (Page & King, 2008), where non-medical clinicians were significantly more likely to use SPC. It is therefore plausible that a medical clinician's specialized training and admission rights to inpatient care may account for this.

USE OF SPC PROCEDURES AND CLINICAL EXPERIENCE

The SPC study data indicated clinicians with less than five years' experience were significantly more likely $\chi2$ (df = 9, n = 297) = 26.06, p = 0.002, V = .17) to have used NSAg in the year prior to the study (Edwards & Sachmann, 2010). Mahrer (1993) and Kroll (2000) suggested exposure to suicidality initially increases SPC use. However, a threshold is reached over time very likely due to increased skill acquisition with a proportional decrease in SPC.

DIFFERENCES IN USE OF SPC PROCEDURES

SPC study data indicated that most participants (n = 317/416; 76 percent) had used verbal NSAg, less so (n = 154/417; 37 percent) for written NSC. In the year prior to the study just over one-third (113/310; 36.5 percent) used NSAg more than 50 percent of the time when consulting a suicidal patient; less so for NSC (22/153; 14.5 percent) (Edwards & Sachmann, 2010).

SUICIDAL BEHAVIOR AND EXPOSURE TO NSAg AND NSC

Noted previously, the SPC study found that almost one half (n = 129/292; 44 percent) of participants recalled a serious attempt or completed suicide when using NSAg. This rate was higher (n = 167/277; 60 percent) when not using NSAg. One-third (n = 49/147; 33 percent) recalled a serious attempt or completed suicide when using NSC, with a higher perceived rate (n = 87/138; 64 percent) when not using NSC (Edwards & Sachmann, 2010). These data are consistent with previous findings (Kroll, 2000; Page & King, 2008), where clinicians reported serious attempts and suicides when using SPC procedures. Again without empirical evidence of effectiveness for SPC, these current data are suggestive that with the greater number of years in practice the likelihood of exposure to serious attempts and suicides increases, irrespective of SPC being in place (Kroll, 2000).

DIMENSIONS OF NSAg AND NSC

SPC study clinicians were asked to describe the dimensions of SPC procedures (table 5.2). Participants using both SPC procedures in their career significantly favored NSC over NSAg when requesting a patient to 'cease specific suicidal behaviors' (Edwards & Sachmann, 2010).

A unique aspect of the SPC study was the differentiation between NSAg and NSC, and the interrogation of each regarding reasons for their use and clinician opinion about their effectiveness. Stanford and colleagues can be credited for making it possible to profile the varieties of SPC using the three lenses of therapeutic, diagnostic and clinico-legal motivations (Stanford, Goetz & Bloom, 1994). Studying two, rather than one SPC procedure, as most previous studies have done, also allowed for a far deeper understanding of SPC, thus helping to establish a more adequate and detailed description of SPC in action.

Table 5.2. Dimensions – NSAg & NSC

Dimensions	*n*	M (SD)[a]	% *Often*[b] (%*Rarely*)[c]
NSAg			
Specify suicidal behaviors cease	313	2.89 (1.34)	33.8 (42.8)
Set a time period for review	313	3.83 (1.13)	67.1 (11.8)
Specify alternatives to suicide	314	4.51 (0.72)	92.4 (1.3)
Include crisis telephone numbers	312	4.37 (1.05)	84 .0 (7.7)
Contact clinician prior to suicide	312	3.43 (1.20)	46.2 (18.6)
Provide clinician's telephone number	314	1.61 (1.23)	10.6 (83.1)
NSC			
Specify suicidal behaviors cease	154	3.13 (1.63)**	41.9 (38.3)
Set a time period for review	154	4.10 (1.18)	72.1 (5.8)
Specify alternatives to suicide	154	4.32 (1.03)	85.1 (3.9)
Include crisis telephone numbers	154	4.33 (1.20)	80.5 (9.1)
Contact clinician prior to suicide	153	3.33 (1.38)	41.2 (22.3)
Provide clinician's telephone number	152	1.60 (1.41)	9.0 (85.5)

Note: [a] Mean and standard deviation for each item; 1 = *'never'* to 5 = *'always'*
[b] % *'often'* = percentage of participants responding 4 = *'often'* and above
[c] % *rarely* = percentage of participants responding 2 = *'rarely'* and below
** $p \leq .01$

DIFFERENCES IN DIMENSIONS, REASONS FOR USE AND OPINION TOWARDS NSAg AND NSC

To clarify perceived differences, an overall two-way unreplicated MANOVA was performed comparing responses from SPC study participants' use of NSAg (with or without the additional use of NSAs) and use of NSC (with or without the additional use of NSAs). The multivariate main effect was significant between procedures (Pillai's Trace (df = 1,105) = 0.568, p = 0.0002 V = .16). An additional three MANOVA tests were conducted with related subsets of items in the questionnaire that measured subjects':

1. emphasis given to the specific dimensions of NSAg and NSC (table 5.3)
2. reasons for use of NSAg and NSC (table 5.4)
3. opinion of the helpfulness of NSAg and NSC (table 5.5)

These data indicate that the perceived differences in the dimensions of NSAg and NSC is largely expressed in 'specifying behaviors to cease' (F =

Table 5.3. Difference in dimensions – NSAg and NSC

Dimensions	*F* statistic	Cramer's *V*	Mean Scores [a]	
			NSAg	NSC
Specify behaviors to cease	9.02	0.18	2.94	3.20**
Specify alternative behaviors	4.11	0.10	4.39*	4.24
Set time period for review	1.03	0.05	3.93	4.01
Specify contacting clinician if suicidal	0.20	0.02	3.27	3.24
Include crisis telephone numbers	0.03	0.01	4.20	4.22
Provide clinician's telephone number	0.02	0.00	1.48	1.49

Note: [a] Mean for each item; 1 = *'never'* to 5 = *'always'*
Participants using no suicide agreements and no suicide contracts (with or without the additional use of no suicide assurances).
** $p \leq .01$, * $p \leq .05$

9.02), with participants perceiving NSC significantly more suited to achieving this outcome. In contrast, NSAg was perceived to be significantly more suitable when 'specifying behaviors alternative to suicide' ($F = 4.11$).

PERCEPTIONS ON SPC'S MAIN FUNCTIONS

Therapeutic Use of NSAg and NSC

Utilizing SPC for mutual therapeutic advantage is the notion that SPC provides an opportunity to establish and strengthen a therapeutic alliance (Selzer et al., 1987, Simon, 2003). In essence, employing SPC is seen to affect the therapeutic outcomes for both a patient and clinician (Stanford et al., 1994). Without exception, all SPC clinician studies have reported various therapeutically oriented reasons for use. In terms of a clinician's therapeutic *reasons for use*, the SPC study found no significant differences between NSAg and NSC (see table 5.4). The study did, however, find significant differences in clinicians' *opinions* regarding the respective therapeutic benefits of NSAg and NSC (see table 5.5).

The SPC study data are consistent with North American data indicating clinicians generally prefer verbal over written SPC procedures where the aim is therapeutic advantage (Mahrer, 1993; Kroll, 2007; Page & King, 2008). For example, the SPC study found that verbal NSAg, and not the written NSC, were seen to be significantly more appropriate for 'communicating a clinician's care and concern', and especially for youth and those at a mild to

Table 5.4. Difference in reasons for use – NSAg & NSC

			Mean Scores [a]	
Therapeutic	*F* statistic	Cramer's *V*	NSAg	NSC
Increase patient sense of safety	3.66	0.10	3.93	3.79
Provide alternatives to suicide	1.48	0.06	4.02	3.93
Increase patient self-responsibility	0.09	0.01	3.94	3.92
Clinico-Legal				
Increase legal protection	14.01	0.20	3.42***	3.13
Lack resources (i.e., inpatient care, psychiatric review, senior consultation)	2.54	0.09	2.74	2.87
Abide by superior's request	1.33	0.05	2.51	2.44
Diagnostic				
Evaluate inpatient vs. outpatient care	4.93	0.13	3.32*	3.13
Assess suicide risk	4.70	0.13	3.32*	3.13
Assess precipitating risk factors	0.01	0.00	2.87	2.88

Note: [a] Mean for each item; 1 = *'never'* to 5 = *'always'*
Participants using no suicide agreements and no suicide contracts (with or without the additional use of no suicide assurances).
*** $p \leq .001$, * $p \leq .05$

moderate risk for suicide (see table 5.5). Instructively to how SPC is understood, the SPC study data are consistent with North American findings indicating clinicians take the view that NSAg and NSC are unlikely to weaken a therapeutic relationship (Page & King, 2008; Davidson et al., 1995).

Diagnostic Use of NSAg and NSC

As we have seen, SPC has been advanced as a tool for the assessment of suicide risk (Drye, Goulding & Goulding, 1973; Hipple & Cimbolic, 1979; Trimble, Jackson & Harvey, 2000; Twiname, 1981; Neville & Barnes, 1985; Stanford et al., 1994; Davidson et al., 1995). What this tool is perceived specifically to assess is the patient's responses to a clinician's request to refrain from suicidal behavior (Range, Campbell, Kovac, Marion-Jones, Aldridge, Kogos & Crump, 2002), and consequently it is used in the assessment aiding patient dispersal decisions (Egan, 1997; Farrow, 2002; Drew, 1999). Yet despite more than a dozen SPC studies, none have found it to be an effective risk assessment tool (Rudd, Mandrusiak & Joiner, 2006, p. 246).

Table 5.5. Difference in opinion items – NSAg & NSC

			Mean scores [a]	
Therapeutic	*F* Statistic	Cramer's *V*	NSAg	NSC
Helpful with youth aged 13 to 19 years	10.37	0.12	2.40**	2.57
Help with mildly suicidal patients	10.07	0.15	1.90**	2.12
Help with moderately suicidal patients	6.67	0.12	2.05*	2.23
Helpful with children < 12 years	4.96	0.10	3.24*	3.38
Communicate care and concern	4.04	0.08	1.95*	2.07
Helpful with adults over 20 years	3.34	0.07	2.08	2.18
Reduce risk for suicide	1.60	0.05	2.46	2.53
Weaken a therapeutic relationship	0.77	0.04	3.78	3.84
Help with severely suicidal patients	0.70	0.05	3.17	3.10
Give patient sense of security	0.10	0.01	2.16	2.18
Strengthen a therapeutic relationship	0.02	0.00	2.20	2.21
Help with chronically suicidal patients	0.01	0.00	2.93	2.92
Offer clinician a sense of security	0.01	0.00	2.50	2.50
Helpful with older adults over 65 years	0.00	0.00	2.50	2.50
Clinico-Legal				
Reduce recriminations from peers	0.00	0.00	(3.10)	(3.10)
Reduce legal liability	0.018	0.00	(3.00)	(3.01)

Note: [a] Mean for each item; 1 = *'strongly agree'* to 5 = *'strongly disagree'*
Participants using no suicide agreements and no suicide contracts (with or without the additional use of no suicide assurances).
** $p \leq .01$, * $p \leq .05$

Research data (as opposed to opinions, of which there are many) relating to the value of SPC for diagnostic clarification is limited. The SPC study confirmed what Mahrer (1993) demonstrated, that SPC is used for diagnostic clarification of suicide risk, including participants using SPC for assessing suicide risk severity and evaluating the need for inpatient or outpatient care. Overall, SPC study participants indicated that they believed verbal SPC procedures are more inherently sensitive than written forms for diagnostic purposes. Perceived differences between the diagnostic aspects of NSAg and NSC were expressed in evaluating types of care ($F = 4.93$) and assessment of risk ($F = 4.70$) (see table 5.4). Unsurprisingly, community-based participants were very highly significantly more likely to utilise NSAg as a dispersal technique χ^2 ($df = 4$, $n = 310$) = 41.00, $p = 0.000$, $V = .36$ than the inpatient cohort.

Clinico-Legal Use of NSAg and NSC

Mahrer's (1993) study of 252 U.S. psychologists was revealing in many ways. The demonstrated use of SPC for perceived clinico-legal protection dates only from Mahrer's study. These psychologists' use of a no suicide contract/agreement was driven in part by the goal to prevent legal liability ('sometimes to often'; *M* = 4.44, SD 1.98:1 = 'Never'; 7 = 'Always'). Expert opinion (Simon, 1999; Simon, 2003, pp. 61–81; Simon & Hales, 2006, pp. 555–557) suggests that SPC has established and retains a quasi-legal status in medical and allied health settings. Other research findings confirm physicians, mental health nurses, social workers and occupational therapists perceive some degree of clinico-legal advantage in the use of SPC (Davidson et al., 1995; Farrow, 2002; Sanders et al., 2006; Page & King, 2008).

In the SPC study, clinicians were using SPC procedures on average 50 percent of the time as a pre-emptive clinico-legal intervention. By differentiating between NSAg and NSC, the study demonstrated, albeit not to a statistically significant level, the probable use of NSC as 'a stop gap measure,' particularly when clinicians lack the resources to adequately respond to suicide risk (see table 5.4). Farrow (2002, p. 216) found a similar use of SPC by crisis nurses. The emphasis placed on NSAg for this reason may relate to some clinicians perceiving that the verbal notation of a patient's willingness to take a degree of responsibility will mitigate future claims of deviation from their duty of care responsibilities.

CONCLUSION

There are multiple commonalities in the profile—comprising practices, beliefs and experiences—of SPC among Australian, North American, Canadian and New Zealand mental health clinicians. (While the use of SPC has been reported in non-Western countries [refer to FAQ, where SPC and cultural influences are discussed], the nature of such use is less understood.) What is also now much clearer than it has been to date is the potential for producing detrimental outcomes when SPC is used on the assumption that it can provide a degree of clinic-legal protection. The practical import of this assumption is that SPC is encouraged in situations where it would otherwise be contraindicated. On page 121, the primary and secondary contraindications of SPC are presented.

6

The Anatomy of Contemporary Suicide Prevention Contracting

It is not the strongest of the species that survives, nor the most intelligent, but the one most responsive to change. —Charles Darwin

KEY POINTS

- A simple stress/coping model characterizes how SPC is activated.
- Contemporary SPC is a multi-dimensional and 'complex system'.
- A provisional SPC nomenclature is clinically useful.

INTRODUCTION

The SPC nomenclature laid out in this chapter is admittedly provisional. It is a task for the future to develop the necessary refinements so that a general consensus may be reached. In the meantime, a degree of caution is needed until further debate can occur. And yet, the task is an urgent one. Bearing in mind the reported concerns about SPC due to the lack of both standard definition(s) and a theoretical or conceptual model that clearly describes the procedure(s) (Rudd, Mandrusiak & Joiner, 2006, p. 245), it is of some importance for clinicians using NSAg or NSC that, at the very least, their practice is directed by an SPC nomenclature—that is, by a definition of its component elements and their interrelationships, resulting in a set of commonly understood and logically defined clinical practice terms.

Integral to the analysis of the largely qualitative data derived from the SPC study was the construction of a conceptual apparatus for SPC, which has come to be titled *The New Vocabulary of SPC*. This conceptual apparatus has two main parts: firstly, *The SPC Decision-Making Schema*, which distils SPC into its essential dimensions and lays bare their interrelationships; and secondly, *The ABC Stress/Defense Model of SPC*, which illustrates how SPC is activated.

THE SPC DECISION-MAKING SCHEMA

Dimensions, Structures and Emerging Nomenclature

Up until now, the nomenclature of SPC has been the subject of sporadic examination or development (Mahrer, 1993; Egan, 1997; Farrow, 2003; Bartlett, 2006). The sheer variety of terms such as 'contracting', 'no suicide promise', 'no suicide contracts', 'contracting for safety', 'no harm contract', 'no suicide agreements' and so forth has done little to define and describe the anatomy (the structure) or the taxonomy (the subtypes) of SPC. The unexamined view has been that SPC is a way of eliciting an agreement from the patient for the sake of their own safety. Because this view is largely one-dimensional, it effectively hides from view not only the other dimensions of SPC, but also the potentially hazardous aspects of SPC which are associated with them.

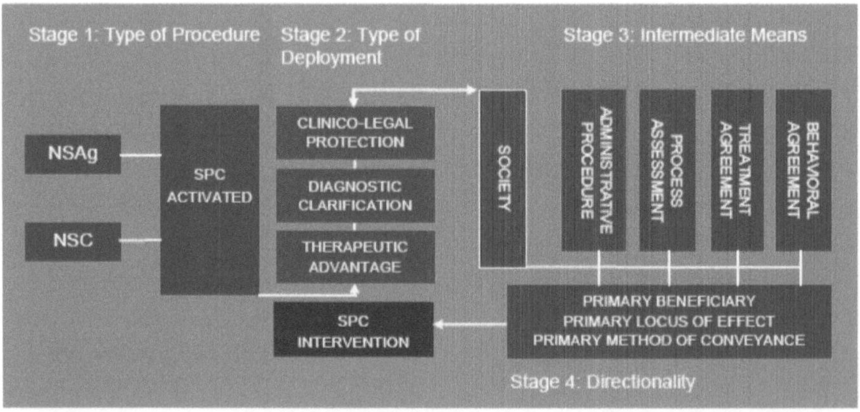

DIAGRAM 6.1
The SPC Decision-Making Schema (DMS)

Diagram 6.1 represents the first part of the anatomy of SPC, titled the *Decision Making Schema of SPC*. Before sketching out the DMS by way of introduction, the attentive reader may wonder why it is so titled. One of the core functions this DMS will hopefully perform is to enable clinicians to determine which enactments of SPC *increase* the potential to create unintended hazards. And the way to do that is to determine which elements of each dimension of the DMS are present in any particular case. (Indeed, the schema could thus also be titled the 'no SPC decision'.)

The SPC Decision-Making Schema (DMS) Evidence Base

Findings derived from the SPC study enabled the development of the component parts of the DMS. You will note the DMS has four dimensions pertaining to the four stages: *(a)* Type of Procedure, *(b)* Type of Deployment, *(c)* Intermediate Means and, *(d)* Directionality.

Types of SPC Procedures

Introduced and defined previously were the two types of SPC procedures. Most participants (n = 317/416; 76 percent) had used NSAg, less so (n = 154/417; 37 percent) for NSC. In the year prior to the study, just over one-third used (n = 113/310; 36.5 percent) NSAg more than 50 percent of the time when consulting a suicidal patient; less so for NSC (n = 22/153; 14.5 percent).

Types of Deployment (Reason for Use)

As described earlier, the study confirmed the presence of previously theorized uses of contemporary SPC (Stanford, Goetz & Bloom, 1994), namely: for perceived therapeutic advantage, for perceived diagnostic clarification, and for perceived clinico-legal protection (See table 6.1).

Between stages 2 and 3 in the DMS is a mediating factor labelled 'society'. While I cannot prove it empirically, the entire intellectual investigation brought to bear on SPC indicates that social pressures impact on the contemporary use of SPC; increased acuity of cases, clinico legal, time and resource pressures facilitating a relentless attempt by clinicians to reconcile competing interests while sometimes struggling within and trying to adapt to an ever-changing complex clinical landscape (See Part IV for a commentary on today's risk society).

Table 6.1. Reasons for use – NSAg & NSC

		NSAg			NSC	
Therapeutic	*n*	M [a]	SD	*n*	M [a]	SD
Provide alternatives to suicide	312	4.10	0.90	115	4.05	1.15
Increase patient self-responsibility	312	3.95	0.90	115	3.98	1.03
Increase patient sense of safety	312	4.00	0.92	115	3.88	1.20
Clinico-legal						
Increase legal protection	312	3.54	1.30	154	3.29	1.52
Abide by superiors request	308	2.32	1.43	155	2.60	1.72
Lack resources (i.e. inpatient care, psychiatric review, senior consultation)	311	2.70	1.31	154	2.93	1.47
Diagnostic						
Evaluate inpatient vs. outpatient care	312	3.50	1.19	155	3.32	1.45
Assess suicide risk	313	3.46	1.19	155	3.21	1.45
Assess precipitating risk factors	308	2.90	1.24	154	3.05	1.65

Note: [a] Mean and standard deviation for each item; 1 = *'never'* to 5 = *'always'*

Intermediate Means

The 'intermediate means' category is a fundamental element in the analytic understanding of SPC. It serves to clarify the nature of the desired outcome of using the procedure by delineating both the type of deployment (reason for use) and its directionality (see over the page). Analysis revealed that the largest proportion of responses referred to use of SPC as a treatment agreement (n = 66/176, 37.5 percent); followed by the administrative procedure (n = 42/176, 24 percent), the process assessment (n = 38/176, 21.5 percent), and the behavioral agreement (n = 30/176, 17 percent).

What is new here are the four types of intermediate means: 'administrative procedure', 'process assessment', 'treatment agreement', and 'behavioral agreement'. Findings from the SPC study's thematic analysis (Tesch, 1990; Boyatzis, 1998) were used to construct the 'intermediate means' and 'directionality' categories, based on participants' (n = 176/420; 42 percent) responses to the only open-ended question in the study:

> Some say that by offering a patient a no suicide contract or no suicide agreement you are acknowledging and encouraging patient self-responsibility. In your view what are some of the theoretical or philosophical reasons why other mental health clinicians use these procedures?

After adapting three TA definitions of patient contracts described by Stummer (2002, pp. 121–123) and utilizing them for the theoretical framework, data from the thematic analysis were categorized under one of four 'intermediate means' categories. The 'administrative procedure' category was deductively derived from the analysis of the data. The four categories are as follows:

- Administrative procedure—a documentation procedure enacted to present the clinician as competent at a future time.
- Process assessment—a procedure used to assess patient permission and assurance for a course of action; it aids the clinician's attunement to a patient and their suicidal thoughts; helps relational impasse checking; is an empathic procedure aiming towards alliance building.
- Treatment agreement—a procedure establishing options for treatment/ clarifying what precipitating factors for suicidality need to be addressed.
- Behavioral agreement—a procedure to effect a course of action; to reinforce new behavior, control symptoms, and offer the patient a sense of mastery over suicidal urges.

Directionality

What is also new here are the DMS structures of directionality and its three substructures, namely *(a)* the 'primary beneficiary', *(b)* the 'primary locus of effect', and *(c)* the 'primary mode of conveyance'.

Primary Beneficiary

The first substructure refers to the intended beneficiary of the SPC intervention. Analysis revealed that the majority (n = 90/176; 51 percent) of responses to the question of the reasons why clinicians use SPC referred to their benefit to the patient; that is, they were *patient* oriented. The other responses were: primarily clinician oriented (n = 66/176; 37.5 percent) and jointly patient/ clinician oriented (n = 20/176; 11.4 percent).

Primary Locus of Effect

The second substructure refers to the time frame for when the effect of the SPC intervention is intended. Analysis revealed that almost one-half (n = 87/176; 49.4 percent) of responses referring to the reasons why clinicians use SPC were solely future oriented. In contrast, the numbers for the other two loci of effect were significantly lower: solely present focused (n = 27/176; 15 percent) and jointly present/future focused (n = 62/176; 35.4 percent).

Primary Mode of Conveyance

The third substructure refers to how the SPC procedure is presented to the patient, specifically whether the SPC is made explicit or remains implicit within the clinician-patient interaction. The analysis revealed that only 19 percent (n = 33/ 176) of responses referred to SPC being conveyed explicitly. Much larger were the numbers of responses indicating that SPC is conveyed implicitly (n = 83/176; 47 percent), or where either an implicit or explicit method of conveyance was possible (n = 60/176; 34 percent).

Some illustrations may be instructive:

Illustration 1:

To amplify diagram 6.2: here the clinician selects NSAg *(type of procedure)* for perceived clinico-legal protection *(type of deployment)*; it takes the form of an administrative procedure *(intermediate means)* and is deployed in order

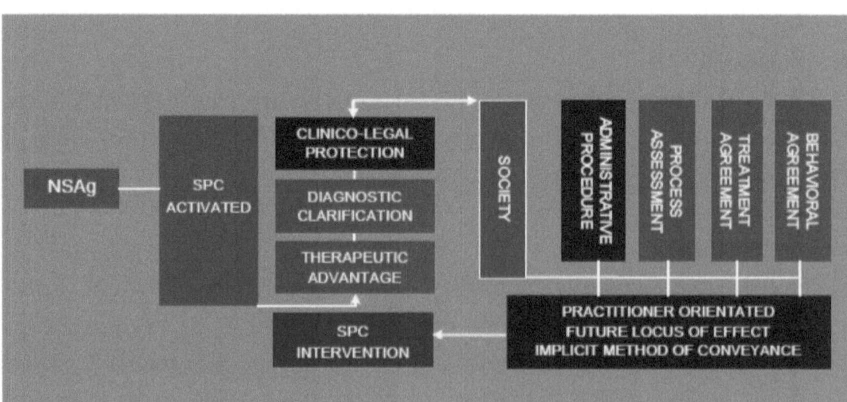

DIAGRAM 6.2
DMS (deploying NSAg for perceived clinico-legal protection)

to present the clinician *(primary beneficiary)* (noting the reason for use and intermediate means) as having acted competently at a future time in the event of an adverse clinical outcome; it is therefore future-focused *(primary locus of effect)* and will be implicitly presented (in contrast to explicit), because the type of deployment is not made clear to the patient *(primary mode of conveyance).*

Illustration 2:
A clinician may employ NSAg as a process assessment in the endeavor to determine a patient's level of assurance for a course of action; perhaps also to evaluate competence or to evaluate the presence of any relational impasses between patient and clinician in light of some observed resistance. To amplify diagram 6.3, the clinician selects NSAg *(type of procedure)* to assess for suicide risk *(type of deployment)*; the *intermediate means* is a process assessment; and the *primary beneficiary* is the clinician; the *primary locus of effect* is the present, where SPC is used as a gauge of any (current) relational difficulties. Lastly, the *primary method of conveyance* is implicit as the patient is not aware of the reason why SPC is being offered and of the potential consequences of his or her responses to it.

Illustration 3:
A clinician may employ NSC to develop a treatment agreement that establishes options for suicide first aid and clarifies what needs to change to reduce

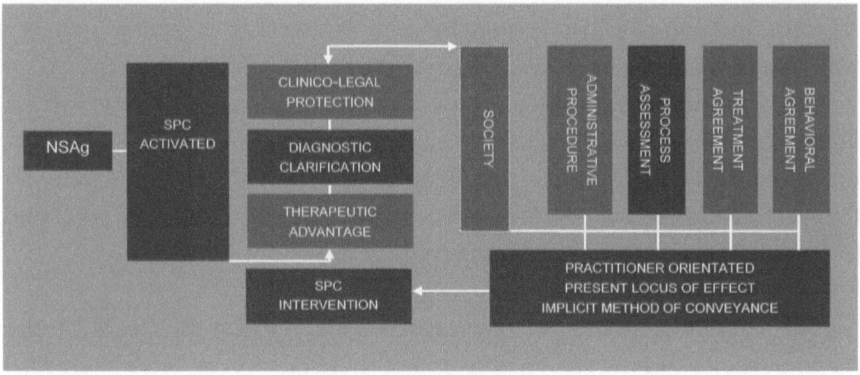

DIAGRAM 6.3
DMS (deploying NSAg to assess for suicide risk)

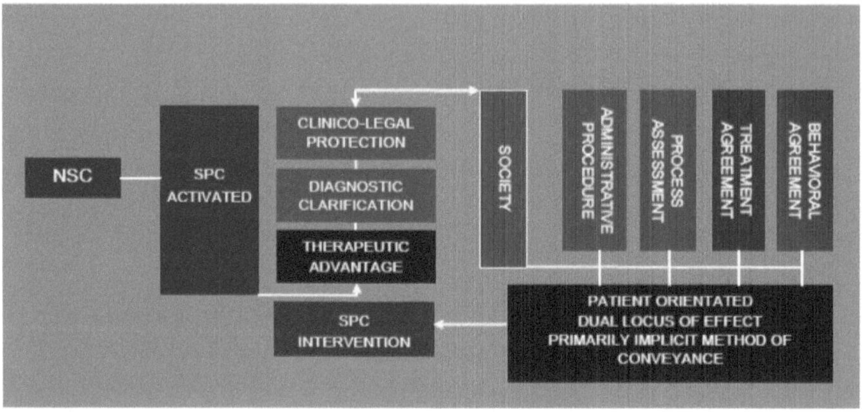

DIAGRAM 6.4
DMS (deploying NSC to increase patient self-responsibility)

a patient's suicide risk status. To amplify diagram 6.4, NSC *(type of procedure)* is selected to increase the patient's self-responsibility during a future crisis *(type of deployment)*; the *intermediate means* is a treatment agreement; the *primary beneficiary* is the patient; the *primary locus of effect* is both the present moment where an assessment is made of the patient's ability to provide consent and also—by way of 'holding' the patient in a moment of future crisis—the future where potentially new coping strategies may lead to the use of SPC as a perceived behavioral agreement; and the *primary method of conveyance* is implicit. (Often, treatment agreements as the intermediate means can be explicit. Here the explicit declaration of the possibility of a punitive response for non-compliance may be seen as useful to assessing a client's willingness to engage in assuring their safety.)

As I think these illustrations show, the interrelationships between these dimensions, their various substructures (summarized in table 6.2), the permutations of the anatomical components of SPC, have the potential to throw the very many subtly different implementations of SPC into sharp relief and to provide some way of assessing its appropriateness or otherwise.

Indeed, I'm reminded of a personal experience in my own life that illustrates the importance of how recognizing one of these factors can have a terminal effect on SPC. In mid 2010, a final-year Chilean student mental health nurse, Ester Redon, who I was supervising in New Zealand, began asking about my

Table 6.2. Dimensions and Structures of SPC

Dimension	Structure
1. Type of Procedure	☐ No Suicide Agreements (NSAg) (verbal) ☐ No Suicide Contracts (NSC) (written)
2. Type of Deployment (reason for use)	☐ Clinico-Legal Protection ☐ Diagnostic Clarification ☐ Therapeutic Advantage *Substructure:* Themes (reasons for use) [1]
3. Intermediate Means	☐ Administrative Procedure ☐ Process Assessment ☐ Treatment Agreement ☐ Behavioral Agreement
4. Directionality	☐ Primary Beneficiary *Substructure:* patient benefit, clinician benefit, mutual benefit ☐ Primary Locus of Effect *Substructure:* present effect, future effect, dual effect ☐ Primary Mode of Conveyance *Substructure:* implicitly conveyed, explicitly conveyed

research. When I told her the topic, she turned and said, "At university, we're told not to use them [SPC]." No follow up explanation, no caveat, no step-by-step rationale, no nothing. When pressed, she simply couldn't add to the reasoning . . . *why not?* Later, it struck me that two things were happening here. Granted, it was good that a lecturer had seen below the waterline and recognized the fractures hidden beyond sight. Yet a clear understanding of the potential hazardous endgame of SPC—the big-picture deep understandings—were left unrealized.

THE ABC-STRESS DEFENSE MODEL OF SPC

How Suicide Prevention Contracting Is Activated

A useful way to understand how SPC is activated, by which I mean how it is selected and employed by the clinician, is to apply a stress and coping analysis to the contemporary use of SPC.[2]

While the naïve view would be that SPC represents an unproblematic, widely accepted standard practice for suicide intervention, the high degree to which the actuality of SPC use conforms to the model of a 'stress/defense' response further reveals its problematic nature.

In what follows I shall demonstrate how *The ABC Stress Defense Model of SPC* operates and how it can help clinicians, clinical supervisors and educators understand the thinking processes of those using SPC.

The ABC Stress Defense Model of SPC proposes that SPC is 'activated' (selected and employed by the clinician) within the following matrix: A (active suicidal behavior) interacts with B (clinician's perceived resources for responding to the crisis), which interacts with C (cognitive appraisal/meaning

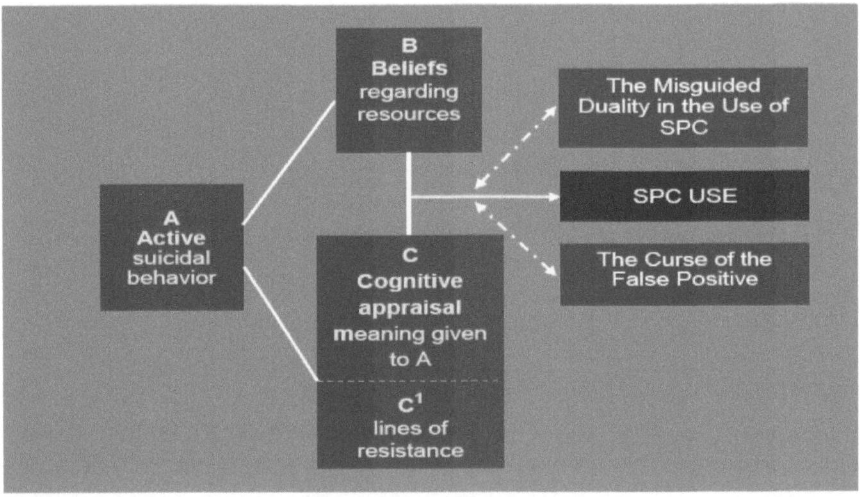

DIAGRAM 6.5
ABC Stress Defense Model of SPC

given to A), which is in turn mediated by C^1 (cognitive appraisal/clinician's pre-existing defense factors for mitigating the injudicious use of SPC) together with two distal factors—essentially the inherent vulnerabilities of SPC: *(a) The Misguided Duality in the Use of SPC*, and *(b) The Curse of the False Positive.*

In diagram 6.5 I've schematized the conceptual links between the component parts and will now elaborate on each.

Active Suicidal Behavior (A)

Active suicidal behavior—defined by the WHO as suicidal thoughts, threats and behavior—produces a multi-faceted response in a clinician that likely includes anxiety, concern for the other, feelings of fearfulness, and for some, threat and a perceived need for self-protection—all of which are factors shaping a response.

Clinician's Beliefs Regarding Resources (B)

The resources available to a clinician to respond to and manage a suicidal crisis are of two kinds: *(a) personal resources*, which can include previous experience of assessing suicidality, positional status/influence and level of training; and *(b) external supports* such as access to inpatient admission, senior peer consultation, cohesiveness and open communication with colleagues within the workplace.

Cognitive Appraisal/Meaning Given to Suicidal Crisis (C)

Generic stress and coping models are based on the premise that under stress, individuals conduct an assessment of their situation and attribute meaning to the event. Three types of assessments are conducted: *(1)* an assessment of the crisis situation, *(2)* the assessment of the individual's ability to cope with the event, and *(3)* an assessment of the social resources available to support or enhance personal resources.

Cognitive Appraisal/Clinician's Lines of Defense (Resistance) (C^1)

The first three components (A, B, and C) provide a model of how contemporary SPC is activated. Yet these three factors alone do not provide a complete picture. Importantly, there also appear to be *lines of defense* preventing the injudicious use of SPC procedures.

They likely consist of four elements: *a)* adherence to core principles of practice, *b)* lines of resistance, *c)* flexible lines of defense, and *d)* internal lines of resistance.[3]

Let me describe each of these in turn.

CORE PRINCIPLES OF PRACTICE

The basic principle of practice is to cause no harm while abiding by professional and legal standards consisting of dictums against the use of procedures with unproven validity and efficacy, and those practices which seek revenge, vindication or private gain (Karasu, 1996). When these basic principles are authentically brought to bear on clinical practice, internal conflicts regarding use of self-serving or unproven procedures (*cf.* SPC) ought to be largely absent.

Lines of Resistance

The lines of resistance that counteract the injudicious use of SPC are those which provide a clinician with constant and stable support. These include a clinician's awareness of and adherence to professional ethics and responsibility to the patient; an experienced clinician's well-developed belief system concerning what constitutes effective and valid treatment procedures (Mahrer, 1993, p. 111); and the effectiveness of a clinician's service level system of care (Peck & Norman, 1999). The kind of extra-personal stressors that can breach the lines of resistance include wider social or political pressures such as conflicting managed care requirements, which potentially compromise good practice or encourage perfunctory practices.

Flexible Lines of Defense

In the case of *The ABC-SPC Stress Defense Model*, flexible lines of defense are dynamic buffers that can potentially prevent injudicious use of SPC. Examples of flexible lines of defense include appropriate and adequate suicide prevention training, access to supervision, and resources enabling adequate and appropriate standards of care.

Internal Lines of Resistance

One part of *The ABC Stress Defense Model of SPC,* internal lines of resistance, are intra-system devices that act to defend against stressors which have permeated the flexible lines of defense. An internal line of resistance may be thought of as a relatively stable compensatory mechanism designed to counteract the effect of an environmental stressor after it has been activated—influencing the cognitive appraisal that might otherwise lead to potentially injudicious uses of SPC. One example would be service-wide decisions regarding a specific use of SPC. Another example of an internal line of resistance would be a 'buddy system' where in the event of a suicide crisis access to a senior colleague for consultation is available—echoing renowned U.S. professor Thomas Gutheil's maxim of 'never worry alone'.

Distal Factors

The steps from (A) an active suicidal crisis, to (B) assessment of resources to cope with the crisis, to (C) assessment of the resources available to support or enhance personal resources, to (C^1) mediation through four resiliency factors, are all fundamental to this stress/coping model. Equally important are two pre-existing vulnerabilities of SPC, which appear to serve as mediating factors in how SPC is activated, if at all.

The Misguided Duality in the Use of SPC

The apparently logical thought process, "How can SPC cause harm when it gives me *some* therapeutic, diagnostic and clinico-legal advantage?", is an example of the *misguided duality in the use of SPC*. The assumption that SPC can provide both patient care and clinician self-protection merely perpetuates its misguided use. SPC is injudicious, in part, because of its untested status and because of its capacity to incorrectly place patients in less secure environments. Also, an overreliance on SPC may come at the expense of a thorough psychiatric evaluation and an ongoing suicide risk assessment process. Such overreliance may lead inexperienced or naïve clinicians to view NSC or NSAg, together with apparent congruent patient body language, as some form of enduring warranty (Jacobs, 1992).

The Curse of the False Positive

The SPC study revealed other assumptions such as this: "I've used SPC with most of my suicidal patients, and I've not lost a patient yet." Unfortunately, as completed suicide has a low base rate, the prediction of completed suicide is vulnerable to relatively high percentages of false positives (Murphy,

1984; Shaffer, Garland, Gould, Fisher & Trautman, 1988, p. 676; Pokorny, 1993). Such "I've never lost a patient . . ." logic likely ascribes practice efficacy and validity to SPC when suicide doesn't occur, yet that it doesn't occur may in reality have little or nothing to do with the actual efficacy of SPC.

These present assumptions about SPC suggest that they function as distal factors that feed into the end stage of *The ABC Stress Defense Model of SPC* process, reinforcing the activation of SPC.

THE VALUE OF AN SPC NOMENCLATURE AND AN UNDERSTANDING OF HOW SPC IS ACTIVATED

The *New Vocabulary for SPC* is intended to provide a language for articulating its manufactured hazards. To illuminate its value in this regard, it may be helpful to apply the *New Vocabulary for SPC* to one of the cases presented in chapter 4. Gaps in our knowledge of this case will be filled by several reasonable hypotheses. Such analysis can demonstrate why similar cases are of concern, even while acknowledging that as a categorizing system the *Vocabulary* has limitations at its current stage of development.

The Florida Social Worker Case

This tragic case of Hope Witsell's suicide, a thirteen-year-old girl who was being cyberbullied highlights better than none other how an apparent over-reliance upon SPC can be implicated in tragic outcomes. The analysis is in two parts: Hypothetically evaluating the case in light of the *ABC Stress Defense Model* (how SPC is activated), followed by evaluating Hope's case using *The Decision-Making Schema* to better understand the manufactured hazards evident.

The Florida school social worker deployed a written no suicide contract, called a *no-harm contract*. In the contract Hope signed, she was to remind herself that she was not to commit suicide under any circumstances; to call 911 if she was in immediate danger; and she was to ring certain numbers if she was not in immediate danger but had suicidal thoughts (Ackerman & Scullin, 2011).

Active Suicidal Behavior

The fact that the social worker deployed a no suicide contract indicated a level of concern she was facing; her distress probably included heightened anxiety, concern for Hope and other transference and countertransference issues potentially compromising their effectiveness, leaving the social worker feeling professionally vulnerable.

Beliefs Regarding Resources

Based on news reports, questions remain whether the social worker had previous experience of and training in assessing suicidality. Furthermore, in one of the news feeds outlining Hope's story, a U.S. professor of social work noted school systems do not always focus upon issues of mental health as they're not seen as core business (Ackerman & Scullin, 2011, p. 1). Hence, Hope's school may not have had protocols for suicidality or how to work alongside mental health service providers in crisis situations.

Cognitive Appraisal/Meaning Given to the Suicidal Crisis

Central to Hope's case is the social worker's omission to contact Hope's parents or apparently any support service once aware of Hope's suicidal ideation. The importance and potential origins of this omission can be seen in the following four domains of C.

Appraisal of the crisis situation

Based on information gathered from interviewing Hope, the social worker's past training experience and in vivo learning, the social worker's assessment of risk for suicidal behavior, indicated the necessity to enact a no suicide contract, yet the risk presented was not sufficient to involve others.

Appraisal of the ability to cope with the event

After the initial assessment, which likely allowed Hope an opportunity to express her thoughts and feelings to the social worker with resultant catharsis, the social worker's omission to involve others is indicative of an appraisal of a low level of threat and the perception of adequate coping ability on the part of Hope.

Appraisal of social resources available to support or enhance personal resources

The social worker's omission to involve others following Hope's disclosure of suicidal ideation indicates that either a low level fear response was evoked or other factors such as the social worker colluding with Hope in not disclosing to others was present. Similarly, the social worker's omission may have been mediated by a 'threat and coping appraisal' where the probability of suicide occurring was assessed as low, the perceived efficacy of NSC was inflated, and by the social worker's belief in her ability to manage alone.

Notwithstanding this, an established stress/coping balance motivated the use of a no suicide contract. Using a *pro forma* no-harm contract (indicating past use of and satisfaction with the procedure), such a response is indicative of the social worker falling foul of the two distal factors: *the misguided duality in the use of SPC* (reliance upon SPC to provide student care *and* worker self-protection), and *the curse of the false positive* (prior use of the no-harm contract without incident, creating a perceived level of efficacy and validity for NSC).

(C[1]) Cognitive Appraisal/Clinician's Lines of Defense (Resistance)

It is less difficult to assess the lines of defense which may have worked against the use of SPC.

Core principles of practice

First, it is regrettable that the social work literature has not rejected outright the use of SPC in their professional standards, or that the social worker apparently wasn't aware of the unproven validity and efficacy of SPC.

Lines of resistance

Second, it remains unclear if the school did indeed have a suicide intervention protocol or endorsed in some way the use of SPC as constituting an effective and valid management procedure.

Flexible lines of defense

Third, was the school social worker appropriately and adequately trained, with access to supervision and resources enabling her to follow a proven standard of care?

Internal lines of resistance

Fourth, with a cognitive appraisal of the crisis and a likely fear/threat balance established influencing the injudicious use of SPC, did the social worker have access to a relatively stable compensatory mechanism designed to counteract the stressor? For example, a school-wide decision regarding the use/non-use of SPC or a 'buddy system' where in the event of a suicide crisis access to a senior colleague for consultation is available.

Distal Factors

Given that the school social worker had Hope read and then sign a *pro forma* no-harm contract (suggesting past use of the procedure) (Ackerman & Scullin, 2011, p. 1), both mediating factors may have influenced the social worker's decision to use NSC.

Turning to the *DMS* to better understand the use of a no suicide contract in Hope's case:

Stage 1 Type of procedure: a written no suicide (no harm) contract was selected and activated.

Stage 2 Type of deployment: without hearing directly from the social worker in question, it is nonetheless plausible to suppose that the no suicide contract was deployed for multiple reasons: for *therapeutic* reasons, to decrease Hope's suicide risk status; for *clinico-legal* reasons, as a means of increasing the social worker's legal protection in the event of an adverse outcome; and as a *diagnostic* tool, to gain clarity about the likelihood for suicide. In a news piece regarding Hope's story, a senior manager of U.S. school psychological services asserted that NSC was used with potentially suicidal students as a conversation tool (Ackerman & Scullin, 2011, pp. 1–2). Does Hope's signing the no-harm contract indicate to the school social worker she is at less risk, which may then explain the lack of parental involvement or apparent omission to involve mental health service providers?

Mediating factor (Society): a potential socially based influence to this case was reported by the U.S. professor of social work's assessment that school systems are sometimes different from clinical settings, where parents need to give their consent for treatment, in this case for SPC (Ackerman & Scullin, 2011, pp. 1–2).

Stage 3 Intermediate means: again, without the social worker present to explain her primary reason(s) for use, at best it is plausible to suppose that she intended all these three: NSC as a likely *behavioral agreement* (perceived as a procedure to effect a course of action); as an *administrative procedure* (a documentation procedure enacted to present the developer as competent at a future time); and as a *process assessment* (using SPC as a procedure utilized to assess an individual's permission and assurance for a course of action—as well as providing attunement [i.e., of the worker] to the student and their suicidal thoughts, and constituting an empathic procedure aimed at alliance building, a conversation tool).

Stage 4 Directionality: the primary beneficiary and locus of effect is unclear, perhaps both for student/worker and for present/future locus of effect respectively. Finally, the no harm contract was conveyed explicitly.

CONCLUSION

The Anatomy of SPC as it presents in clinical practice across many Western countries is an overly complicated and, at times, ill-fitting system. And it's this potential for ill fit that was a critical endpoint of the SPC study. The sometimes ill fit and fine detail of the system merely reflects the stark lack of attention SPC has received in the last forty years or more. Here, then, I offer this detailed anatomy of SPC for careful consideration, debate and revision as needed.

III

THE POTENTIAL-TO-CAUSE-HARM PROFILE OF SUICIDE PREVENTION CONTRACTING

The *social contract* is prominent in Western philosophy, where it is regarded as the bedrock of political life and justice. It is the basis of democracy where individuals considered equal in capacity agree to give up the private use of force and to respect another's property in exchange for peace and security (Nussbaum, 2006, p. 10). The core moral code in the tradition of social contracting is that of mutual advantage and reciprocity among people who make such a contract (Ibid., p. 16). More than a structural signifier of the relationship between government (i.e., ruler) and those governed (i.e., subjects), the social contract defines the day-to-day intercourse of individuals who tacitly agree to the mutual ethical obligations it entails.

North American philosophy professor Martha Nussbaum (2006) contends that not everyone can easily be included in social contractual arrangements, as embodied in the classical tradition (e.g., those with mental disabilities, refugees, non-human animals). Disadvantage precludes those afflicted from being party to the design of the contractual arrangement, such as to make it exclusive of those individuals lacking certain capacities (e.g., language, rationality) (Ibid., p. 16). Essentially, Nussbaum cites the 'problem' of the social contract for those lacking the pre-requisites of exchange between 'equals' for 'mutual advantage'.

Australian anthropologist professor Ghassan Hage (2000) suggests that the contemporary social contract has been reinterpreted through neo-liberal economics. It has shifted from the ethical obligation involved in a mutual honoring of the individuals in the exchange to a mutual obligation where the *return* is more important than the *gift* made possible by an ethical society. Hage suggests the 'honorable society' has been eroded and the nature of the social and moral obligation has become devoid of the ethical component—leaving the importance of the social contract only in maintaining individuals as practically and effectively committed to it (p. 32).

These philosophical illuminations of contemporary society and the ties that bind individuals perhaps also reveal the apparent tensions evident within the often contested milieu of health and social services and, specific to this book, how and why SPC has been recast from its early beginnings as a relationship-based technique to one that appears to be used in contemporary practice to meet a range of quite different objectives. The SPC study findings suggest that clinicians perceive that SPC valorizes the existence of the patient by being a means for expressing their care and concern for them and that SPC re-establishes the patient to reciprocity of mutual obligation by returning a degree of self-responsibility. However, just as the contemporary social contract is lacking the compulsion of ethical reciprocity, contemporary SPC appears to be lacking a higher level of ethical consciousness. In short, contemporary SPC has been undermined by the tensions of legality, expedience and a perceived duty of care requirement, and it appears to be most valued merely for its capacity to secure the commitment of patients to it.

7

How Suicide Prevention Contracting Can Compromise Treatment

Clinicians seek easy solutions to the difficult issue of suicide . . . "Easy steps for little feet."

—Edwin Shneidman maxim

KEY POINTS

- The perceived validity and effectiveness of SPC is challenged by fundamental difficulties in the contemporary logic of its use.
- Evaluating the 'right patient type' to offer SPC is highly problematic.
- The apparent values-base of SPC obscures the potential hazards of SPC.

Integral to SPC's propensity to manufacture hazardous clinical situations is a series of pre-existing deficits, which I call the *Four Fatal Flaws of SPC*. The SPC study demonstrated that in every case of NSAg and NSC activation one or more of three reasons for use are at play (perceived clinico-legal, therapeutic, diagnostic advantage), irrespective of which procedure is used. And, at the same time, each of these motivations for use brings with it a set of troubling inter-related notions and assumptions about the perceived nature and power of SPC which, when examined closely, show themselves to be deeply problematic, as I explain in the pages that follow. (We met two of these in the previous chapter as the two distal factors in the *SPC Decision-Making Schema* [*DMS*]).

FOUR FATAL FLAWS OF SPC

Fatal Flaw #1: All Things to Some People

The first of these is that clinicians using SPC appear to simultaneously seek therapeutic, clinico-legal and diagnostic advantage (Stanford, Goetz & Bloom, 1994; Davidson, Wagner & Range, 1995; Page & King, 2008; Edwards & Sachmann, 2010), SPC hereby representing an *all things to some people* 'shotgun' type approach to suicide intervention.

Fatal Flaw #2: The Curse of The False Positive

The second stems from the perceived efficacy of SPC by some clinicians generated, in part, when no serious suicide attempts or completed suicides occur when SPC is used. In other words, in comparison to the number of times an intervention is used, adverse outcomes are low, thereby giving the impression of general success to the intervention. The fact is, because serious suicide attempts and completed suicides are a relatively rare event, the prediction and prevention of suicide is therefore plagued by high rates of false positive evaluations (Murphy, 1984; Shaffer, Garland, Gould, Fisher & Trautman, 1988; Pokorny, 1993; Shneidman, 1993). The result is that low base rates and high false positive rates can generate a false sense of security in clinicians in respect to treatment modalities and management strategies. I've titled this *the curse of the false positive,* which amounts to attributing validity and efficacy to SPC when seemingly as a result of SPC suicidal behavior is averted.

Fatal Flaw #3: The Misguided Duality in the Use of SPC

The third, what I came to know as *the misguided duality in the use of SPC*, comprises using SPC *simultaneously* for 'communicating care and concern' to a patient *and* the clinician's clinico-legal self-protection (Weiss, 2001; Page & King, 2008; Edwards & Sachmann, 2010), as if the second had no impact on the first.

No matter how we phrased it, the basic idea of *the misguided duality in the use of SPC* was the same: *The Each Way Bet.* In other words, because of the ever-present possibility of an adverse outcome when dealing with suicidal patients, SPC is sometimes simultaneously employed as a merely *prudential* strategy. The logic of this strategy is that, on the one hand, SPC might reduce the risk of suicide occurring, but just in case it fails, on the other hand, it's perceived by some nonetheless to offer protection—when it can be shown that a patient assumed a degree of self-responsibility by agreeing to a agreement or contract—against the threatening consequences of that failure—potential litigation and possible recriminations from peers.

Fatal Flaw #4: Quasi-Legal Status of SPC

Fourth is the *quasi-legal status of SPC*, where clinicians presume that using an SPC procedure provides them with a degree of legal protection (Simon, 1999; Simon & Hales, 2006; Garvey, Penn, Campbell et al., 2009).

Yet the practical and clinical outcomes of such motivations can include: placing patients in a less restrictive setting having obtained a no suicide agreement or contract (Jones & O'Brien, 1990); SPC replacing a thorough assessment and management response (Rudd 1996); viewing a patient promise, and apparent 'congruent for safety' body language, as some form of guarantee of safety or diagnostic warranty (Jacobs, 1992, p.164); using SPC for perceived clinico-legal protection when clinically contraindicated (Simon, 1999; Simon & Hales, 2006). The use of an SPC procedure in each of these clinical scenarios is not helpful and has the potential to actually compromise treatment.

SPC as a Second or Third Backup Safety System

During a suicidal crisis, clinicians appear to *hardwire* everything that can be hardwired: increase patient supervision, consult with a senior colleague, employ a standardized risk evaluation tool, consider hospitalization, and remove everything that can't be, for example, reducing access to means. And at the same time, akin to air safety standard operating procedures, clinicians will often make a "second backup system" by providing crisis telephone numbers, and sometimes a third backup system in the form of SPC.

The logic of this practice is embedded in some of the comments we heard from clinicians: "I'll do a risk assessment and all that—I know they [SPC] may not help medico-legally but will note them anyway,"[1] "They [SPC] are a last resort to risk management,"[2] "They [SPC] give a ray of hope; it's [SPC] a kind of bonding to a stranger who cares; it's a last hope to cling to,"[3] And lastly, "More of a last resort."[4]

Now, you might be thinking: "But we should expect that. Of course, clinicians will do just about anything within reason to keep a patient safe. What's wrong with that?"

Here's what's wrong.

First, when you have what is perceived as a second or third backup system—in this case SPC, being used, in some cases as a first-order response, clinicians can incorrectly extrapolate from a positive response to SPC, thinking, "Hey, if they agree, then I don't need to *fully* consider hospital, or perform a thorough evaluation, or undertake other safety measures." It's no more complicated than what has likely already been happening for decades: on-the-job training in SPC informed—in some settings—unwittingly by *The Curse of the False Positive*. Second, most clinicians understand that complex cases are difficult to manage, and almost all suicidal crises are complex. Worse—*and this is the critical point*—the compounding of treatment "systems" into systems of systems results in more unwieldy complexity. Consider, for example (and, back to our air safety example) hydraulic, propulsion, lift surface, life support, navigation and other systems of aircrafts all tend to introduce new complexities in the form of unexpected overlaps of parts and unexpected behavior of previously well-behaved flight systems. For clinicians, the net result of introducing SPC into an already complex system is simply a rising level of complexity, potentially compromising treatment. In our case, unexpected overlaps occur such as introduced by *Miller's Paradox-The3Cs*, and unforeseen consequences such as *Simon's Paradox, The One in Four Concept*, all of which I will now explain.

THE FIVE PARADOXES OF SPC

And what, after all, is a paradox? A paradox commonly takes the form of a pair of statements about the one phenomenon that both appear to be true but which are nonetheless inconsistent with each other. There is something puzzling and seemingly nonsensical about the juxtaposition of the two sides of a paradox; you scratch your head and wonder: How on earth can this be? Paradoxes leave you with the impression that, contrary to impressions, both sides *cannot* be true; there must be some hidden error in one of them at least. One example is the commonly heard statement: "You're damned if you do, [and at the same time] you're damned if you don't." (Maybe you even feel this way about SPC—that you're damned if you do employ it because you're no longer convinced of its efficacy to prevent suicide; and you're damned if you don't because of the status it has achieved, in some settings, as the expected standard of care in some clinical settings.)

Indeed, a central point of this chapter, and a critical point of the entire book, is that the fundamental paradox of SPC use, which each of the following five paradoxes are a testament to, is this: while the purpose and intent of SPC is to protect (either patient or clinician), the effect of its practice is in fact threatening (to either or both patient and clinician). Just how and when this can be so will quickly become clear.

The SPC study data and wider literature led us to develop the following five paradoxes, established when SPC is activated resulting in the unintended consequence of establishing a potential for compromising treatment.

1. Simon's Paradox
2. Miller's Paradox-The 3Cs (including the One in Four Concept)
3. Mahrer's Paradox
4. McArdle's Paradox
5. Farrow's Paradox (including the Central Values Paradox of SPC and the Ethics of Expedience)

#1 SIMON'S PARADOX[1]

Studies have found unequivocal use of SPC procedures for perceived clinico-legal clinician self-protection in the anticipated event of litigation following a serious attempt or completed suicide (Mahrer, 1993; Davidson, Wagner & Range, 1995; Farrow, 2002; Sanders, Ting, Power & Jacobson, 2006; Page &

> Indeed, we came to understand the use of SPC as a somewhat Machiavellian construct. The contemporary practice of SPC made gains—establishing itself in the psychiatric lexicon since the 1980s—by manipulating the belief systems (*a Fear/Threat Balance*) of those pressured clinicians faced with active suicidal behavior and working in an environment characterised by uncertainty, the concealed apparent (in this case suicide) and the hidden (in this case perceived litigation and/or peer recriminations).

King, 2008). This reason for use was similarly illustrated in the SPC study data (Edwards & Sachmann, 2010), where more than one-half (n = 173/312; 55.5 percent) reported they *often to always* used NSAg for clinico-legal protection; less so for NSC (n = 74/154; 48 percent). The results from a MANOVA statistical test indicated significant differences (Pillai's Trace (df = 1, 105) = 0.223, p = 0.002 V = .17) between use of NSAg and NSC for clinico-legal protection. Subsequent ANOVA testing indicated significant univariate effect, where NSAg were significantly favored (F = 14.01) over NSC for 'increasing legal protection'.

According to professor Robert I. Simon (Simon, 1999, pp. 447–448), clinician claims of clinico-legal protection from a patient 'breaching' a suicide prevention contract are not likely to be upheld for the following four reasons:

- The parties to the contract must be legally competent—questions arise when one of the parties is mentally ill or suicidal and the other party has reason to know of this condition.
- The agreement or contract must include a value consideration, an inducement for each party to carry out his or her part of the bargain—any fee paid to the clinician is in exchange for the promise to provide competent services. In agreeing to SPC no additional consideration is provided by the patient.
- A mutual obligation must be imposed on each party—in SPC, the patient is the only party agreeing not to do something he or she is under no legal obligation to give up. The clinician may agree to call the patient; however, this is an extension of the duty of care already owed to the patient. Therefore the clinician's obligation in SPC is superfluous. Moreover, the significant power differential between clinician and patient would likely nullify the legal validity of a suicide prevention contract.
- The contract must not contravene public policy—a clinician may not enforce contract terms that would relieve them from liability for any harm caused by their negligence.

The opinions of an Australian Queens Legal Counsel and a State Coroner are consistent with Simon's (ibid.) North American opinion:

> I have never heard of a case dealing with the subject of no suicide contracts or no suicide agreements . . . while such contracts may have some therapeutic

value, I have considerable doubt as to whether their use would provide any immunity whatsoever from action by the dependents of a deceased patient who died by suicide if a breach of duty by the clinician who sought to rely upon the agreement could otherwise be established. (*Personal correspondence from Mr. Peter Semmler, Queens Legal Counsel, Sydney, Australia.)*

I am aware of mental health professionals asking persons at risk for self-harm to enter into a no suicide contract or no suicide agreement. I have never understood this was intended to be some form of legal arrangement, rather I have understood that it was intended by these techniques to reduce the likelihood that a person at risk from self-harm would take his or her own life. The way it has been explained at inquest hearings is that the technique is intended to create a relationship where, if the person does take his or her own life, then that would be contrary to the agreement and, therefore, in breach of the trust and expectation of the mental health professionals. As I understand the situation the technique is only helpful to place an impediment in the way of a person otherwise minded to take his or her own life. And it is not realistically seen as a reliable defense against any legal action. *(Personal correspondence from Mr. Alastair Hope, Queens Legal Counsel, State Coroner of Western Australia [retired].)*

Nevertheless, due to the ever-present possibility of an adverse outcome when dealing with suicidal patients, the data indicates SPC adherents' reasoning uses a risk and insurance calculation as its general principle. The paradox arising from using SPC for perceived clinico-legal protection is this: SPC "can

SIMON'S PARADOX

Routine use of SPC procedures for perceived clinico-legal protection *AND*, at the same time, over-reliance on SPC procedures, thereby replacing or moderating accepted standards of care, leaving clinicians open to legal and professional claims of negligence.

falsely offer clinicians a method for relieving their clinico-legal anxieties, potentially lessening their vigor and attention to other intervention modalities" (Simon, 1999, p. 446). Contemporaneously, if a clinician overly relies on SPC at the expense of accepted standards of care "it can serve as an indictment of his or her clinical judgment rather than offering protection" (ibid., p. 449), thereby potentially *increasing* liability (we coined this advise *Simon's Rule*):

Litigation after a Suicide

A concise commentary on suicide risk and suicide litigation comes from an interview with Dr. Phillip Resnick, MD, professor of psychiatry and director of the division of forensic psychiatry at Case School of Medicine in Cleveland by Susan Kweskin reporting for the *Psychiatric Times* (Resnick, 2011). Malpractice law expects the clinician to take reasonable precautions with regards to suicide risk. It must be shown that the clinician has violated the standard of care and didn't act reasonably. In the eyes of the law, there are two types of errors: an error of fact, and an error of judgment. Error of fact boils down to failing to gather relevant data such as assessment of suicidal intent, past history of suicidality, substance abuse, and so forth. Essentially for us, with regard to SPC, if it can be shown that employing an SPC was the primary assessment or management intervention, this could indicate negligence on the part of the clinician due to a lack of attention to their duty of care responsibilities. Let's say a clinician jumps in early and secures a contract or agreement—essentially accepting a patient's disavowal of intent to engage in suicidal behavior solely based on a patient agreeing to SPC—and fails to move onto completing the reasonable standard of care—thorough assessment, treatment and management interventions in line with the presented risk. Here they run the real risk of being seen to have failed in their duty of care.

For a plaintiff, four elements of proof are necessary for a malpractice case to prevail. The trier of fact examines the case for potential negligence based on what is often cited as The 4Ds:

1. Plaintiff must show the clinician had a Duty to the patient; duty is usually established with the clinician/patient relationship, and the
2. plaintiff must show a Dereliction in that duty of care; a deviation from the standard of care and that,

3. a deviation from such a standard of care Directly caused Damages: in our case most often physical injury or death resulting from a self-inflicted injury by the patient.

In sum, it needs to be shown that no prudent clinician would engage in these acts of omission or commission committed by the clinician under scrutiny. *Note*: Readers should bear in mind that legal practice cited here may differ from the practices in their own country.

#2 MILLER'S PARADOX-THE 3Cs[2]

Miller's Paradox is subtitled 'The 3Cs' because it centers on the current state that clinicians use SPC to 'communicate their care and concern' to the suicidal patient. Previous North American studies have identified a central theme of SPC, that it is believed to 'communicate a clinician's care and concern' to the patient asked to agree to SPC (Mahrer, 1993; Davidson et al., 1995; Page & King, 2008). This finding is consistent with the psychiatric literature postulating the utility of SPC in positively affecting a therapeutic alliance (Stanford, Goetz & Bloom, 1994; Range, 2005; Gutheil, 1992; Miller, Jacobs & Gutheil, 1998). Simlarly, findings from the SPC study were supportive of a perception that SPC communicates a clinician's care and concern. More than three-quarters (n = 269/312; 86.5 percent) '*agreed to strongly agreed*' that NSAg communicated their care and concern to a patient with only 6.1 percent (n = 18), stating they '*disagreed to strongly disagreed*' that NSAg achieves this. Similarly, (n = 128/155; 82.6 percent) '*agreed to strongly agreed*' for NSC, with 4 percent (n = 14) stating they '*disagreed to strongly disagreed*' that NSC achieves this.

It is sobering, then, to examine, albeit severely limited, the patient-focused research that demonstrates such unequivocal support for SPC communicating care and concern is questionable. Critically, these studies indicate that rather than conveying *positive* messages, the deployment of SPC with some patients has the probability of communicating negative messages.

A patient-focused study by Tony L. Farrow, PhD (New Zealand) found patients perceived that a decision to agree to SPC had adversely affected their relationship with the crisis team clinician who some participants felt was "just doing their job by securing a no suicide contract, and thereafter were given less attention" (Farrow, Simpson & Warren, 2002, p. 244). A U.S. study of college students found they were largely positive about SPC, except for those with a history of psychotherapy who believed that SPC would reduce a clinician's clinico-legal liability compared to students without past psychotherapy (Decant & Range, 1997), again making it plausible some patient cohorts view SPC negatively.

Steven Davis, MSc, and colleagues (from the United States) found patients with a history of multiple suicide attempts, on average, rated the therapeutic features of SPC lower than did patients without a multiple history of suicidal presentations (Davis, Williams & Hays, 2002). Citing the wider literature where patients with a multiple history of suicide attempts likely present with higher levels of psychopathology and lower problem-solving abilities (Linehan, Goodstein, Nielsen & Chiles, 1983; Rudd, Joiner & Rajab, 1996; Scott, House, Yates & Harrington, 1997), Davis suggests patients with a multiple history of suicide attempts may in fact perceive any intervention less favourably (p. 61). It seems possible to me, and fits the frequently heard clinical "wisdom," that requesting patients with a multiple suicide attempt history to sign, for example, a no suicide contract prior to day leave and alike has little benefit.

Obviously more patient-focused research is required to determine for sure the extent to which SPC conveys anti-therapeutic messages potentially compromising treatment by negatively impacting a therapeutic relationship. Nonetheless, I think it not premature to say that, on the basis of the currently known data, it would certainly appear that SPC are likely to communicate a negative message to some patients.

MILLER'S PARADOX

A clinician deploys SPC to communicate their care and concern to a patient, thereby strengthening a therapeutic alliance, *AND,* at the same time, the patient perceives SPC is used for clinician self-protection—increasing a potential to weaken the therapeutic alliance and strengthen risk for suicide.

The data and clinical wisdom behind Miller's Paradox indicates SPC users and a specific patient cohort may have a diametrically opposite conception of SPC. In short, the clinician believes SPC strengthens the therapeutic alliance, while patients may experience it as weakening the therapeutic alliance. In the end, clinicians use SPC to reduce suicide risk, and Miller's Paradox suggests the inherent potential of SPC to increase it.

The One in Four Concept

Naturally, the danger of Miller's Paradox doesn't apply in every case. Yet the question of whom it most obviously doesn't apply to is a critical question. What *the one in four concept* (determining quadrant of four patients) attempts to clarify theoretically is the 'right patient type' to offer SPC. Based upon research findings and speculation presented in Miller's Paradox, four variables appear in the four quadrants of the one in four matrix below. In only one of those possibilities is SPC not contraindicated—that is, when the factor of a patient's limited or no history of suicidal behavior is combined with their positive belief about SPC. According to the 1:4 matrix, in every other case SPC is contraindicated.

There would be no issue if clinicians were able to screen patients for their suitability for entering into an SPC. However, what evidence exists demonstrates that clinicians were largely indiscriminate about whom they offered

1. No previous suicidal behavior + negative belief about SPC = SPC contraindicated	2. Multiple suicide attempts + negative belief about SPC = SPC contraindicated
4. No previous suicidal behavior + positive belief about SPC = ?	3. Multiple suicide attempts + positive belief about SPC = SPC contraindicated

DIAGRAM 7.1
The One in Four Matrix

SPC procedures to. Essentially, clinicians did not individually evaluate patients for their suitability to enter into verbal NSAg or written NSC (Mahrer, 1993).

The One in Four Concept is a theory-based algorithm. Unfortunately, the set of rules behind the algorithm that could be used to evaluate which patient is suitable for SPC remain, for the most part, unknown. Consider firstly, for example, whether a clinician can accurately determine what constitutes a 'limited history' of suicidal behavior on an individual basis. Secondly, can a clinician accurately evaluate whether a patient is truly judging an offer for SPC positively? Thirdly, can a clinician prevent a patient's initially positive judgment changing from hour to hour, day to day, week to week, and from clinician to clinician? On all three scores, the potential disparity between appearance and reality makes the endeavor to reliably evaluate someone as being 'the right type' for using SPC a futile exercise. In the end, then, the theoretical value of the one in four matrix fails to translate into practical utility, and we are no closer to identifying for SPC a legitimate, that is, hazard-free, domain of applicability.

#3 MAHRER'S PARADOX[3]

Simple logic would indicate that if SPC was valid and effective in reducing risk for suicide, clinicians—rather than using it less over time—would use

Table 7.1. Suicidal patients seen in previous year afforded an SPC procedure by clinician's length of service status

Length of service	*n* (M) SD[a]	
	NSAg	NSC
Less than 5 yrs	43 (2.74) 1.25 **	14 (1.64) 1.15
Between 6 & 10 yrs	61 (2.20) 1.16	29 (1.79) 1.69
Between 11 & 20 yrs	89 (1.96) 1.10	49 (1.27) 0.63
More than 20 yrs	104 (2.03) 1.14	55 (1.49) 0.99

Note: [a] Mean and standard deviation for each item; 1 = *'Between 0 and 25% of the time'* to 4 = *'Between 76 and 100% of the time'*
** χ^2 ($df = 9$, n = 297) = 26.06, $p \leq .01$ $p = 0.002$, $V = .17$)

MAHRER'S PARADOX

Less experienced clinicians likely use SPC procedures more, *AND*, at the same time, more experienced clinicians use SPC procedures less.

SPC more. Yet, the evidence doesn't support such a hypothesis. In separate studies, clinical psychologist Jonathon Mahrer, PhD, and psychiatrist Jerome Kroll, MD, examined some five hundred psychiatrists' and psychologists' use of SPC (Mahrer, 1993; Kroll, 2000). The studies reported what has been described as "a time by use curve" (Mahrer, 1993, p. 111), whereby exposure to suicidality initially increases SPC use. However, a threshold is reached over time where after proportional usage decreases. According to Jon Mahrer, this threshold is likely reached as a clinician gains more clinical practice experience (i.e., years of service), after which proportional use of SPC decreases (ibid.). Consistent with these U.S.-based studies, clinicians in the SPC study with less than five years' experience were significantly more likely ($\chi 2$ [df = 9, n = 297] = 26.06, $p \leq .01$, $p = .002$, $V = .17$) to have used NSAg in the year prior to the study (See table 7.1).

In sum, contrary to expectations for an effective set of interventions, newer clinicians with likely fewer practice skills and knowledge appear to use SPC procedures more often, whereas more experienced and likely knowledgeable clinicians use SPC procedures less.

#4 MCARDLE'S PARADOX[4]

Given the existence of two SPC procedures (NSAg, NSC), an *ad hoc* assumption can be that clinicians use each procedure for different diagnostic reasons, situations, and patient presentations. Such an assumption has not yet been examined in prior SPC research. The SPC study found participants (n = 163/313; 52 percent) *often to always* preferred NSAg for assessing suicide risk

MCARDLE'S PARADOX

Clinicians using no suicide contracts according to suicide risk severity to increase safety, *AND,* at the same time, none of the SPC procedures offering any evidence of effectiveness according to risk levels, whichever way they may be utilized.

and to evaluate the need for inpatient or outpatient care ($n = 168/312$; 53.8 percent). However, participants used NSC more often when assessing precipitating risk factors ($n = 51/154$; 43.1 percent). Significant differences between the perceived diagnostic aspects of both SPC procedures were expressed in a preference for NSAg when considering dispersal options ($p \leq .05$, $F = 4.93$) and in assessment of risk ($p \leq .05$, $F = 4.70$).

When we lined up several of the NSAg and NSC data with No Suicide Assurances (NSAs) data, what appeared was a plausible pattern indicating an apparent 'use-by-risk' phenomenon. In that most participants ($n = 355/417$; 85 percent) used NSAs significantly more ($p \leq .001$) than NSAg for 'assessment of suicide risk'; NSAg were used significantly more ($F = 4.11$, $p \leq .05$) when 'specifying alternatives to suicide'; whereas NSC were used significantly more ($F = 9.02$, $p \leq .01$) when 'specifying specific suicidal behavior to cease'.

These data indicate a potential clinical practice situation where (1) NSAs represent a universal assessment intervention for all patients, (2) NSAg represent a specific intervention suggesting alternatives to suicidal behavior, and (3) NSC are perceived to offer clinicians a specialized intervention aimed at deterring specific suicidal behaviors with the highest risk patients.

#5 FARROW'S PARADOX[5]

Arising directly out of the use-by-risk proposition in McArdle's Paradox is *Farrow's Paradox*. The notion is simply this:

FARROW'S PARADOX

Those patients who are less likely to be able to give informed consent are more likely to be offered a procedure requiring the ability to give informed consent, that is, NSC or NSAg, *AND*, at the same time, those at less risk, who are more likely to be able to give informed consent, are less likely to be offered NSC or NSAg, both of which require it.

Central Values Paradox of SPC

Published work on the ethics of SPC has been largely confined to considering whether SPC is consistent with the legal and ethical doctrine of informed consent (Farrow, 2002; Farrow, Simpson & Warren, 2002; Farrow & O'Brien, 2003; Farrow, 2003). Tony Farrow's New Zealand–based study concluded that nurses felt their independent assessment alone of a patient's risk would not be seen as sufficient to accurately determine risk. Fearing future claims of negligence for not having used SPC led crisis nurses to secure NSAg or NSC with a majority of their patients (Farrow, 2002, pp. 215–218). It would appear such motivation has little to do with ethical considerations and more to do with expedience.

The perceived ethical foundations of SPC were explored in the SPC study using Thematic Analysis described by Boyatzis (1998). Unlike the closed-ended questions contained in the questionnaire where participants were asked to describe their own use and perceptions of SPC, the open-ended question asked participants for their understanding about how *other* clinicians use SPC. It was expected that by wording this question in such a way—a convention adopted from family therapy—participants would feel less threatened and therefore be able to respond more openly. These data ($n = 176/420$; 41 percent) indicated that SPC was regarded something like an ethical two-way street. SPC was seen to both serve as a vehicle for communicating fundamental values to patients *AND*, at the same time, used to engender a similar response in patients. Some examples may be clarifying.

The following quotes are representative statements from the study's clinicians who were asked to describe the theoretical and philosophical reasons for SPC use. Next to each statement are the core value(s) that perhaps best reflect their responses. The value-centered reasons why clinicians use SPC included:

- "[SPC] shows care and concern for client safety and prevents hospitalization when not necessary"[5] Clinical psychologist with four years' experience (*Concern*)
- "[SPC] shares burden of care with patient"[6] Occupational therapist with six years' experience *(Concern)*
- "[SPC] highlights the reciprocal nature of the relationship"[7] Social worker with thirty years' experience (*Consideration*)
- "[SPC] supports informed consent/assists with problem solving via modeling"[8] Mental health nurse with twenty years' experience *(Truthfulness, Respect)*
- "[SPC] expresses care and concern—[and is used for] instituting behavioral and treatment approaches"[9] Social worker with five years' experience (*Concern*)
- "In most cultures giving your word and keeping it are important; a verbal agreement is more important than a written one"[10] Mental health nurse with thirty-one years' experience (*Honesty, Respect*)
- "[SPC is] associated with Carl Rogers's client-centred approach of empathy, unconditional regard and congruence" [11] Social worker with nine years' experience *(Concern, Respect)*
- "[SPC is used] to communicate to the patient the importance which the worker places on both *a)* how despairing the patient is feeling and *b)* how seriously the workers want the patient to be safe"[12] Clinical psychologist with twenty years' experience (*Respect, Concern*)
- "Thinking it [SPC] is required by their service; 'doing everything possible'."[13] Registered medical officer with twenty years' experience (*Duty*)

As mentioned, the thematic analysis showed that SPC was used not only as a way to embody the clinician's values, but to elicit an enactment by the patient of values such as respect, duty, obedience and responsibility. SPC's use appears to be understood as a vehicle for requesting enactment of these values, thereby creating a climate where compassion and kindness is shown, and the patient's sense of obligation and self-responsibility is fostered. These findings are reflective of early expert opinion likening SPC to a badge of honor, or what Stone (1980, p. 65) describes as a "patient's written pledge" where the therapeutic alliance established with a clinician was used to appeal to a patient's sense of honor. These second set of representative statements highlight how clinician's seek to engender patient-directed values when offering SPC. The patient-directed values that are why clinicians offer SPC included:

- "I use these as a way of engaging the patient's sense of obligation to refrain from suicide through the relationship between therapist and client." [14] Social worker with twelve years' experience *(Patient Obedience, Responsibility, Duty)*
- "SPC encourages patient self-responsibility, but does not reduce risk."[15] Mental health nurse with thirty years' experience *(Patient Responsibility)*
- "Encourage [patient] accountability and responsibility."[16] Mental health nurse with thirty-three years' experience *(Patient Obedience, Responsibility)*
- "Theory of duty of care, sanctity of life argument; self-determination and autonomy; rights and responsibility towards suicide ideation; religious beliefs"[17] Mental health nurse with forty-one years' experience *(Patient Duty, Respect, Responsibility)*
- "Trust—I take their word as meaning something; it can look paternalistic but I view it as more humanistic"[18] Mental health nurse with fifteen years' experience *(Patient Trust & Honesty, Kindness, Responsibility)*
- "Ownership of behavior given to patient"[19] Clinical psychologist three years' experience *(Patient Responsibility)*
- "I think they work extremely well in the community and give credibility to the therapeutic process"[20] Mental health nurse with thirty years' experience *(Patient Honesty & Trust)*

It should be evident that the apparently ethical foundation of SPC rests on its being seen to embody both the clinician's personal and professional values, as well as its capacity to encourage the patient to also act according to objective values. Whether such appearances really do fall under the broad rubric of genuinely ethical practice is open to debate, given that SPC has been shown to be used as an administrative procedure for clinico-legal protection, and the consequences of not agreeing to SPC (e.g., involuntary admission) is often implicitly rather than explicitly communicated to the patient. On the face of it, the concerns about informed consent and the unintended consequences of SPC use render its ethical foundations deeply problematic.

CONCLUSION

This largely theoretical approach to reviewing primarily qualitative research findings illustrates the breadth and depth of the potential hazards with SPC. It is evident that positive clinician reports regarding their attitudes towards, satisfaction with, and use of SPC procedures are in likely opposition to a cohort of patients. More patient studies are required. It is apparent that the potential hazards are more potent when SPC is used as a first-line or stand-alone intervention. The demystification of SPC and potential to compromise treatment has been made possible by viewing SPC as a multi-dimensional set of procedures. Caution is nonetheless needed regarding the limitations of the presented data, namely, drawing definitive conclusions from qualitative data.

8

The Role of No Suicide Assurances in Clinical Practice

People are pretty much alike. It's only that our differences are more susceptible to definition than our similarities.

KEY POINTS

- NSAs are qualitatively different to NSAg/NSC and not a form of SPC.
- Used under specific criteria, NSAs are not subject to the same problems and paradoxes of NSC and NSAg.
- The conflation of NSAs with NSAg and NSC has hampered clear debate and hindered research about SPC.

No suicide assurances (NSAs) have been defined as a brief verbal exchange (a single question and answer process) where a patient is asked to assure the evaluator that they are able to refrain from suicidal behavior (Edwards & Sachmann, 2010, p. 291). For example, a patient is asked directly: "Are you able to refrain from suicidal behavior?" or "Are you able to control your suicidal urges?"

Due to the limited current understanding of and lack of nomenclature for SPC, there is neither debate nor consensus regarding the differences and similarities between NSAs and NSC/NSAg. The SPC study data suggested that NSAs were used as a routine suicide risk assessment procedure. Granted, as was the case for NSC and NSAg, routine use of any procedure by a majority of clinicians is no proof of its validity and efficacy. Yet the broader scholarship indicates that deployment of a no suicide assurance type procedure in the context of a broader and ongoing evaluation, treatment and management protocol by a trained clinician to provide a subjective measure of patient suicide risk represents sensible practice (Mahrer & Bongar, 1996; Shea, 1999, p. 182; Range, Campbell, Kovac, Marion-Jones, Aldridge, Kogos & Crump, 2002; Brent, 1997, p. 283).

THE NATURE OF NO SUICIDE ASSURANCES

The SPC study involved an initial survey of the literature, followed by a series of unstructured interviews conducted with a group of mental health clinicians with the aim to inform the development of a semi-structured interview format. These second series of interviews comprised twelve semi-structured interviews with a separate group of mental health clinicians. The data obtained from these interviews indicated clinician's utilize three types of procedures. This assumption was tested by dividing the SPC study's questionnaire into three sections asking clinicians' their use of, attitudes towards and satisfaction with NSAs, NSAg and NSC.

Findings show that most participants (n = 355/417; 85 percent) had used NSAs. NSAs were used by 45 percent of clinicians (n=157/349) 50 percent of the time when consulting a suicidal patient, which may suggest a standard of care. More than one-half (n = 194/350; 55 percent) reported they '*often to always*' used NSAs for clinico-legal protection (M = 3.48, SD 1.33). Just over one half (n = 182/352; 52 percent) of clinicians '*often to always*' used NSAs to 'assist the therapeutic process' (M = 3.50, SD 1.04; 1 = '*never*' to 5 = '*always*'), with 14.5 percent (n = 51) stating they '*rarely to never*' used NSAs for this reason. Nearly two-thirds (n = 212/354; 60 percent) reported they '*often to always*' used NSAs for 'diagnostic clarification' of suicide risk (M = 3.66, SD 1.11), with 13 percent (n = 46/354) stating they '*rarely to never*' used NSAs for this reason. In fact, clinicians significantly favored NSAs over NSAg for 'assessing suicide risk' (Wilcoxon signed ranked test n = 140, z = –3.33, p = .001, two tailed; NSAs: M = 3.68, SD =1.03; NSAg: M = 3.45, SD = 1.05: 1 = '*never*' to 5 = '*always*').

These data are suggestive that while some clinicians understand NSAs to represent a brief yes/no verbal exchange, likely used as an adjunct to a thorough evaluation, to establish a subjective measure of self-reported suicide risk, others may well conflate NSAs with NSAg and NSC. With NSAs typically grouped with NSAg and NSC, this is not only an error, because of the qualitative different, it has also hidden their benefits under specific conditions.

The Judicious Use of NSAs

To recap, while data from the SPC study showed some clinicians understand a degree of clinico-legal protection in the use of NSAs, it is also apparent clinicians see NSAs as both a risk assessment question and, by raising the issue of suicidality in the form of a no suicide assurance, may well offer the patient an opportunity for human connection and cathartic release. Redefining how clinicians think about and talk about NSAs will affect how it is used and will likely reduce unintended adverse consequences from SPC. To quickly grasp the reasoning for this, consider the following vignette when a no suicide assurance is implemented strictly in accordance with what has been titled *Fenner's Rule.*[1]

The key point here is that *within the conditions specified by Fenner's Rule, and only within those conditions, there is nothing militating against the safe use of NSAs.* But where those conditions are not met, NSAs cannot be relied upon to provide clinico-legal, therapeutic or diagnostic advantage.

Case Example of NSAs in Practice

Over the initial sessions with a depressed patient, a 'treatment agreement' is developed; a mutually conducted procedure is undertaken to clarify the maintaining and precipitating factors that need to be addressed, and to establish

> **FENNER'S RULE**
>
> Within a comprehensive and ongoing evaluation and suicide risk management response (medical, psychological and/or social), the routine use of a no suicide assurance aims to gain a subjective level of risk for suicidal behavior.

options for treatment. The benefits and risks of all considered treatment interventions, including no treatment, are presented to the patient, whose informed consent is sought. During the treatment phase it becomes clear that a specific troubling behavior, for example struggling with compliance to methadone treatment for heroin addiction, is having a negative effect on treatment outcomes. A 'contingency contract,' also called a 'behavior agreement,' is established. This is a procedure that capitalizes on the patient-clinician relationship by involving the patient in treatment decision-making to affect a course of action aimed at reinforcing new behavior, controlling symptoms and offering the patient a sense of mastery over their addictive behaviors. During this stage of treatment, the patient experiences distressing levels of suicidal thinking.

At each subsequent session a routine suicide risk assessment is undertaken. As part of the suicide risk evaluation a 'no suicide assurance' is used, where the patient is asked directly: *"Are you able to refrain from suicidal behavior until I see you again?"* or *"Are you able to control your suicidal urges until next we meet?"* Here, the evaluator is seeking to establish the level of suicide risk, albeit subjectively, on the basis of the patient's self-assessment (i.e., by listening for a simple 'yes' or 'no', and vocal and physical congruence or otherwise, questioning further any inconsistencies). Having subjectively gauged the level of risk—and recording this in their risk evaluation—the clinician then completed their risk assessment and moved from the no suicide assurance (hence not exposing either patient or clinician to the detrimental aspects of either a no suicide agreement or no suicide contract) to developing and deploying one of the alternative procedures to SPC, as necessary.

Finally, prior to ending each session, a Crisis Plan Response (CPR) is developed and agreed upon. The process for obtaining emergency assistance and/or enacting other pre-arranged safety steps in times of suicidal crises are discussed and even rehearsed. Decisions are made regarding the patient having access to the clinician in times of suicidal crises. The CPR is reviewed at each subsequent session where suicide risk is noted. (Such a process is described in chapter 10 as Alternative #1.)

Comparison of SPC and NSAs

To summarize, NSAs comprise a brief verbal exchange (a single question and answer process) where a patient is asked to assure the evaluator they are able to refrain from suicidal behavior. For example, a patient is asked directly:

Table 8.1. Comparison of SPC and NSAs

Dimensions of SPC	SPC (NSAg/ NSC)	NSAs
Historical and conceptual basis	SPC is a confluence of theoretical notions; representing a procedural admixture of competing clinician demands for clinical advantage prone to cultivating a false sense of advantage.	NSAs operating under *Fenner's Rule* are one element of a standard suicide risk assessment/ management protocol.
Anatomy of SPC (see SPC Decision Making Schema; Farrow's Paradox)	The desired effect of SPC is often future focused and frequently implicitly conveyed to a patient bringing into question a clinician's adherence to duty of care and raises other ethical questions.	NSAs are a present focused 'point-in-time' patient-directed evaluation explicitly conveyed.
Clinico-legal protection (see Simon's Paradox)	SPC reliance can moderate accepted standards of care, leaving clinicians open to legal and professional claims of negligence.	NSAs operating under *Fenner's Rule* shifts focus from SPC as a stand-alone evaluation or management procedure to a *subjectively* calibrated indicator of risk for suicidal behavior.
Therapeutic advantage (see Miller's Paradox)	SPC's apparent and contradictory advantages evoke patient's perceptions of clinician's retreating to self-protection, potentially weakening alliances.	NSAs as a point-in-time overtly communicated subjective assessment of risk evaluation are congruent with establishing a therapeutic alliance.
Diagnostic clarification (see McArdle's Paradox)	SPC used as a dispersal procedure, as a calibrated predictive or evaluative measure is prone to placing severely suicidal in unsafe environments increasing risk.	NSAs offer a subjective assessment of risk within the confines of a broader evaluation process.
Contraindications (see One in Four Concept; primary and secondary contraindications)	SPC's evaluation for patient appropriateness is unreliable; prone to variance between appointments.	NSAs are indicated for the majority of patients with suicidal ideation.

"Are you able to refrain from suicidal behavior?" or *"Are you able to control your suicidal urges?"* This brief procedure can provide a subjective appraisal of the patient's self-assessed level of suicide risk. To harness an already established level of therapeutic alliance, asking the question towards the end of the evaluation process is preferable. The essential step about utilizing NSAs is that it must be understood as the *subjective evaluation component* of a comprehensive assessment and management approach (*cf.* Fenner's Rule).

When NSAs are employed according to Fenner's Rule, the clinician places no *therapeutic or clinico-legal burden* on the patient's assurances. The clinical utility of NSAs is strictly confined to its purpose of gaining a subjective measure of current risk. The therapeutic, clinico-legal and diagnostic burden continues to be carried by the other supportive processes put in place by the clinician and, in part, shared with the patient.

Here you may be wondering: "Why don't NSAs fall foul of the practical, legal and other fundamental flaws which undermine the reasons for using SPC?" To understand the qualitative differences of NSAs and NSAg/NSC in clinical practice, a comparison may be instructive. Table 8.1 lists the fundamental flaws in SPC procedures (as elaborated upon in the previous chapter), and explains why and how the use of NSAs (only according to Fenner's Rule) avoids manufacturing the unintended consequences of SPC procedures.

CONCLUSION

Findings from reported SPC studies offer little to confirm the diagnostic or therapeutic benefits of NSAs. So then, at this point in time, the other and more important question is whether or not the use of NSAs lies within the realms of good practice. The answer to this question is almost invariably yes, not solely because it is not a stand-alone modality, likely on occasion divorced from other response strategies, but because it can (and should) function as a minor adjunct to a comprehensive assessment process. When the aggregated findings regarding SPC procedures are considered, far less of the potential for compromising treatment present for SPC exist in relation to NSAs operating under *Fenner's Rule.*

9

Contraindications for Suicide Prevention Contracting

Everything should be made as simple as possible, but not simpler. —Albert Einstein

KEY POINTS

- More patient-perspective SPC research is required to better understand its contraindications.
- Primary and secondary contraindications disqualify most of the therapeutic, diagnostic and clinico-legal reasons for using SPC.

Before describing the alternative techniques, procedures and protocols to SPC in chapter 10, it may be instructive to provide in condensed form the factors working against contemporary SPC as described in previous chapters. In the remainder of this chapter are summarised the primary and secondary contraindicated factors for SPC.

As a general rule, the primary contraindicated factors—those developed from the key findings of the SPC study—are first-order questions a clinician or supervisor needs to consider prior to developing, activating or recommending either NSAg or NSC. The following are the primary contraindications to SPC. They also represent pre-deployment questions to determine the appropriateness of SPC. As a general rule: SPC is contraindicated if any question is answered in the affirmative.

- Mahrer's Paradox—is the clinician inexperienced, without training in SPC or suicide prevention generally?
- McArdle's Paradox—is the clinician considering SPC with a patient assessed at a moderate to high risk for suicide?
- Miller's Paradox (The 3C's)—is the clinician considering SPC in order to communicate their care and concern to a patient they have minimal knowledge of or with whom a minimal therapeutic alliance has been developed?
- The One in Four Concept—is the clinician considering SPC with a patient who has a prior history of suicidal behavior and/or a negative or ambivalent regard for SPC?
- The Quasi-Legal Status of SPC (Simon's Paradox)—is the clinician considering SPC with a patient for clinico-legal self-protection?
- Farrow's Paradox—is the clinician considering SPC with a patient unlikely to be able to give informed consent to the procedure, or unaware of the consequences (e.g., involuntary admission) if declined?
- Right-Minded Values in the Injudicious Use of SPC—is the clinician considering SPC for value-centered reasons such as trust, honesty, and respect? *AND, at the same time,* seeking to engender patient-directed values such as obedience, responsibility, and duty by using SPC?
- Curse of the False Positive—is the clinician considering SPC due to past use without adverse outcomes?
- Misguided Duality in the Use of SPC—is the supervisor recommending/the clinician considering SPC simultaneously for patient care and clinician self-protection?

The secondary contraindications go to the heart of a clinical presentation—the nature of a therapeutic alliance, and the elements in clinical settings which are considered, according to expert opinion, adverse to employing any form of SPC. You will notice in examining the following list that the secondary contraindications have one or more key findings from the study next to each factor, indicating its likely activation if SPC is used in a contraindicated fashion.

Patient & Caregiver

- SPC is ill advised with patients who have made suicide the central theme of their lives; where heavy use of alcohol and/or drugs is present; who are intellectually impaired (Drye, Goulding & Goulding, 1973)—McArdle's Paradox

- SPC is ill advised with severely suicidal patients due to psychotic illness and/or those assessed as chronically suicidal (Mahrer & Bongar, 1996)—McArdle's Paradox, Farrow's Paradox
- SPC is ill advised with patients experiencing an escalation of suicidal risk (Clark & Kerkhof, 1993, 1997)—McArdle's Paradox
- SPC is ill advised with patients assessed as not interpersonally responsive; as characterlogically maladaptive; as impulsive; as chronically suicidal (parasuicidal); as extremely paranoid; the patient is a child or an adolescent; assessed as significantly alcohol and/or drug dependent; the evaluating clinician is not from (or is unfamiliar with) the suicidal patient's culture (Mahrer, 1993, p. 43)—Miller's Paradox, One in Four Concept, McArdle's Paradox, Farrow's Paradox
- SPC is ill advised when the caregiver(s) of a child or adolescent patient is absent and/or caregiver(s) are assessed as not being able to adequately supervise its implementation (Brent, 1997)—Ethics of Expedience, Farrow's Paradox, All Things to Some People

Inappropriate Therapeutic Alliance

- SPC is ill advised where the deployment of SPC is secondary to a therapeutic rupture (i.e., a clinician offers SPC as a means of repairing an alliance) (Jacobs, 1992)—Miller's Paradox, One in Four Concept
- SPC is ill advised when a therapeutic relationship between clinician and patient has not developed or is attenuated (i.e., has become weaker) (Simon & Hales, 2006; Miller, 1999)—Miller's Paradox, One in Four Concept

Non-Conducive Clinical Environment

- SPC is ill advised within an emergency setting. For example, in the hospital emergency department setting or community crisis setting where a therapeutic relationship may not develop or is weak; where a clinical environment making assessment of competence over time is unlikely (Simon & Hales, 2006; Miller, 1999; Rudd, Mandrusiak & Joiner, 2006; Reid, 2005)—Miller's Paradox, One in Four Concept
- SPC is ill advised when used in isolation from a robust assessment and management plan (Weiss, 2001)—Mahrer's Paradox

CONCLUSION

While no large-scale patient research exists demonstrating the importance of these primary and secondary contraindications for SPC, large-scale clinician surveys (Mahrer, 1993; Page & King, 2008; Edwards & Sachmann, 2010) and expert opinion are consistent, and may be sufficient to justify SPC's contra-indicated factors per se.

IV

ALTERNATIVES TO SUICIDE PREVENTION CONTRACTING

German philosopher Ulrich Beck (1992, 1999, 2000) describes today's society as the *risk society* due, in large part, to the unintended consequence of a neo-liberal free-market vision and its implementation. He describes how the modernization of the post-industrialized world has undermined the foundations of society, changing traditional social, economic and political frames of reference. As such, the task of institutions in contemporary society is to 'manage' these self-induced consequences (*risks*) of rapid technological advancement by making them socially calculable, and their potential consequences controllable. Beck (2000) understands that contemporary society is characterized by projections of fearful realities, which are balanced by evidence of the ability to control the unanticipated through "a dialectic of risk and insurance calculation providing the cognitive and institutional apparatus (p. 76)."

Not surprisingly, the communication of this sense of present and future risk and the potential for hazard is not a mere statement of possibilities. Risks contain a theoretical and normative element. Beck (1992) contends that manufacturing prospects for terrible consequences in itself has the potential for making those consequences real/bringing those consequences about—manufacturing of a terrible consequential reality can be enough to create its inevitability or 'truth'. Thus, even as conjecture, risks are threats to the future, which develop a 'practical relevance to preventative actions'

(p. 34). In this way risk can be constantly imagined, implied to be true and believed by the vast majority. The imagined threat of clinico-legal litigation, for example, assumes almost literary proportion with its own plotline (e.g., adverse clinical outcome and consequences) and dramatic narrative outcome (e.g., litigation).

10

Seven Alternatives to Suicide Prevention Contracting

Sow a Thought, Reap an Action; Sow an Action, Reap a Habit; Sow a Habit, Reap a Character; Sow a Character, Reap a Destiny. —A Character Maxim

KEY POINTS

- Developers of alternatives to SPC cite the crucial necessity for informed consent.
- Careful suicide risk assessment and management process is routine practice when using any alternative to SPC.
- One of the alternatives to SPC has an emerging evidence base.

Granted, all those who use SPC procedures will not overly rely upon them at the expense of a thorough assessment, treatment and management process. Yet there remains the clear reality that SPC is seen by some to replace or that it compromises other responses such as detailed and ongoing risk assessment, removal of lethal means, senior peer consultation or hospitalization. One clinical practice axiom that emerged for us from the SPC study was that "the risks of using SPC obviously outweigh the benefits." To this can be added a second: "that any benefits lost by not using an SPC procedure can be recovered by using alternative interventions that carry less potential risk."

The following seven alternatives to SPC are based on good practice protocols. Some are discrete techniques within a broader, theory-driven treatment process; others derive variously from a brief contingency planning approach, a structured CBT-inspired methodology, a blend of the principles of informed consent and the therapeutic contract, to a multi-modal approach comprising assessment, management planning and consultation.

#1 CRISIS PLAN RESPONSE

In my work with suicidal children and youth, I have observed numerous methods for documenting management, treatment, safety and crisis plans. While again not wanting to belabor and detail all the types of CPR templates possible, re-stating the critical distinction is necessary: why a CPR is not an SPC procedure. First and foremost, a CPR does not explicitly request, either verbally or in writing, a patient to agree not to engage in suicidal behavior for a specified time period. There are several common elements of a CPR evident:

1. A CPR for suicidal behavior sometimes includes the patient's risk status, known risk factors (e.g., nature of current mental illness, current plans, previous attempts and means, access to current means), protective factors, the recorded factors likely to increase risk (e.g., alcohol use), and a list of clinicians and significant others and their contact details who are able to assist in a future suicidal crisis. This CPR is useful when sharing the document with others involved in increasing the patient's safety. A condensed version (see Safety Plan) may be seen as more appropriate for individual patients.
2. A CPR for suicidal behavior usually includes a list of actions a patient (partner or caregiver in the case of child and adolescent patients) should enact in times of elevated suicide risk. For example, trying a graded response from using pre-defined coping strategies, contacting designated crisis lines, or attending the emergency center.
3. A CPR for suicidal behavior usually includes what the attending clinician will do in times of elevated patient suicide risk. For example, a statement regarding times the clinician is available to be contacted is included.

A CPR framework provides one powerful example of how all of the available resources (i.e., the patient's, clinician's, practice setting's, caregivers' and significant other resources) can be mobilized and brought to bear on reducing the future risk for patient suicidal behavior.

Safety Planning

Perhaps less so than with the lack of nomenclature surrounding SPC, there exists a variety of terms for categorizing the steps taken to increase a suicidal patients' safety. That said, the term "safety planning" appears to have taken hold, and related emerging work presents useful response strategies in negotiating and collaborating with the suicidal patient and caregiver(s) rather than seeking an "ironclad" agreement (Rudd, Joiner & Rajab, 2001; Samra & Bilsker, 2007; Brent, Poling, & Goldstein, 2011; Stanley & Brown, 2012; Jobes, 2012). Though fully describing some of these recent works is beyond the scope of this chapter, an introductory review of some may be instructive.

U.S. suicidologist David A. Jobes, PhD, (2006, 2012) has devised an evidence-led psychotherapeutic approach to managing suicide risk (both inpatient and outpatient focused) titled the Collaborative Assessment and Management of Suicidality (CAMS). Within the CAMS approach Jobes (2006) recommends clinicians use the multipurpose assessment, treatment planning, tracking and outcome tool titled a Suicide Status Form (SSF), a widely used seven-page instrument (Range, 2002). Refer to Jobes (2006) to gather a full understanding of the approach with access to the SSF and the associated Safety Plan.

To summarize, a Safety Plan for suicidal patients is a brief step-by-step list of contingencies jointly developed between the clinician, the patient and any competent present caregiver(s) (in case of minors) or partner/caregiver (in case of adults) aimed at increasing safety by reinforcing pre-defined coping behaviors, and, in turn, better controlling suicidal thoughts and behavior, which offers the patient and caregiver a sense of mastery over their distress. In practice, on completion of the suicide risk assessment, the clinician then works with the patient and caregiver on developing their Safety Plan. Younger children may have a one-point plan of telling the caregiver when they have suicidal thoughts, with the remaining list of contingencies developed with and for the caregiver. Developing a Safety Plan is one part of the clinical process: a procedure that capitalizes on the patient-clinician relationship by actively involving patients and caregivers in treatment decision-making to affect a course of action. A Safety Plan is not a stand-alone procedure. The steps in the planning, when enacted, are intended to reduce the frequency and intensity of suicidal crises and to increase patient safety during such crises.

Safety Plan

If you have thoughts of hurting yourself, start at Step 1. Go through each step until you are safe. Remember: Suicidal thoughts can be very strong. It may seem they will last forever. With support and time, these thoughts will usually pass. When they pass, you can put energy into sorting out problems that have contributed to you feeling so badly. The hopelessness you may feel now will not last forever. It is important to reach out for help and support. You can get through this difficult time. Since it can be hard to focus and think clearly when you feel suicidal, please copy this and put in places where you can easily use it, such as your purse, wallet or by the phone.

1. Do the following activities to calm/comfort myself:

2. Remind myself of my reasons for living:

3. Call a friend or family member:	Name:
	Phone:
4. Call a backup person if person above is not available:	Name:
	Phone:
5. Call a care provider (psychologist, psychiatrist, therapist):	Name:
	Phone:
6. Call my local crisis line:	Phone:

7. Go somewhere I am safe:

8. Go to the Emergency Room at the nearest hospital.

9. If I feel that I can't get to the hospital safely, call [ ] and request transportation to the hospital.

They will send someone to transport me safely.

FIGURE 10.1
Safety Plan template[1]

One version of a Safety Plan is that presented by Samra & Bilsker (2007) (See figure 10.1).

Somewhat similar, is another version developed by Stanley & Brown (2012) (See figure 10.2). The Safety Plan proforma is designed to offer patients and caregivers a graded process they can use moving from step 1 through 5 until a strategy responds adequately to the level of suicidality:

SAFETY PLAN

Step 1: Warning signs:

1. ____________________
2. ____________________
3. ____________________

Step 2: Internal coping strategies - Things I can do to take my mind off my problems without contacting another person:

1. ____________________
2. ____________________
3. ____________________

Step 3: People and social settings that provide distraction:

1. Name________________ Phone________
2. Name________________ Phone________
3. Place____________________
4. Place ____________________

Step 4: People whom I can ask for help:

1. Name________________ Phone________
2. Name________________ Phone________
3. Name________________ Phone________

Step 5:Professionals or agencies I can contact during a crisis:

1. Clinician Name______________ Phone________
   Clinician Pager or Emergency Contact #____________
2. Clinician Name______________ Phone________
   Clinician Pager or Emergency Contact #____________
3. Suicide Prevention Lifeline: 1-800-273-TALK (8255)
4. Local Emergency Service ________________
   Emergency Services Address________________
   Emergency Services Phone ________________

Making the environment safe:

1. ____________________
2. ____________________

Stanley, B. & Brown, G. K. (2012). Safety planning intervention: A brief intervention to mitigate suicide risk. *Cognitive and Behavioral Practice, 19*, 256-264

FIGURE 10.2
Safety Plan Sample

Step 1: Warning Signs

Knowing what types of situations, images, thoughts, feelings or behaviors triggers the patients' suicidality will help the individual understand when they need to use their Safety Plan.

Step 2: Internal Coping Strategies

Strategies the patient can do on their own before contacting another, such as pre-rehearsed self-soothing techniques or physical activity. Consider the likelihood of the patient undertaking this step in a suicidal crisis and problem solve what may get in their way from trying it.

Step 3: Social Contacts That May Distract the Patient from a Crisis

Coach the patient/caregiver to use step 3 if step 2 didn't help to reduce thoughts of suicide. Together with the patient, write down safe places they can go to be around people or a person they can be around who knows them and cares about them. If the patient is unable to think of safe people or safe places, problem solve as appropriate. Again, consider the likelihood of the patient undertaking this step in a suicidal crisis and problem solve what may get in their way from trying it.

Step 4: People Whom I Can Ask for Help

Coach the patient/caregiver to use step 4 if step 3 didn't help to reduce thoughts of suicide. Help the patient to write down several names in case one is not contactable. These are people they can go and tell when in crisis. It's best to role play this in session and, if the patient is unable to nominate people, problem solve as appropriate.

Step 5: Professionals and Agencies to Contact for Help

Coach the patient/caregiver to use step 5 if step 4 didn't help to reduce thoughts of suicide. Work with the patient to write down the names and telephone numbers of these crisis and other professional services they can call. It's best to role play this in session and, if your patient is unable to do this, problem solve as appropriate. If appropriate, write down what days you're available to take your patients' call if they ring during business hours.

Making the Environment Safe (Reducing Access to Means)

Together, work out ways to make the patient's environment safer by removing means they may use in a suicidal crisis, such as medications. It's best to arrange this in session, assessing the likelihood if the patient can do this step, and discuss the outcome with the caregiver or partner. In the case of children and adolescents, assess the likelihood that the caregiver/partner will do this step. If they are unable or unwilling to reduce access to means, consider increasing the child's risk rating and adjust their management plan accordingly.

#2 THE SAFETY AGREEMENT

In 2001, U.S. nurse practitioners clinical professor of nursing, Mertie L. Potter and Ann M. Dawson, RN, devised an alternative to SPC specific to inpatient-based nursing care (Potter & Dawson, 2001). The Safety Agreement is a questioning and evaluation process to confirm a nurse's clinical observations of a patient, which assists in assessing and obtaining a hospitalized patient's cooperation and participation in an agreement for safety.

Under the rubric of Orlando's nursing theory, the Safety Agreement aims to reduce patient distress and increase collaboration and communication between the patient and nurse. The Safety Agreement comprises an initial screening of a patient's cognitive state, having already established the presence or absence of psychosis and dementia.

Following screening, a scripted set of questions contained in the Safety Agreement tool is asked to enable a nurse to examine more closely their perceptions of a patient's apparent levels of emotional distress. A scoring instrument comprising a series of Likert scales are included in the Safety Agreement, which further assists a nurse to assess a patient's distress levels. Once these patient observational data have been collated, the nurse enters into an open discussion with the patient. In this discussion, the nurse describes their perceptions to the patient, and describes which interventions can be used to maintain patient safety, including an explanation of the nurse's rationale for recommending a specific treatment (See Appendix A, pages 210–211, for an example of a Safety Agreement[2]).

3 THE COMMITMENT TO TREATMENT STATEMENT

CTS involves a mutual verbal and written agreement between patient and clinician for a course of treatment and commitment to living facilitated by open discussion regarding all aspects of the treatment process, including suicidal risk, and is grounded within a comprehensive assessment, management and crisis plan response (Rudd, Mandrusiak & Joiner, 2006). The CTS developers, U.S. suicidologists M. David Rudd, PhD, Jan Mandrusiak, PhD, and Thomas T. Joiner, PhD, recommend a structured approach in the form of a CTS which is a blending of the therapeutic alliance with informed consent. As part of a broader treatment plan, the CTS, as an alternative to SPC, is seen as an agreement between patient and clinician, wherein the patient is to make a commitment to the treatment process and to living.

The CTS comprises:

1. Identification of the roles, obligations, and expectations of both parties
2. A commitment to open, two-way communication about all the aspects of treatment, including a patient's negative perceptions about treatment
3. A commitment to living evidenced by the patient agreeing to engage fully in treatment (e.g., attending scheduled appointments, goal setting, compliance with prescribed medications and planned homework tasks such as structured problem-solving and experimenting with new ways of coping)
4. A commitment to activating a pre-defined CPR during crises
5. A mutually agreed-upon review date for the CTS

Commitment to Treatment Statement[3]

I, __________________, agree to make a commitment to the treatment process. I understand that this means that I have agreed to be actively involved in all aspects of treatment, including:

(1) attending sessions (or letting my therapist know when I can't make it),
(2) setting goals,
(3) voicing my opinions, thoughts, and feelings honestly and openly with my therapist (whether they are negative or positive, but most importantly my negative feelings),
(4) being actively involved *during* sessions,
(5) completing homework assignments,
(6) taking my medications as prescribed,
(7) experimenting with new behaviors and new ways of doings things,
(8) and implementing my crisis response plan when needed (see the attached crisis response plan card for details).

I also understand and acknowledge that, to a large degree, a successful treatment outcome depends on the amount of energy and effort I make. If I feel like treatment is not working, I agree to discuss it with my therapist and attempt to come to a common understanding as to what the problems are and identify potential solutions. In short, *I agree to make a commitment to living.* This agreement will apply for the next three months, at which time it will be reviewed and modified.

Signed: ______________________________
Date: ________________________________
Witness: _____________________________
(Rudd, Mandrusiak, and Joiner, 2006)

M. David Rudd and colleagues stress that a CTS should always be handwritten, thereby avoiding the less collaborative and more bureaucratic approach that patients may perceive in the perfunctory use of printed forms. The patient needs to sign the CTS, and space is included for a witness, usually a significant other who is also involved in the treatment process. Both the patient and clinician should retain a copy of the CTS. In sum, the CTS not only acknowledges a reality that there will be suicidal crises and periods of ideation, but critically the patient is committing to living, which is essential for the treatment to have a positive effect (ibid.).

#4 THE ALLIANCE FOR SAFETY

The Alliance for Safety uses a functional treatment alliance based upon informed consent embedded within a comprehensive assessment and management process (Miller, 1999; Miller, Jacobs & Gutheil, 1998). Advanced specifically as an alternative to SPC, the Alliance for Safety entails that clinicians share the therapeutic burden—both the uncertainty and the responsibility—with their patients by way of a blend of an established therapeutic alliance and the practice of informed consent (Miller, 1999, p. 473). In short, the Alliance for Safety makes SPC redundant by means of a therapeutic contract subsumed under the doctrine of informed consent.

To illustrate the point, a clinician reviews the variety of treatment options with the patient, spelling out the risks and benefits of each option. By fully examining and explaining each option, a clinician is then able to facilitate the full and voluntary participation of the patient in mutually agreed-upon treatment goals. In this alternative to SPC, the potential risk of suicidal behavior, as well as other risks, that are often associated with a decrease in patient autonomy—such as involuntary hospitalization—are examined and made clear.

In outlining the Alliance for Safety alternative to SPC, U.S. psychiatrist Michael Craig Miller, MD, details the process of decision-making involved in assessing a patient's ability to give informed consent.

Give the patient adequate instruction regarding the following:

- Diagnosis, treatment proposed, purpose of treatment, likelihood of success, side effects and risks of treatment, alternatives proposed, including no treatment,
- Assess their understanding of the instruction, and their ability to think and use the data rationally,
- Assess the emotional impact of the illness and treatment proposed,
- Consider evaluating the patient at several different times to establish competence over time;
- Finally, consider using alternative evaluators (ibid., p. 476).
- The patient's ability to collaborate in the treatment is critical to managing suicide risk; the assessment of the patient's ability to work competently with the clinician toward developing a reasonably safe treatment plan is arguably a key feature of that work (ibid.).

#5 NO SUICIDE ASSURANCES WITH CAREGIVERS OF CHILDREN AND ADOLESCENTS

The lack of empirical data attesting to the therapeutic and diagnostic utility of alternatives to SPC for children and adolescents requires us to turn to clinical wisdom. In the late 1990s, U.S. professor of child and adolescent psychiatry, David Brent, MD, described how a no suicide assurance—largely used for diagnostic reasons—can form an adjunct to the treatment planning phase when working with the caregivers of suicidal children and adolescents—specifically, to subjectively assess caregivers' competency in how the family is able, or not, to contain the child's suicidal behaviors in their home environment (Brent, 1997, p. 283).

To illustrate this modification, an example may be clarifying.

Over the initial evaluation sessions with a thirteen-year-old boy, a provisional diagnosis of PTSD as a result of the boy witnessing and experiencing violence in the home is established. Concerning levels of low mood and a negative thinking style, low self-esteem and evidence of hopelessness and suicidal thoughts are evident. In subsequent sessions a 'treatment agreement' and 'crisis plan response' is developed. As part of this treatment planning phase, a 'no suicide assurance' (caregiver version) is employed:

Clinician (Seeking a no suicide assurance [caregiver]): "Based on my assessment, [assessment is explained] I am concerned your son is at risk for suicidal behavior. Can you agree that until our next appointment you [caregiver(s)] are willing and able to follow the Safety Plan [critical Safety Planning steps are re-stated] we have agreed upon?"

Parent/carer: "Yes/No/Unsure."

By inspection, the evaluator, with a developing sense of the abilities and willingness of the caregiver(s) to effectively collaborate in treatment, is further seeking to establish a subjective level of competence of the caregiver(s): is the family able or not to contain the child's future suicidal behaviors in their home environment? By listening to their responses to a no suicide assurance, and vocal and physical congruence or otherwise; and by exploring any presented qualifications such as "I'm not sure," "Only if my husband leaves the house," or "If I can stop drinking," additional systemic assessment information can be obtained.

An important caveat is required here. David Brent and colleagues have since revised this procedure in their clinical work, and while retaining the basic principle that you negotiate and collaborate with the patient and caregiver(s) have moved to adopting the approach of "safety planning" in line with work by Samra & Bilsker, 2007; Stanley & Brown, 2012 (Brent, 2013 personal correspondence).

#6 BONGAR'S RULE[4]

Within an established therapeutic relationship, as part of a suicide risk assessment and management plan, and in the context of an appropriate (e.g., noncrisis) clinical environment, a clinician seeks an assurance from the patient who has been previously assessed to be competent that if he or she feels unable not to act upon suicidal urges, he or she will contact the clinician. Importantly, contingency measures are agreed regarding the limits of the clinician's availability and when the clinician is unavailable to take their call.

Bongar's Rule, as I've come to know it, involves the clinician inviting the patient to establish contact during a suicidal crisis. This provision is grounded within a comprehensive assessment and management approach with a patient previously assessed as appropriate for such a strategy. There are two versions of Bongar's Rule. In the first version, clinicians seek an assurance from the patient that if he or she feels unable not to act upon suicidal urges, he or she will contact the clinician. In the second version, the clinician requests the patient—again with the preconditions in place—to contact the clinician to say goodbye prior to suicide (Mahrer & Bongar, 1996, p. 288). Both approaches provide an expression of care for the professional relationship as well as an opportunity for the clinician to have contact in a crisis time.

Here, recalling Shneidman's (1993) wisdom is instructive:

> What do suicidal patients and treating clinicians want more than almost anything else? They want the psychological pain leading the patient to suicide to be reduced, and ultimately to stop. In crises, the clinician wants to widen the patient's constricted vision and hope. The patient wants the confusion and distress to cease. Bongar's Rule simply provides an opportunity for clear and unambiguous open expression of care for the professional relationship, as well as for the clinician to share the burden of pain by having the patient contact them in a suicide crisis.

Is Bongar's Rule practicable for clinicians in the public health and social services field? The SPC study found 83 percent ($n = 261/314$) of participants '*rarely to never*' provided their telephone number, preferring to provide patients with crisis line details, indicating Bongar's rule is likely to be more suited to clinicians in private clinical settings.

7 CRITICAL ELEMENTS IN THE MANAGEMENT OF SUICIDAL BEHAVIOR

In 2005, U.S. nurse researchers Jeane B. Lee, PhD, and Mary L. Bartlett, PhD, collated what they regarded to be the critical elements of suicide management (Lee & Bartlett, 2005).

Essentially, these are a series of actions that simultaneously potentially provide patients with emotional and physical protection and provide clinicians with the confidence of being grounded in current best practice. In sum, theirs is a comprehensive assessment and management approach grounded in consultation with an experienced colleague—again echoing U.S. professor Thomas Gutheil's maxim of 'never worry alone'.

The twelve-step clinician actions detailed by the authors offer a comprehensive alternative to SPC:

Presuicide Crisis:

1. be familiar with current laws and ethical standards
2. comply with relevant written policies and procedures
3. receive adequate and ongoing training in recognizing and responding to suicidal behavior
4. be proficient in documentation
5. establish a sound network of clinical resources

During Suicide Crisis:

6. conduct an ongoing, rigorous risk assessment process—facilitated by proforma assessment tools which specifically assesses for suicide intent
7. remove access to means
8. consider hospitalization
9. develop a management plan—strengthen patient supervision by increasing clinician contact and the involvement of significant others
10. involve family members or a significant other; consider breaking confidentiality in cases where family support and other supports are indicated to manage patient risk
11. consult with other experienced colleagues
12. document agreed-upon plans, when treatment was commenced, and the rationale for the clinician's actions, including the level of risk assessed at each point in time

Lee and Bartlett omitted one element during the postsuicide crisis (postvention) phase. It is generally acknowledged, dependent upon the clinician role and setting, to check that agreed-upon plans were enacted and to consider and respond to others affected by the suicide crisis (Edwards, 2000).

THE 4Rs FOR RECOGNIZING AND RESPONDING TO YOUTH SUICIDAL BEHAVIOR

Assessing and managing patients with suicidality is a demanding and complex task and not all in the helping professions will have the capacity to offer ongoing treatment and management. Lee and Bartlett's (2005) twelve critical elements in the management of suicidal behavior represent good practice. Nonetheless, during the suicidal crisis phase some clinicians, particularly those non-mental-health trained, will find this stage demanding, often experiencing transference and countertransference issues which can compromise their effectiveness. To work towards mitigating these challenges, a gold standard is that all in the helping professions (Goldney 2010, p. 47) have an ability to undertake what's sometimes called suicide first aid: recognizing the signs, raising the issue, risk assessing, and responding adequately to the suicide risk presented.

In the early 1990s, one of the authors (SE) developed a simple mnemonic for recognizing and responding to various public health risks. The approach was later revised for suicidality (Edwards, Gostelow, Pfaff, Baily, Hyde, Follett & Leung, 1995) and piloted with a group of primary care physicians (McKelvey, Davies, Pfaff, Acres & Edwards, 1998). A follow-up cohort study sought to determine the effectiveness of The 4Rs training program for primary care physicians in recognising and responding to psychological distress and suicidal ideation in young people (Pfaff, Acres & McKelvey, 2001). The study utilized a pre/post test design to audit consecutive young patients presenting in the six weeks before and the six weeks after the primary care physicians trained in The 4Rs; participants consisted of twenty-three primary care physicians and 423 patients aged fifteen to twenty-four years who presented to the primary care physicians' surgeries (203 prior to The 4Rs training day and 220 post The 4Rs workshop). Outcome measures included three patient self-report inventories (General Health Questionnaire-12 [GHQ-12], Center for Epidemiological Studies Depression Scale [CESD] and Depressive Symptom Inventory-Suicidality Subscale [DSI-SS]); a clinician questionnaire for each patient summarising presenting complaint(s); psychological assessment and a brief management plan.

After being trained in The 4Rs, the primary care physicians demonstrated increased recognition rates of psychologically distressed patients scoring above the cut-offs of the GHQ-12 (48 percent increase; odd ratio [OR], 1.748; 95 percent Cl, 0.904–03.381) and CES-D (39.5 percent increase; OR, 2.067; 95

percent Cl, 1.031–4.143); raising the issues of suicidal ideation increased by 32.5 percent (OR, 1.483; 95 percent Cl, 0.929–2.366); and recognizing suicidal patients (determined by DSI-SS score) increased by 130 percent (OR, 3.949; 95 percent Cl, 1.577–9.888).

The 4Rs Guide

For many reasons, including an increasing desire for independence and autonomy, young people do not easily seek professional assistance. The majority will not openly present any thoughts of suicide. Yet the opportunity to recognize and respond to suicidal youth appears achievable when data indicate up to 83 percent of completed suicides have had contact with a primary care physician within a year of their death and up to 66 percent within a month (Mann, Apter, Bertolote, Beautrais et al., 2005, p. 2065). It is therefore necessary for the clinician to have an 'attitude of respectful inquisitiveness' during appointments with youth, and remain open-minded to the real possibility that the concerns presented may potentially be risk factors for suicidality.

The following is a condensed version of The 4Rs package presented here to assist educators to develop a training programme along similar lines. The 4Rs mnemonic was developed to assist clinicians to evaluate an individual by outlining the four key steps of recognizing and responding to suicidality. The four stages provide a simple and straightforward guide during a consultation. While individuals may disclose information at various points during a consultation, it is suggested that the evaluator move from recognizing the signs, to raising the issue, to risk assessment, and finally, to responding.

1. **Recognizing the signs**—Identify the risk factors/warning signs for suicide
2. **Raising the issue**—Encourage disclosure of psychological distress and suicidal ideation
3. **Risk assessment**—Determine the level of risk and urgency for intervention
4. **Responding**—Provide appropriate response to the risk presented (continuity of care)

1. Recognizing the Signs

For young people, a psychosocial review of their situation is at least as important as the physical exam. One approach is the HEADDSS method of

Table 10.1. HEADDSS psychosocial youth screening interview format[5]

H = *Home & health* Unstable housing – parental, financial or drugs problems – low parental or other supports – abuse or conflict – recent or impending crisis – parental separation or divorce – chronic health problems.	☐ Tell me about things at home. ☐ Does home life make you feel nervous, worried or angry? ☐ Do you like where you live? ☐ Have you any health problems?
E = *Education, employment & eating* Bullying – school avoidance or poor performance – recent suspensions – recent transition between schools – socially isolated – unemployed.	☐ Tell me about things at school. ☐ Does school sometimes make you feel nervous, worried or angry? ☐ Do you like school? Why? ☐ Have you recently changed schools? Tell me about this. ☐ Are you working? ☐ Are you worried about losing your job?
A = *Activities* Limited social contacts – conflict with friend(s) – criminal activities.	☐ Tell me about your friends? Who are they? What do you do with them? ☐ Do you worry or avoid meeting and talking with people you don't know? ☐ Is there someone you talk with, who knows you well?
D = *Drugs* Problems with relationships – police/ legal, work, finances, health.	☐ Do you use alcohol or other drugs? Why do you use drugs? ☐ Do you sometimes use alcohol or other drugs as a way to cope with problems? How often? How much each time? ☐ Does your drug use encourage anxious, depressed or paranoid feelings? ☐ Has anyone ever told you that your alcohol or drug use is a problem? ☐ Do you have weird or paranoid thoughts hard to get out of your head?
D = *Depression* Depressed mood – loss of interest in pleasurable activities – feeling slowed down – feeling bored – irritable – social withdrawal – increased anger – alcohol or other drug use.	☐ Have you or a family member ever been depressed? ☐ Tell me about a time when you have felt really down, more than just sad. ☐ Do you think you are depressed?
S = *Sexuality* Sexual abuse – sexuality conflict or confusion – sexual discrimination.	☐ Are you in a romantic relationship? Tell me about it. ☐ Have you ever been touched or looked at in a way that made you feel uncomfortable? ☐ Do you worry about your sexual orientation – being gay or lesbian?
S = *Suicide* Own thoughts, threats, plans or attempts – past or current DSH (e.g. cutting) – aware of another's suicide threats, attempts or completion.	☐ Have you ever felt like life is not worth living? [If yes] Do you feel like that now? ☐ Do you sometimes have depressing thoughts that are hard to get out of your head? Tell me about them? ☐ Have you ever hurt yourself or tried to kill yourself?

interviewing (Goldenring and Cohen, 1988). The risk factors presented under each heading are to remind the clinician that, if present, they can affect a person's mental health.

The HEADDSS interviewing approach proceeds naturally from predictable and less threatening questions to more personal and intrusive questions, allowing the evaluator to establish a degree of trust and rapport with the young person before asking the most difficult questions in this psychosocial interview.

Yet depending on your circumstance and role, you may not be able to follow the HEADDSS format. Alternatively, over the page are some categories of risk factors and warning signs. Some of these will seem common to many young people, and consequently, may not be seen as warning signs. The key is to remember: the greater number of risk factors, the greater the risk. Recognizing the signs means exploring those factors that singly may lead to suicidal behavior, and in tandem greatly increase the risk because of their mutually reinforcing effect.

Risk Factors and Warning Signs

Health

- Diagnosed or suspected mental illness; chronic or recent physical health problem (e.g., epilepsy, glandular fever)

Suicidality

- Current suicide thinking, threats or behavior
- Past suicide attempt(s)
- History of DSH

Social Difficulties

- Academic failure
- Social isolation
- Legal problems
- Relationship conflict
- Recent loss/change of personal status such as 'coming out' as gay or lesbian or school bullying

Family Problems

- Abuse or neglect
- Family history of mental ill health or suicide
- Cultural conflict (adult/young person)

Contributing Factors

The presence of contributing factors does not necessarily place an individual at risk for suicide. They may, however, affect their ability to bounce back from difficulties and when combined with risk factors can increase the likelihood of suicidal behavior.

- Sexual identity conflict
- Lacking functional coping skills
- Exposure to (social) media messages about DSH or suicide
- Limited social supports
- Access to firearms or other lethal means

2. Raising the Issue

The success of *Raising the issue* of psychological distress and suicide, in part, depends upon the responder's attitudes and beliefs about suicide and its prevention. Clinicians may unwittingly believe one of the many myths about suicide and downplay the severity of a situation (e.g., just a cry for help), thus masking the need to take action. Lang, Ramsay, Tanney, & Tierney (1989) demonstrated that personal attitudes and beliefs in the context of suicide and its prevention have an influence on outcomes.

Using The 4Rs, *Raising the issue* of suicide utilizes the symptomatology identified in the *Recognising the signs* stage relating to psychological distress, suicidal thoughts and behavior. Ridsdale, Mandalia, Evans, Jerrett, & Osler (1999) described a similar approach in primary care physicians' practice in utilizing presented symptomatology as a 'ticket of entry' for opportunistically raising the issue of a difficult topic with a patient.

1. "I'm concerned about how you are feeling [reflect back symptoms]; I think you're pretty down right now. I think you may be depressed!"
2. "When people get depressed, they can sometimes think life's not worth living."
3. "Have you been thinking about hurting yourself, about suicide?"

To be clear, if you don't ask, you won't know. If you don't know, you are less able to assist and your/their situation becomes more demanding. Importantly, any damage caused to the clinician/patient relationship by the clinician 'disclosing-without-consent' remains a secondary concern to ensuring their safety by involving others.

3. Risk Assessment

If the clinician recognized risk factors/warning signs and the individual has acknowledged suicidal thoughts, assessing and realizing the current level of risk for suicide is the next step. The key is: when determining an individual's suicide risk is to gauge the degree and urgency of an intervention required (see table 10.2).

Hockberger and Rothstein (1987) reported significant statistical associations between any one of the following four items on the SAD PERSONS scale indicating the need for hospitalization: 'Depression, hopelessness', 'Rational thinking loss', 'Organized plan/serious current attempt,' 'Stated future attempt'. The flexibility of The 4Rs package allows the clinician to include the addition of other suicide intent and depression assessment tools, such as the newly developed Columbia Suicide Severity Rating Scale (C-SSRS) (Posner, Brown, Stanley, Brent, et al., 2011).

Protective Factors

Many individuals experiencing suicidal thoughts and depression do not attempt or complete suicide. Those with adequate problem solving skills and external protective factors may be deterred from acting on their thoughts to harm themselves. The presence of protective factors can give the clinician 'time' to secure professional assistance. No amount of protective factors, however, should deter the clinician from discussing their assessment with a more experienced colleague.

The following are some protective factors that can reduce the need for immediate professional assistance. Importantly, protective factors can lose their ability to shield the person and need to be reassessed at follow-up appointments.

The suicidal individuals':

- Problem-solving abilities
- Willingness to receive assistance

Table 10.2. Modified SAD PERSONS scale[6]

S = Sex	Males have higher rates for completed suicide; female have higher rates for attempting suicide and DSH
A = Age	In non-indigenous populations, DSH and suicidality is rare in pre-pubertal children
D = Depression, hopelessness	Diagnosed or suspected depressive illness; loss of interest, feelings of helplessness, poor sleep, appetite and concentration
P = Previous attempts or psychiatric care	Previous inpatient or outpatient psychiatric care
E = Excessive alcohol or drug use	Addiction or recent heavy use
R = Rational thinking loss	Organic brain syndrome or psychosis
S = Separated, divorced, widowed or recent relationship breakdown	
O = Organized plan/ serious current attempt	Well thought out plan (access to means) or recent "life threatening" suicide attempt
N = No social supports	Real or perceived lack of family, friends; another who knows them well and cares or active religious affiliation
S = Stated future attempt	Current intent, unremorseful/ ambivalent

Degree & urgency of assistance indicated?

Imminent suicide risk = Immediate assistance required

Less serious risk = Assistance required within 24 hours

- Religious and other personal beliefs against suicide
- Hope for the future
- Responsibility to friends, family, a pet
- Belief another truly understands and cares about them

Formulation of Suicide Risk

A suicide risk formulation should address how serious, imminent, changeable and specific the risk is and how effective the risk management plan is likely to be in addressing it.

Consider:

- Nature and degree of suicide risk identified. How likely is it to occur?
- Relationship between risk and mental ill health, current social circumstances or other contextual factors.
- Factors increasing risk and protective factors that reduce risk. Also, other previously helpful interventions
- Client's, caregivers' and other's view of the suicide risk. Include any gaps in information (level of confidence)
- Changeability and assessment confidence

Consider: Changeability

Changeability of risk status, especially in the immediate period, should be assessed and high changeability should be noted. While risk status is by nature dynamic and requires re-assessment, highly changeable risk status is worth identifying as it will guide clinicians as to the safe interval between risk assessments.

Consider: Assessment Confidence

The clinician should consider the confidence he/she has in the risk assessment. Several factors may indicate low assessment confidence, including factors in the social environment representing an impending loss such as a court case, divorce with child custody dispute; individual factors such as impulsivity, likelihood of drug or alcohol abuse, present intoxication, an inability to engage and, factors in the clinician's assessment such as incomplete assessment, inability to obtain collateral information. Low assessment confidence will influence the need for careful re-assessment to occur, for example, within twenty-four hours. A more vigilant management is adopted with respect to the safety of the person in the light of the gaps in information or rapport.

Example of a Suicide Risk Formulation

Client .... is currently assessed to present a potential risk for suicide (note nature and means if known). The level of suicide risk is heightened by .... (specify situations and risk factors increasing risks). Individual protective factors (including interventions), which reduce risk, appear to be .... Currently the risk appears to be .... (increased, lowered, stable, etc.) because .... The clinician's level of confidence with the formulation is (low, adequate) because .... The changeability status is .... (low, high) because .... If high, the clinician will .... (e.g., increase the frequency of follow-up sessions from forty-eight hours to twenty-four hours).

4. Responding

Imminent Suicide Risk

If the clinician believes the individual is at imminent suicide risk, assertive action is required. This always begins by involving others who are able to provide advice and direction to the clinician, increasing already the supervision of the individual. Some other practical safety steps include:

- Reducing the individuals' access to the means for suicide
- Provide reassurance and listen; be with the person
- Seeking consultation from a senior colleague
- Increasing the level of supervision, usually by involving their caregivers
- Consider hospitalization (usually during the senior colleague consult)
- Maintain contact with the individual (usually until another professional takes over the situation)

Less Serious Risk

If the clinician, in consultation with a senior colleague believes the individual is at less imminent suicide risk, assertive action is still required. Again, this always begins with involving others more experienced in suicide management. They will be more able to determine the current risk and provide advice and direction about increasing the individual's safety. The key here is: assess and understand the reasons why the individual is suicidal and formulate a plan that attempts to identify the factors able to be reduced or removed. Mann, Apter, Bertolote, Beautrais et al. (2005, p. 2071) concluded that an effective chain of care—follow up and continuity of care—following suicidal behavior may improve compliance with treatment and decrease new attempts.

S.A.F.E. Care Approach

When a less serious suicide risk is presented, The 4Rs *Responding* stage explores the role of clinicians in ensuring continuity of care at subsequent appointments under a S.A.F.E. care approach:

- *Safety* of the patient—schedule frequent appointments and re-assess risk while also checking levels of supervision and potency of any previously identified protective factors. Develop and/or review Safety Plan.
- *Assistance* with meeting the individual's practical needs and in seeking additional psychological care, when indicated.
- *Follow-up* on progress with pre-agreed plans, including problem-solving strategies.
- *Exploration* of the underlying reasons—once these are known, empathic support and assistance can do much to reduce their influence.

CONCLUSION

All of these seven alternatives to SPC are recommended to operate within a careful assessment and management process; such protocols have been shown to reduce re-admissions rates of DSH (Goldney 2010, p. 50). Obviously, careful assessment, diagnosis, treatment and management will never be an exact science under any set of standard procedures. But there is now no need to actually create hazards by the use of inadequate clinical practices.

Conclusion

'Where do you hurt?' 'How can I help you?' —Edwin Shneidman

KEY POINTS

- A range of alternatives to SPC are known and available for use.
- On balance, SPC is not helpful and can compromise treatment.
- When responding to suicidality, adopting and documenting accepted standards of care undertaken will provide clinicians clinico-legal protection.

CONSIDERATIONS

It is no longer acceptable to state categorically that SPC procedures universally strengthen a patient/clinician therapeutic relationship, or that it does no harm. Yet it is unrealistic to expect its complete eradication when SPC "seems to hold the promise that the strength of a relationship of a particular patient to a particular clinician will make the critical difference in keeping a person from taking the final steps in a long chain of visualized and possibly rehearsed scenarios of self-destruction" (Kroll, 2007, p. 1). Thankfully, there are a number of alternative approaches which present similar opportunities for communicating care, compassion and concern while seeking personal connection and human relatedness to reduce a patient's suicidality.

When all the pieces come together the story of Suicide Prevention Contracting exemplifies a series of perceived dualities. When the data was lined up a number of clinical factors, specifically clinicians seeking therapeutic, diagnostic and clinico-legal advantage, are associated with SPC. A duality of thought whereby SPC is regarded as able to contribute simultaneously to patient care and clinician self-protection contributed to its wide appeal. Although desirable, if it could be achieved without the associated ethical dilemmas, the accurate assessment of which patients will benefit from SPC and who will experience it as undermining their sense of support and ultimately safety is largely beyond the realm of practicability. The theoretical analysis of clinicians' use of, attitudes towards, and satisfaction with SPC have identified and clarified multi-dimensional difficulties in the form of potentially dangerous paradoxes when SPC is activated. Therefore, the emerging SPC nomenclature is useful in determining from where its compromising treatment effects may arise. And it should now be appreciated that there are primary and secondary contraindications for SPC indicating a far narrower scope of use, if at all. It is important to reiterate that completed suicide has a relative low base rate, making the prediction of completed suicide vulnerable to relatively high percentages of false positive assessments, leaving clinicians vulnerable to perceiving practice efficacy in NSAg and NSC.

Clinicians understand that complex cases are difficult to manage, and almost all suicidal crises are complex. It is now apparent that introducing SPC into cases of suicidality results in more unwieldy complexity in the form of unexpected overlaps such as introduced by *Miller's Paradox*, *The One in Four Concept* and unforeseen consequences such as *Simon's Paradox*. At the very least, when the Critical Elements in Suicide Management are followed (see chapter 10) the patient is provided with the best possible response. And in the end, when the clinician is undertaking what later can be assessed to represent best possible practice, clinician anxiety relating to potential clinico-legal issues that may arise in the event of an adverse clinical outcome will rightly lessen.

SIX WAVES IN THE RESURGENCE OF SPC

The Exploitation of the Mental Health Recovery Doctrine

Without vigorous debate and evaluation, SPC has careered across four decades of the mental health movement in 'five waves'. As we saw in chapter 2, the first wave was the development of Redecision Therapy and the creation of no-suicide decisions, leading some to ascribe the same therapeutic foundations to contemporary SPC. The second wave was the explosion of telephone crisis centers using an adapted form of no-suicide decisions now called no suicide contracts, and so forth. The third wave occurred when SPC seemingly met inpatient and outpatient nursing demands of patient management, discharge and admission. The fourth wave saw SPC get the upper hand in apparently supporting behavioral and cognitive approaches to managing suicidality. And in the fifth wave SPC has been used in an attempt to mitigate the demands of an over-stretched clinical practice environment that is acutely mindful of litigation.

This brings me to the possibility of a sixth wave that might once again lift SPC onto the shores of many clinical practice settings. The predicted motivation in this case is a misguided use of the mental health recovery doctrine. In some countries a recovery approach is being promoted as the preferred philosophy of service delivery to which all mental health services should adhere. The core principles of the recovery model are to encourage service users to take active responsibility for their own self-care and journeys of recovery. Here there is the clear potential for SPC to be seen by the naïve or permissive clinician as an "easy way out." For example, a distorted view of recovery can lead clinicians to expect more of patients than they are capable, particularly when unwell. Consider a potentially frequent circumstance where this may lead the clinician to decide against admitting a person to hospital, instead seeking to increase a patients' self-determination, self-responsibility and empowerment by placing them under SPC. The point here is this: SPC is again perfectly positioned to be not helpful and compromise treatment under the current right-minded recovery philosophy to mental health care.

SPC ALTERNATIVES WITHIN A CULTURE OF SAFETY, NOT FEAR

Clinicians who are drawn to safe clinical practices with suicidal patients—who 'hardwire' for safety—increase patient supervision, consult with a senior colleagues, employ a standardized suicide risk evaluation tool, reduce access to means and consider hospitalization—rather than use untested, pre-emptive and defensive practices—will likely be driven less by either fear or the threat of repercussions (following a patient's serious attempt or completed suicide in their care). Nor will they operate according to a 'production line' *modus operandum* based on an *ethics of expedience*. They won't be plagued by countertransference fears of recriminations from peers. They won't be driven by fear and doubt of not following a superior's request to use SPC. They won't be driven by fear of insecurity when finding out about a serious attempt or completed suicide in their care.

In short, if we diligently apply the critical elements in the management of suicidal patients—without the use of SPC, mindful of the core concepts presented here—you will have amassed the best possible resource desirable in the prevention of suicide at the front line of health care and social services.

When I look over the SPC study findings, the one image that keeps coming to mind is jet airliner SOP. Never was there a better example of 'hardwiring' (literally) for safety than what occurred in the development of the commercial jet industry. Imagine had it been otherwise: if five decades ago, Boeing had settled on a culture of uncertainty, even fear, rather than a culture of clarity and safety when they built the first 707 and started transporting tens of thousands of passengers around the world. Imagine Boeing executives burying their heads in the sand and out of fear, threat, mere expedience or a surface-level understanding, settling on quasi-legal safeguards analogous to "contracts and agreements" rather than developing a universal SOP, including operational definitions and measureable key terms for commercial jet safety *(cf. New Vocabulary of SPC)*. Imagine Boeing flying poorly tested commercial jet planes under the highest-risk weather conditions (*cf. McArdle's Paradox*). Add to this horror scenario the fact that pilots who are less able to bring to bear sound decision-making when flying during the highest-risk weather conditions being more likely to be offered those flights; and, conversely, those pilots more able to offer clear decision-making less likely to be offered flight time during the highest-risk weather conditions (*cf. Farrow's Paradox*). Now imagine that less experienced Boeing pilots were using untried emergency protocols, procedures rejected outright by more experienced Airbus pilots (*cf. Mahrer's Paradox*). Disaster would soon follow if Boeing pilots used one call-sign for landing on an eastern runway, a call-sign perceived by some air traffic controllers as the call sign for landing on the western runway (*cf. Miller's Paradox-The 3Cs*). To make matters even worse, Boeing pilots have a 'one in four chance' of sitting next to a competent co-pilot when flying during the highest-risk weather conditions (*cf. The One in Four Concept*).

These are silly analogies, granted.

We all know what the outcome would be if, rather than hardwiring for safety, Boeing was ambiguous about safety SOPs or worse driven merely by fear and the threat of repercussions; or by simple expedience, in a resource-poor environment. Corners would get cut, and sooner or later a major disaster would occur. The enormity of the danger might not even be obvious. Every flight that landed safely would merely add to a false sense of security *(cf. The Curse of the False Positive).* The procedures and protocols in place would seem to receive confirmation every time a journey ended without incident. Faith in their adequacy, their capacity to stave off disaster, might even be widespread *(cf. All Things to Some People).* When these two distal factors come together it can even be difficult to perceive any more that there is a problem.

When all these pieces came together, the key, we learned, is the perceived symbiotic relationship between these two phenomena—the very fact that SPC has become *All Things to Some People* and *The Curse of the False Positive*—explains why clinicians in many parts of the world appear to have embraced SPC as an *uncomplicated value-driven prescription for a multi-factored problem.* Many seem to be swayed, to some degree, by the many 'magical powers' that SPC would seem to possess.

Still, you might argue that if a foolhardy or fascinated clinician is so keen to use SPC procedures that they fail to watch out for their potential for harm, this hardly constitutes clinician negligence. Indeed, negligence doesn't enter the equation. I think it not premature to say that, on balance their potential to compromise treatment is now a fact of clinical practice life, and SPC procedures have been superbly positioned to do so without the potential having been entirely obvious. Whilst we're currently unable to affect the false positive rate until more sensitive evaluation protocols are developed, we can now modify the *All Things to Some People* side of the SPC equation. And that means challenging SPC use: dispelling widespread myths about it, communicating to others its paradoxes, and exposing its fatal flaws.

Of course, jet airliners still come down despite decades of hardwiring for safety; no system of safety is foolproof. Similarly, medications, inpatient care, and increased supervision, no matter how well pulled together, can never guarantee to prevent high-risk individuals from completing suicide. No procedure or policy will completely compensate for limited resources or experience, for human error, or soothe good enough clinician anxiety in the face of today's complex clinical presentations. No prescribed practices will achieve the communication of a clinician's care and concern to every patient all the time, or instill in patients a faith in a talking therapy's effectiveness. Diagnosis will never be an exact science under any set of standard procedures. But there is now no need to actually *create* hazards by the use of inadequate clinical practices prone to compromise treatment.

What is needed now and what this book calls for are advocates, champions for a culture of safety, and for an ending to a malignant culture of fear—maintained by a dialectic of risk and insurance calculation—yes, even in one of the biggest risk arenas of professional practice—suicide intervention/prevention. So I advocate for the alternatives described earlier, to replace a set of treatment-compromising procedures that are inherently unstable and frankly ultimately unnecessary.

Notes

INTRODUCTION

1. *Rules for type of procedure*

Explicit rewards (like tokens, cash or social benefits) may or may not be present. Patient contracts include self-management, providing that self-management is supported by a form of contracting (Ibid.).

Sub-rules for type of procedure

If a clinician's intervention doesn't comprise a mutual agreement between two or more parties, that action(s) will be done by both or either parties, it is not considered a form of patient contracting. For example, clinician instructions, education, incentives or reminders are not considered forms of patient contracting (Ibid., pp. 3–5).

2. *Rules for diagnostic deployment*

(i) There are two distinct ways in which patient contracting is used for diagnostic purposes. The first is when patient contracting is a point-in-time assessment of the therapeutic alliance. Here, using *Directionality* sub-structures, patient contracting is characteristically a present-focused, and implicitly presented, process assessment (*Intermediate Means* sub-structure) designed to seek a patient's assurance for a course of action. Alternatively, it can be used to assess patient competence, or used to assess the presence of any relational impasses between patient and clinician, i.e., therapeutic ruptures.

(ii) The second is when specific patient contracting such as SPC is used for a subjective point-in-time assessment of risk for suicide. Here SPC represents an

implicit documentation process, recording the patient's verbal and non-verbal responses to a request to enter into SPC.

Rules for therapeutic deployment

(i) Table 1 indicates most types of patient contracts are perceived to have moderate to high therapeutic advantage. In order to identify a therapeutic deployment in any particular case, locate and establish the one or both of the *Intermediate Means*, namely: *(a)* the treatment agreement—patient contracting is used with either a present or a future focus to establish options for treatment and to clarify what needs to change. And *(b)* the behavioral agreement—patient contracting is used with a future focus to effect a cure or instigate a course of action, to reinforce new behaviors, to control symptoms or offer patients a sense of mastery. A therapeutic deployment is interchangeably either present or future focused, implicitly or explicitly presented, and for either patient or clinician advantage.

Granted, on the surface this last point looks illogical; i.e., how can a therapeutic deployment of a patient contract be anything other than of sole advantage to the patient? Yet, this is not the case. Put simply, SPC study participants indicated contracting was used to relieve clinician anxiety, which is a clinician-oriented therapeutic deployment. Similarly, in the case of a difficult patient contract, staff will likely have a sense of security if the disruptive incidents decrease while the individual is 'under contract'.

3. *Sub-rule for type of deployment*

(i) More often than not, it will be possible to locate and establish simultaneously *all* three (clinico-legal, diagnostic, therapeutic) reasons for using a SPC procedure in any specific suicidal crisis presentation.

Suppose someone came along and asked, "What was the one big 'what for' reason why clinician X used SPC in the Y case?" Even in the most ideal case of, say, interviewing X directly following deployment—including an MRI scan of X's fear response across the amygdala during deployment—at this point in the understanding of SPC you wouldn't be able to conclusively answer the question: Was it for therapeutic advantage? Diagnostic evaluation? Clinico-legal protection?

No! Based upon our findings, it's often *all* of these reasons added together in an overall admixture of effort applied in a largely misguided fashion. I say misguided—and this is a critical point of the entire book—simply because of the sheer weight of counterbalancing factors—manufactured hazards—activated when SPC procedures are deployed, irrespective of type, deployment, means or directionality. (Throughout the book, when I mention the manufactured dangerousness or compromising factors of SPC, I am usually referring to the Four Features of SPC, Six Core

Concepts and The Four Fatal Flaws of SPC. See Teaching Tools for a summary.) Yes, some clinicians may confirm a 'what for' greater than another, but any single *Type of Deployment*—no matter how well identified and established—likely reflects only one part of the whole anticipated cumulative effect—what is 'hoped for' when using SPC.

CHAPTER 6

1. Table 6.2 Dimensions and structures of SPC/ Type of deployment/ *Substructure*: Themes (reasons for use): Diagnostic clarification—'assesses risk', 'assesses willingness to engage in process'; Therapeutic advantage—'facilitates therapeutic alliance', 'clarifies communication'- [care/concern], 'reduces clinician anxiety', 'encourages collaboration', 'increases patient self responsibility', 'offers alternatives to suicide'; Clinico-legal—'transfers accountability to patient', 'abiding by service's regulations', 'provides legal protection', 'demonstrates duty of care'.

2. Perhaps the most cited model for understanding how stress impacts on thoughts, feelings and ultimately behavior (coping) is the ABCX Model developed by University of Minnesota professor Reuben Hill in 1947. See: McCubbin, H, I. & Patterson, J. M. (1983). The family stress process: The double ABCX model of adjustment and adaptation, *Marriage and Family Review*, 1, (2), 7–37.

3. Credit for the notion of a clinician's *defenses* which can be considered as resilience qualities that counterbalance environmental stressors leading to—in this case—the use/ no use of SPC goes to UCLA nursing professor Betty Newman. Since the 1970s professor Newman's teachings have served to train thousands of graduate nurses worldwide in the fundamentals of sound nursing practice.

CHAPTER 7

1. Since the early 1990s, Emeritus professor Robert I. Simon, MD, past President of the *American Academy of Psychiatry and the Law* has commentated on the pseudo-legal position of SPC.

2. In 2000, Michael Craig Miller, MD, a Harvard Medical School Lecturer commentated on the possibility for SPC to, in fact, retard patient/clinician communication rather than facilitating it and, in turn, adversely affect a therapeutic alliance. Prior to Miller, John Ewart, MD, reporting in the American *Comprehensive Textbook of Psychiatry* (1967 edition), raised similar cautions about the procurement of a patient promise not to suicide adversely effecting a patient's ability to discuss their distress.

3. Credit for the notion of a link between increasing clinical practice experience and decreasing use of SPC goes to U.S. psychologist Jon Mahrer, PhD; Mahrer, J. 1993, *The Use of No-Suicide Contracts and Agreements with Suicidal Patients,* Dissertation, Palo Alto, California, Pacific Graduate School of Psychology. In his study, Jon Mahrer raised the idea that as practitioners gain more experience their use of SPC is less prevalent.

4. Recruited in the final stages of the SPC study to undertake additional statistical analysis, associate professor Brian McArdle, DPhil, from the Department of Mathematics at the University of Auckland first realized the particularly strong pattern in the findings suggestive of a use-by-risk phenomenon.

5. Credit for teasing apart some of the ethical considerations with SPC goes to Tony L. Farrow, PhD, a New Zealand nurse practitioner. In a review of the ethics of SPC (Farrow, T.L. & O'Brien, A. (2003). No Suicide Contracts' and Informed Consent: An Analysis of Ethical Issues, *Nursing Ethics,* 10, pp. 201–207) Dr Farrow drew out the ethical basis for the dangers of SPC for clinicians and patients.

CHAPTER 8

1. Australian consultant psychiatrist Stephen Fenner, MD, first alerted the Western Australian SPC study team to the possibility of NSAs operating in clinical practice, and to the nature of its potential for judicious use.

CHAPTER 10

1. Samra, J. & Bilsker, D. (2007). Coping with Suicidal Thoughts, Consortium for Organizational Mental Health (COMH;www.comh.ca), Faculty of Health Sciences, Simon Fraser University, Vancouver, BC. http://summit.sfu.ca/item/1115, retrieved 29.06.2013.

2. Potter, M. L., Vitale-Nolen, R. & Dawson, A. M. (2005). Implementation of Safety Agreements in an Acute Psychiatric Facility. *Journal of the American Psychiatric Nurses Association*, 11, 144–155.

3. Rudd, D., Mandrusiak, M. & Joiner, T. (2006). The Case Against No suicide Contracts: The Commitment to Treatment Statement as a Practice Alternative. *Journal of Clinical Psychology*, 62, 243–251.

4. Bruce Bongar, PhD, is a U.S.-based clinical psychologist and suicidologist who along with Jon Mahrer, PhD, were the first to fully research the use of contemporary SPC and offered rudimentary alternatives to NSC and NSAg.

5. Adapted with permission from Goldenring & Cohen, 1988; Edwards, S. J. (2001) Getting into Adolescent HEADDSS. In *Thinking on your feet: Tough Decisions in General Practice. University Program for General Practitioners.* Sydney, Merck Sharp and Dohme.

6. Hockberger, R. S. & Rothstein, R. J. (1987). Assessment of Suicide Potential by Nonpsychiatrists Using the SAD PERSONS Scale. *The Journal of Emergency Medicine,* 6, 99–103.

References

PREFACE

Goin, M. (2003). The suicide-prevention contract: A dangerous myth. *Psychiatric News,* 38 (14), 3–4.

INTRODUCTION

American Psychiatric Association. (2003). *Practice Guidelines for the Assessment and Treatment of Patients with Suicidal Behavior*. New York: American Psychiatric Association.

Australian & New Zealand College of Psychiatry. (2004). Clinical Practice Guidelines for the Management of Adult Deliberate Self-Harm. *Australian & New Zealand Journal of Psychiatry*, 38, 868–884.

Bosch-Capblanch, X., Abba, K., Prictor, M. & Garner, P. (2009). Contracts between patients and healthcare practitioners for improving patients' adherence to treatment, prevention and health promotion activities. *Cochrane Database of Systematic Reviews,* 2, 1–71.

Corden, J., & Preston-Shoot, M. (1987). Contracts or Con Trick? A Reply to Rojek and Collins. *British Journal of Social Work*, 17, 535–543.

Dunbar, J. M., Marshall, G. D. & Hovell, F. (1979). Behavioral strategies for improving compliance. In: Haynes, T. B., Taylor, D. W. & Sackett, D. L. (Eds). (pp. 174–90), *Compliance in health care.* Baltimore: Johns Hopkins University Press.

Edwards, S. J. (2008). *No Suicide Contracts, No Suicide Agreements and No Suicide Assurances: An exploratory study of their nature, utilization and perceived effectiveness.* Dissertation. Perth, Western Australia: Discipline of Social Work and Social Policy, University of Western Australia.

Edwards, S. J. & Harries, M. (2007). No Suicide Contracts, No Suicide Agreements and No Suicide Assurances: A controversial life. *Australaisan Psychiatry*, 15, 484–489.

Edwards, S. J., Harries, M. & Kumar, R. (2006). *No Suicide Contracts, Agreements and Assurances. Preliminary Findings from an Exploratory Study Investigating their Nature, Frequency of Use and Perceived Effectiveness*: (Poster) presented at the 42nd Congress of the Australian and New Zealand College of Psychiatry: Perth, Western Australia.

Edwards, S. J. & Sachmann, M. D. (2010). No Suicide Contracts, No Suicide Agreements and No Suicide Assurances. A Study of Their Nature, Utilization, Perceived Effectiveness, and Potential to Cause Harm. *Crisis: Journal of Crisis Intervention & Suicide Prevention,* 31, (6), 290–302.

Garvey, K., Penn, J., Campbell, A., Esposito-Smythers, C. & Spirito, A. (2009). Contracting for safety with patients: clinical practice and forensic implications, *Journal of the American Academy of Psychiatry and the Law*, 37, 363–70.

Goldney, R. D. (2005). Suicide Prevention: A Pragmatic Review of Recent Studies. *Crisis: The Journal of Crisis Intervention and Suicide Prevention,* 26, (3), 128–140.

Goldney, R. D. (2010). *Suicide Prevention.* New York: Oxford University Press.

Hariharan, J., Lamb, G. C. & Neuner, J. M. (2007). Long-term opioid contract use for chronic pain management in primary care practice: A five year experience. *Journal of General Internal Medicine,* 22, (4), 485–90.

Harris, P. S., Duermeyer, M., Ehly, C., Hartig-Toth, S., Hayes, S., Holsapple, L., et al. (1999). The Impossible Patient: Organizational response to a clinical problem. *The Journal of Clinical Ethics*, 10, (3), 242–44.

Hollis, F. (1970). The Psychosocial Approach to the Practice of Casework. In J. Roberts, & P. MacNee (Eds). *Theories of Social Casework.* Chicago: University of Chicago Press.

Lieber, S. R., Kim, S. Y. & Volk, M. L. (2011). Power and control: contracts and the patient–physician relationship. *International Journal of Clinical Practice*, 65, 1214–1217.

Maluccio, A. & Marlow, W. D. (1974). The Case for the Contract. *Social Work,* 19, (1), 28–36.

Sackett, D. L., Straus, S. E., Richardson, S. W., Rosenberg, W. & Haynes, B. R. (2000). *Evidence Based Medicine: How to practice and teach EBM.* Edinburgh: Churchill Livingstone.

Sacopulos, M. & Segal, J. (2009). Limiting exposure to medical malpractice claims and defamatory cyber postings via patient contracts. *Clinical Orthopaedics and Related Research,* 467, (2), 427–33.

Stanford, E., Goetz, R. & Bloom, J. (1994). The No Harm Contract in the Emergency Assessment of Suicidal Risk. *Journal of Clinical Psychiatry,* 55, 344–48.

Starrels, J. L, Becker, W. C., Alford, D. P., Kapoor, A., Williams, A. R. & Turner, B. J. (2010).

Systematic review: treatment agreements and urine drug testing to reduce opioid misuse in patients with chronic paIn *Annuals of Internal Medicine,* 52, (11), 712–20.

Volk, M. L., Lieber, S. R., Kim, S. Y., Ubel, P.A. & Schneider, C.E. (2012). Patient Contracting in Clinical Practice. *Lancet,* 379, 9810, 7–9.

CHAPTER 1

Potter, M. L., Vitale-Nolen, R. & Dawson, A. M. (2005). Implementation of Safety Agreements in an Acute Psychiatric Facility. *Journal of the American Psychiatric Nurses Association,* 11, 144–155.

Stanford, E., Goetz, R. & Bloom, J. (1994). The No Harm Contract in the Emergency Assessment of Suicidal Risk. *Journal of Clinical Psychiatry,* 55, 344–48.

CHAPTER 2

Assey, J. (1985). The Suicide Prevention Contract, *Perspectives in Psychiatric Care,* 23, 99–103.

Badger, J. M. (1995). Reaching out to the suicidal patient, *Advanced Journal of Nursing,* March, 24–32.

Bergson, H. In Harris, T. A. (1967). *I'm OK-You're OK: a Practical Guide to Transactional Analysis.* (p. 97), New York, Harper Perennial.

Bradley, V. & Shawler, C. (1993). One emergency department's guidelines for the care of suicidal patients, *Journal of Emergency Nursing,* 19, (5), 393–95.

Bongar, B. (1991). *The Suicidal Patient: Clinical Challenges and Standards of Care.* Washington, DC: American Psychiatric Association.

Busch, K. A., Clark, D. C., Fawcett, J. & Kravitz, H. M. (1993). Clinical Features of Inpatient Suicides, *Psychiatric Annals*, 23, 256–62.

Butcher, J. & Maudal, G. (1976). Crisis Intervention. In I. Werner (Ed.), *Clinical Methods in Psychology.* (pp. 591–648), New York: Wiley-Interscience Publications.

Corden, J. & Preston-Shoot, M. (1987a). Contracts or Con Trick? A Reply to Rojek and Collins. *British Journal of Social Work*, 17, 535–543.

Corden, J. & Preston-Shoot, M. (1987b). *Contracts in Social Work.* Aldershot: Gower.

Corden, J. & Preston-Shoot, M. (1988). Contracts or Con Trick? A Postscript. *British Journal of Social Work*, 18, 623–634.

Cautela, J. R. (1973). *The modification of behavior that influences the probability of suicide in elders.* Unpublished manuscript, Boston College.

Davidson, M., Wagner, W. G. & Range, L. M., (1995). Clinicians' Attitudes Toward No Suicide Agreements. *Suicide & Life-Threatening Behavior*, 25, 410–414.

Decant, J. & Range, L. M. (1997). No Suicide agreements: College students' perceptions. *College Student Journal*, 31, (2), 238–24.

Drye, R. C. Goulding, R. L. & Goulding, M. E. (1973). No Suicide Decisions: Patient Monitoring of Suicidal Risk, *American Journal of Psychiatry*, 130, (2), 171–74.

Duffy, D. (1993). Prevention suicide, *Nursing Times,* 89, (31), 28–31.

Egan, M. (1997). Contracting for Safety: A Concept Analysis. *Crisis: Journal of Crisis Intervention & Suicide,* 18, (1), 17-23.

Ewart, J. R. (1967). Other Psychiatric Emergencies, In A.F.H. Kaplin (Ed.), (pp. 1179–87), *Comprehensive Textbook of Psychiatry,* Baltimore, Williams and Wilkins.

Goldney, R. D. (1998). Suicide Prevention is Possible: A Review of Recent Studies. *Archives of Suicide Research*, 4, 329–39.

Goulding, R. L. & Goulding, M. E. (1978). *The Power of the Patient,* San Francisco, TA Press.

Goulding, R. L. & Goulding, M. E. (1979). *Changing Lives Through Redecision Therapy,* New York, Brunner Mazel.

Green, J. S. & Grindel, C. G. (1996). Supervision of Suicidal Patients in Adult Inpatient Psychiatric Units in General Hospitals. *Psychiatric Services*, 47, 859–863.

Hatton, V., Valente, S. & Rink, A. (1984). *Suicide Assessment and Intervention,* Norwalf, CT: Appleton Century Crofts

Hillard, J. R. (1990). (Ed.). *Manual of Clinical Emergency Psychiatry*, Washington, DC: American Psychiatric Press.

Hipple, J. & Cimbolic, P. (1979). *The Counselor and the Suicidal Crisis.* Illinois: Charles C Thomas.

Hirsch, S. (1981). A Critique of Volunteer-Staffed Suicide Prevention Centers. *Canadian Journal of Psychiatry,* 26, (6), 406–410.

Hollis, F. (1970). The Psychosocial Approach to the Practice of Casework. In J. Roberts, & P. MacNee (Eds). *Theories of Social Casework.* Chicago: University of Chicago Press.

Hollis, F. (1972). *Casework: A Psychosocial Therapy*. New York: Random House.

Jacobs, D. G. (1989). Evaluation and Care of Suicidal Behavior in Emergency Settings. In D. Jacobs and H. Brown (Eds.), *Suicide: Understanding and Responding, Harvard Medical School Perspectives,* (pp. 363–379), Connecticut: Universities Press.

Jacobs, D. G. (1992a). Evaluating and Treating Suicidal Behavior in the borderline patient. In D. G. Jacobs (Ed.). *Suicide and Clinical Practice,* (pp. 115–131), Washington DC: American Psychiatric Press.

Jacobs, D. G. (1992b). *Suicide and Clinical Practice.* New York: American Psychiatric Publishing, Inc.

Janz, N. & Hartman, P. (1988). Contingency Contracting to Enhance Patient Compliance: A review. *Patient Education and Counseling*, 5, (4), 165–178.

Jones, R. N. & O'Brien, P. (1990). Unique Observations for Child Inpatient in Psychiatry. *Journal of Psychosocial Nursing and Mental Health Care*, 28, 29–31.

Jones, R. N. O'Brien, P. & MacMahon, W. M. (1993). Contracting Status for Lower Precaution Status for Child Psychiatric Patient. *Journal of Psychosocial Nursing and Mental Health Care*, 31, 6–10.

Liberman, R. P. & Eckman, T. (1981). Behavior therapy vs insight-oriented therapy for repeated suicide attempters. *Archive of General Psychiatry*, **38**, (10), 1126–1130.

Loomis, M. (1985). Levels of Contracting, *Journal of Psychosocial and Mental Health Nursing*, 23, 9–28.

MacEnany, G. & Teschler, J. (1985). Contracting for Care, *Journal of Psychosocial Nursing and Mental Health Care,* 24, 11–18.

MacGee, R. (1974). *Crisis Intervention in the Community,* Baltimore: University Park Press.

Mahrer, J. (1993). *The Use of No Suicide Contracts and Agreements with Suicidal Patients.* Dissertation, Palo Alto, California: Pacific Graduate School of Psychology.

Maltsberger, J. (1988). Suicide danger: Clinical estimation and decision, *Suicide and Life Threatening Behaviors*, 18, 47–54.

Maluccio, A. & Marlow, W. D. (1974). The Case for the Contract. *Social Work,* 19, (1), 28–36.

McLean, A. (1995). Empowerment and the Psychiatric Consumer/ Ex-Patient Movement in the United States: Contradictions, crisis and change. *Journal of Social Science and Medicine*, 40, (8), 1053–1071.

McNeel, J. (1999). Redecision Therapy as a process of new belief acquisition. *Journal of Redecision Therapy,* 1, 103–115.

Miller, M., Jacobs, D. G. & Gutheil, T. G. (1998). Talisman or Taboo: The Controversy of the Suicide-Prevention Contract. *Harvard Review of Psychiatry*, 6, 78–87.

Mishara, B.L. & Daigle, M. S. (1997). Effects of Different Telephone Intervention Styles with Suicidal Callers at Two Suicide Prevention Centers: An Empirical Investigation. *American Journal of Community Psychology*, 25, 861–885.

Mothersole, G. (1996). Existential Realities and No Suicide Contracts. *Journal of Transactional Analysis,* 26, (2), 151–159.

Neville, D. & Barnes, S. (1985). The Suicidal Phone Call, *Journal of Psychosocial Nursing and Mental Health Care,* 23, 14–18.

O'Farrell, T., Goodenough, D. & Cutter, H. (1981). Behavioural Contracting for Repeated Suicide Attempts. *Behavior Modification*, 5 (2), 255–272.

Perlman, H. H. (1970). The Problem-Solving Model in Social Casework. In J. Roberts, & P, Mac Nee (Eds.), *Theories of Social Casework*. Chicago: University of Chicago Press.

Quarneri, K. (1997). *Gender Differences Among Clinical Psychologists in the Assessment of Suicidality*. Dissertation. Palo Alto, California: Pacific Graduate School of Psychology.

Rapoport, L. (1970). Crisis intervention as a mode of treatment. In R. W. Roberts & R. H. McNee (Eds.), *Theories of Social Casework*. Chicago: University of Chicago.

Rudd, D., Mandrusiak, M. & Joiner, T. (2006). The Case Against No Suicide Contracts: The Commitment to Treatment Statement as a Practice Alternative. *Journal of Clinical Psychology*, 62, 243–251.

Shneidman, E. S. & Farberow, N. L. (1957). *Clues to Suicide*. New York, McGraw-Hill.

Simon, R. (1991). *Review of Clinical Psychiatry and the Law*, (2), Washington DC: Psychiatric Press, Inc.

Smith, D. (1974). The Free Clinic Movement in the United States. *The Medical Journal of Australia*, 2, 34–36.

Stanford, E., Goetz, R. & Bloom, J. (1994). The No Harm Contract in the Emergency Assessment of Suicidal Risk. *Journal of Clinical Psychiatry*, 55, 344–48.

Stewart, I. & Joines, V. (1987). *TA Today*. Nottingham: Lifespace Publishing.

Stone, M. H. (1980). The Suicidal Patient: Points Concerning Diagnosis and Intensive Treatment. *Psychiatry Quarterly*, 52, 52–70.

Stummer, G. (2002). An Update on the Use of Contracting. *Journal of Transactional Analysis*, 32, (3), 121–123.

Thomas, A. (1970). Social Case Work: A Behavioral Approach. In J. Roberts, and P, Mac Nee (Eds.), *Theories of Social Casework*. Chicago: University of Chicago Press.

Twiname, B. G. (1981). No Suicide Contracts for Nurses, *Journal of Psychiatric Nursing Mental Health Services*, 19, 11–12.

Weiss, A. (2001). The No Suicide Contract: Possibilities and Pitfalls. *American Journal of Psychotherapy*, 55, (3), 414–19.

CHAPTER 3

Assey, J. (1985). The Suicide Prevention Contract, *Perspectives in Psychiatric Care,* 23, 99–103.

Bartlett, M. L. (2006). *The Efficacy of No Suicide Contracts with Clients in Counseling on an Outpatient Basis.* Dissertation, Auburn, Alabama: Graduate facility of Auburn University.

Clark, D. & Kerkhof, Ad. J. F. M. (1997). No Suicide Contracts and No suicide Decisions. *Crisis: Journal of Crisis Intervention and Suicide,* 18, 1–2.

Egan, M. (1997). Contracting for Safety: A Concept Analysis. *Crisis: Journal of Crisis Intervention & Suicide,* 18, (1), 17–23.

Goldney, R. D. (2010). *Suicide Prevention.* New York: Oxford University Press.

Joiner, T. (2011). Understanding and Overcoming the Myths of Suicide: What Goes On in the Minds of Whose Who Attempt Suicide. *Psychiatric Times,* 28, (1), http://www.psychiatrictimes.com/suicide/content/article/10168/1780274: Retrieved 24.01.2011.

Maris, R. (2002). Suicide. *Lancet,* 360, 319–327.

Miller, M. (1999). Suicide-Prevention Contracts: Advantages, Disadvantages, and An Alternative Approach. In D. J. Jacobs (Ed.), *The Harvard Medical School Guide to Suicide Assessment and Intervention.* (pp. 463–481), San Francisco: Jossey-Bass Publishers.

Miller, M., Jacobs, D. G. & Gutheil, T. G. (1998). Talisman or Taboo: The Controversy of the Suicide-Prevention Contract. *Harvard Review of Psychiatry,* 6, 78–87.

O'Carroll, P., Berman, A., Maris, R., Moscicki, E., Tanney, B. & Silverman, M. (1996). Beyond the Tower of Babel: A nomenclature for suicidology. *Suicide and Life Threatening Behavior,* 26, (3), 237–252.

Potter, M. & Dawson, A. (2001). From Safety Contract to Safety Agreement. *Journal of Psychosocial Nursing & Mental Health Services,* 39, (8) 38–46.

Rudd, D., Mandrusiak, M. & Joiner, T. (2006). The Case Against No Suicide Contracts: The Commitment to Treatment Statement as a Practice Alternative. *Journal of Clinical Psychology,* 62, 243–251.

Twiname, B. G. (1981). No Suicide Contracts for Nurses, *Journal of Psychiatric Nursing & Mental Health Services,* 19, 11–12.

CHAPTER 4

Ackerman, A. & Scullin, J. (2010). Hillsborough schools' suicide policy questioned. *The Tampa Tribune*, (14th April 2011) (http://www2.tbo.com/content/2011/apr/14/hillsborough-schools-suicide-policy-questioned/news-breaking/) Retrieved 22.04.2011.

American Psychiatric Association. (2003). *Practice Guidelines for the Assessment and Treatment of Patients with Suicidal Behavior*. New York: American Psychiatric Association.

Australian Psychological Society. (1999). *Suicide*: An Australian Psychological Society Discussion Paper.

Australian & New Zealand College of Psychiatry. (2004). *Clinical Practice Guidelines for the Management of Adult Deliberate Self-Harm*. Australian & New Zealand Journal of Psychiatry, 38, 868–884.

Boyatzis, R. E. (1998). *Thematic Analysis and Code Development: Transforming Qualitative Information*. Thousand Oaks: Sage Publications.

Brent, D. (1997). The After Care of Adolescents with Deliberate Self Harm. *Journal of Child Psychiatry*, 38, 277–286.

Brent, D. & Kolko, D. (1990). Suicide and suicidal behavior in children and adolescents. In B. D. Garfinkel, G. Carlson & E. Weller (Eds.), *Psychiatric disorders in children and adolescents*. (pp. 372–391). Philadelphia: W. B. Saunders Company.

Cantor, C. M. & MacDermott, P. (1994). Suicide Litigation: From Legal to Clinical Wisdom. *Australian & New Zealand Journal of Psychiatry*. 28, 431–437.

Clark, D. and Kerkhof, Ad. J. F. M. (1993). No Suicide Decisions and Suicide Contracts in Therapy. *Crisis: Journal of Crisis Intervention and Suicide*, 14, (3), 98–99.

Clark, D. & Kerkhof, Ad. J. F. M. (1997). No Suicide Contracts and No Suicide Decisions. *Crisis: Journal of Crisis Intervention and Suicide*, 18, 1–2.

Cummings, L. (2010). Charmaine had 'suicide contract' with doc. *The Sydney Daily Telegraph*, (18th March) (http://www.dailytelegraph.com.au/news/nsw-act/charmaine-had-suicide-contract-with-doc/story-e6freuzi-1225842377663) Retrieved 20.11.2010.

Davidson, M., Wagner, W. G. & Range, L. M. (1995). Clinicians' Attitudes Toward No Suicide Agreements. *Suicide & Life-Threatening Behavior*, 25, 410–414.

Davis, S., Williams, I. S. & Hays, L. W. (2002). Psychiatric Inpatients' Perceptions of Written No Suicide Agreements: An Exploratory Study. *Suicide & Life-Threatening Behavior*, 32, (1), 51–61.

Decant, J. & Range, L. M. (1997). No Suicide Agreements: College students' perceptions. *College Student Journal*, 31, (2), 238–243.

Detre, T. & MacDonald, M. C. (1997). Managed Care and the Future of Psychiatry. *Archives of General Psychiatry*, 54, 201–204.

Edwards, S. J. & Harries, M. (2007). No Suicide Contracts, No Suicide Agreements and No Suicide Assurances: A controversial life. *Australasian Psychiatry*, 15, 484–489.

Edwards, S. J. & Sachmann, M. D. (2010). No Suicide Contracts, No Suicide Agreements and No Suicide Assurances. A Study of Their Nature, Utilization, Perceived Effectiveness, and Potential to Cause Harm. *Crisis: Journal of Crisis Intervention & Suicide Prevention*, 31, (6), 290–302.

Egan, M. (1997). Contracting for Safety: A Concept Analysis. *Crisis: Journal of Crisis Intervention & Suicide*, 18 (1), 17–23.

Ewart, J. R. (1967). Other Psychiatric Emergencies, In A.F.H. Kaplin (Ed.), (pp. 1179–87), *Comprehensive Textbook of Psychiatry*, Baltimore, Williams and Wilkins.

Farley, F. (2006). In conversation with Aaron T. Beck. *American Psychological Association* 114th Convention, New Orleans, August 12th 2006, Retrieved 20th November 2008. (http://www.fenichel.com/Beck2006.shtml)

Farrow, T. (2002). Owning Their Expertise: Why Nurses Use "No Suicide Contracts" Rather Than Their Own Assessments. *International Journal of Mental Health Nursing*, 11, 214–219.

Farrow, T. (2003). No Suicide contracts in community crisis situations: a conceptual analysis. *Journal of Psychiatric and Mental Health Nursing*, 10, 199–202.

Farrow, T. & O'Brien, A. (2003). No Suicide Contracts' and Informed Consent: An Analysis of Ethical Issues. *Nursing Ethics*, 10, 201–207.

Farrow, T., Simpson, A. & Warren, H. (2002). The Effects of the Use of No Suicide Contracts in Community Crisis Situations: The Experience of Clinicians and Consumers. *Brief Treatment and Crisis Intervention*, 2, (3), 241–246.

Gavazzi, J. D. (2010). *No Suicide Contracts: Is a No Suicide contract an effective strategy?* Pennsylvania Psychological Association, Ethics Committee, Blog: http://www.papsyblog.org/2011/07/nosuicide-contracts.html (Retrieved 10.05.2012).

Hillard, J. R. (1990). (Ed.). *Manual of Clinical Emergency Psychiatry*. Washington, DC: American Psychiatric Press.

Hipple, J. & Cimbolic, P. (1979). *The Counselor and the Suicidal Crisis*. Illinois: Charles C Thomas.

Jacobs, D. G. (1992). Evaluating and Treating Suicidal Behavior in the Borderline Patient. In D. G. Jacobs (Ed.). *Suicide and Clinical Practice*, (pp. 115–131), Washington DC: American Psychiatric Press.

Kroll, J. (2000). Use of No Suicide Contracts by Psychiatrists in Minnesota. *American Journal of Psychiatry*, 157, 1684–1686.

Kroll, J. (2007). No Suicide Contracts as a Suicide Prevention Strategy. *Psychiatric Times*, 24, (8), 1–2.

Lewis, M. (2007). No-Harm Contract: A Review of What We Know. *Suicide and Life Threatening Behaviors*, 37, (1), 50–57.

Linehan, M. M., Goodstein, J. L., Nielsen, S. L. & Chiles, J. A. (1983). Reasons for staying alive when you are thinking of killing yourself. *Journal of Consulting and Clinical Psychology*, 51(2), 276–286.

Mahrer, J. (1993). *The Use of No Suicide Contracts and Agreements with Suicidal Patients.* Dissertation. Palo Alto, California: Pacific Graduate School of Psychology.

Mick, J. (2010). Foxconn Makes Employees Promise Not to Kill Themselves, *Daily Tech*, 27th May 2010 (blog) (http://webcache.googleusercontent.com/search?q=cache:rYjBezVyBTIJ:www.dailytech.com/Foxconn percent2BMakes percent2BEmployees percent2BPromise percent2BNot percent2Bto percent2BKill percent2BThemselves/article18526.htm+Foxconn+Chinese+to+sign+a+no+suicide+contract.+Daily+Tech+28th+May+2010+suicide+apple&cd=2&hl=en&ct=clnk&gl=au) Retrieved 20.11.2010.

Miller, M. (1999). Suicide-Prevention Contracts: Advantages, Disadvantages, and An Alternative Approach. In D. J. Jacobs (Ed.), *The Harvard Medical School Guide to Suicide Assessment and Intervention.* (pp. 463–481), San Francisco: Jossey-Bass Publishers.

Miller, M., Jacobs, D.G. & Gutheil, T.G. (1998). Talisman or Taboo: The Controversy of the Suicide-Prevention Contract. *Harvard Review of Psychiatry*, 6, 78–87.

O'Hare, P. (2010). Boy's act of despair shocks school: Mother blames bullies after 8-year-old allegedly jumps off balcony in suicide try, *Houston Chronicle*, (27th March): (http://www.chron.com/disp/story.mpl/metropolitan/6932149.html) Retrieved 20.11.2010.

Page, S. & King, M. (2008). No Suicide Agreements: Current Practices and Opinions in a Canadian Urban Health Region. *The Canadian Journal of Psychiatry*, 53, (3), 169–76.

Potter, M. L., Vitale-Nolen, R. & Dawson, A. M. (2005). Implementation of Safety Agreements in an Acute Psychiatric Facility. *Journal of the American Psychiatric Nurses Association*, 11, 144–155.

Range, L., Campbell, C., Kovac, S. H., Marion-Jones, M., Aldridge, H., Kogos, S. & Crump, Y. (2002). No Suicide Contracts: An Overview and Recommendations. *Death Studies*, 26, (1) 51–74.

Reid, W. H. (2005). Contracting for Safety Redux. *Journal of Practical Psychiatry and Behavior,* 11, (1), 54–57.

Rudd, M. D. (1996). The Role of No Suicide Agreements in the Treatment of Suicidal Ideation and Behavior. *Suicide & Life-Threatening Behavior,* 26, 216–217.

Rudd, M. D., Joiner, T. & Rajab, M. H. (1996). Relationships among suicide ideators, attempters, and multiple attempters in a young-adult sample. *Journal of Abnormal Psychology*, 105, (4), 541–550.

Scott, J., House, R., Yates, M. & Harrington, J. (1997). Individual risk factors for early repetition of deliberate self-harm, *British Journal of Medical Psychology*, 70, 387–393.

Simon, R. I. (1999). The Suicide Prevention Contract: Clinical, Legal, and Risk Management Issues. *Journal of the American Academy of Psychiatry & the Law*, 27, 445-450.

Simon, R. (2003). *Assessing and Managing Suicide Risk. Guidelines for Clinically Based Risk Management.* Washington, D.C: American Psychiatric Publishing.

Simon, R. & Hales, R. (2006). *Textbook of Suicide Assessment and Management.* Washington, DC: American Psychiatric Publishing, Inc.

Stanford, E., Goetz, R. & Bloom, J. (1994). The No Harm Contract in the Emergency Assessment of Suicidal Risk. *Journal of Clinical Psychiatry*, 55, 344–48.

Twiname, G. (1981). No Suicide Contracts for Nurses. *Journal of Psychiatric Nursing & Mental Health Services,* 19, 11–12.

CHAPTER 5

Colucci, E., Kelly, C. M., Minas, H., Jorm, A. F. & Nadera, D. (2010). Mental Health First Aid guidelines for helping a suicidal person: a Delphi consensus study in Philippines. *International Journal of Mental Health Systems*, 4:32. doi: 10.1186/1752-4458-4-32. (http://www.biomedcentral.com/content/pdf/1752-4458-4-32.pdf) Retrieved 01.07.2012.

Colucci, E., Kelly, C. M., Minas, H., Jorm, A. F. & Chattwejee, S. (2010). Mental Health First Aid guidelines for helping a suicidal person: a Delphi consensus study in India. *International Journal of Mental Health Systems*, 4:4. doi: 10.1186/1752-4458-4-4. (http://www.ijmhs.com/content/4/1/4) retrieved 01.07.2012.

Colucci, E., Kelly, C. M., Minas, H., Jorm, A. F. & Suzuki, Y. (2011). Mental Health First Aid guidelines for helping a suicidal person: a Delphi consensus study in Japan. *International Journal of Mental Health Systems*, 4:12. doi:10.1186/1752-4458-5-12. (http://www.biomedcentral.com/content/pdf/1752-4458-5-12.pdf) retrieved 01.07.2012.

Davidson, M., Wagner, W. G. & Range, L. M. (1995). Clinicians' Attitudes Toward No Suicide Agreements. *Suicide & Life-Threatening Behavior*, 25, 410–414.

Drew, B. (1999). No Suicide Contracts to prevent suicidal behavior in psychiatric inpatients settings. *Journal of the American Psychiatric Nurses Association*, 5, 23–28.

Drew, B. L. (2001). Self-Harm Behavior and No Suicide Contracting in Psychiatric Inpatient Settings. *Archives of Psychiatric Nursing*, 15, 99–106.

Drye, R., Goulding, R., & Goulding, M., (1973). No Suicide Decisions: Patient Monitoring of Suicidal Risk. *American Journal of Psychiatry*, 130, 171–74.

Edwards, S. J. (2008). *No Suicide contracts, No Suicide Agreements and No Suicide Assurances: An exploratory study of their nature, utilization and perceived effectiveness.* Dissertation, School of Social Work & Social Policy, University of Western Australia.

Edwards, S. J. & Harries, M. (2007). No Suicide Contracts, No Suicide Agreements and No Suicide Assurances: A controversial life. *Australaisan Psychiatry*, 15, 484–489.

Edwards, S. J. & Sachmann, M. D. (2010). No Suicide Contracts, No Suicide Agreements and No Suicide Assurances. A Study of Their Nature, Utilization, Perceived Effectiveness, and Potential to Cause Harm. *Crisis: Journal of Crisis Intervention & Suicide Prevention,* 31, (6), 290–302.

Egan, M. (1997). Contracting for Safety: A Concept Analysis. *Crisis: Journal of Crisis Intervention & Suicide,* 18, (1), 17–23.

Farrow, T. L. (2002). Owning Their Expertise: Why Nurses Use "No Suicide Contracts" Rather Than Their Own Assessments. *International Journal of Mental Health Nursing,* 11, 214–219.

Farrow, T., Simpson, A. & Warren, H. (2002). The Effects of the Use of No Suicide Contracts in Community Crisis Situations: The Experience of Clinicians and Consumers. *Brief Treatment and Crisis Intervention,* 2, (3), 241–246.

Hage, G. (2000). On the Ethics of Pedestrian Crossings: Or Why Mutual Obligation Does Not Belong in the Language of Neo-Liberal Economics. *Meanjin*, 4, 27–37.

Hansen, A., Heath, M. A., Williams, M., Fox, Jay, Hudnall, G. A. & Bledsoe, C. (2012). No-Suicide Contracts with Suidcidal Youth: Mental Health Professional's Perceptions and Current Practice. *Contemporary School Psychology*, 16, 145–159.

Hipple, J. & Cimbolic, P. (1979). *The Counselor and the Suicidal Crisis*. Illinois: Charles C Thomas.

Hiroto, I., Kawano, K., Kawashima, D. & Kawanishi, C. (2008). Responses to patients with suicidal ideation among different specialties in general hospitals. *General Hospital Psychiatry*, 30, (6), 578–80.

Kroll, J. (2000). Use of No Suicide Contracts by Psychiatrists in Minnesota. *American Journal of Psychiatry*, 157, 1684–1686.

Kroll, J. (2007). No Suicide Contracts as a Suicide Prevention Strategy. *Psychiatric Times,* 24, (8), 1–2.

Mahrer, J. (1993). *The Use of No Suicide Contracts and Agreements with Suicidal Patients.* Dissertation. Palo Alto, California: Pacific Graduate School of Psychology.

Miller, M. C., Jacobs, D. G. & Gutheil, T. G. (1998). Talisman or Taboo: The Controversy of the Suicide-Prevention Contract. *Harvard Review of Psychiatry*, 6, 78–87.

Neville, D. & Barnes, S. (1985). The Suicidal Phone Call. *Journal of Psychosocial Nursing and Mental Health Care*, 23, 14–18.

Page, S. & King, M. (2008). No Suicide Agreements: Current Practices and Opinions in a Canadian Urban Health Region. *The Canadian Journal of Psychiatry*, 53 (3), 169–176.

Potter, M. L., Vitale-Nolen, R. & Dawson, A. M. (2005). Implementation of Safety Agreements in an Acute Psychiatric Facility. *Journal of the American Psychiatric Nurses Association*, 11, 144–155.

Range, L., Campbell, C., Kovac, S. H., Marion-Jones, M., Aldridge, H., Kogos, S, & Crump, Y. (2002). No Suicide Contracts: An Overview and Recommendations. *Death Studies*, 26, (1), 51–74.

Rudd, D., Mandrusiak, M. & Joiner, T. (2006). The Case Against No Suicide Contracts. The Commitment to Treatment Statement as a Practice Alternative. *Journal of Clinical Psychology*, 62, 243–251.

Sanders, S., Ting, L., Power, J. & Jacobson, J. (2006). Social Worker's Views of No Suicide Contracts. *Social Work in Mental Health*, 4, 51–66.

Selzer, M., Koenigsberg, H. & Kernberg, O. (1987). The Initial Contract in the Treatment of Borderline Patients. *Journal of Psychiatry*, 144, (7), 927–930.

Simon, R. (1999). The Suicide Prevention Contract: Clinical, Legal, and Risk Management Issues. *Journal of the American Academy of Psychiatry & the Law*, 27, 445–450.

Simon, R. (2003). *Assessing and Managing Suicide Risk. Guidelines for Clinically Based Risk Management.* Washington, DC: American Psychiatric Publishing.

Simon, R. & Hales, R. (2006). *Textbook of Suicide Assessment and Management.* Washington, DC: American Psychiatric Publishing, Inc.

Stanford, E., Goetz, R. & Bloom, J. (1994). The No Harm Contract in the Emergency Assessment of Suicidal Risk. *Journal of Clinical Psychiatry*, 55, 344–48.

Trimble, L., Jackson, K. & Harvey, D. (2000). Client Suicidal Behaviour: Intervention, and Implications for Psychologists. *Australian Psychologist*, 35, 227–232.

Twiname, G. (1981). No Suicide Contracts for Nurses. *Journal of Psychiatric Nursing Mental Health Services*, 19, 11–12.

Volk, M. L., Lieber, S. R., Kim, S. Y., Ubel, P. A. & Schneider, C. E. (2012). Patient Contracts in Clinical Practice. *Lancet*, 379, 9810, 7–9.

Wittgenstein, L. (1953). *Philosophical Investigations*, 125.

CHAPTER 6

Ackerman, A. & Scullin, J. (2011). Hillsborough schools' suicide policy questioned. *The Tampa Tribune*, (14th April); retrieved 16th May 2012. http://www2.cohpa.ucf.edu/social/documents/hillsborough-schools-a.leon-quoted.pdf

Bartlett, M. L. (2006). The Efficacy of No Suicide Contracts with Clients in Counseling on an Outpatient Basis. Dissertation, Auburn, Alabama: Graduate facility of Auburn University.

Brent, D. (1997). The After Care of Adolescents with Deliberate Self Harm, *Journal of Child Psychiatry*, 38, 277–286.

Boyatzis, R. E. (1998). *Thematic Analysis and Code Development: Transforming Qualitative Information*. Thousand Oaks: Sage Publications.

Edwards, S. J. (2008). *No Suicide Contracts, No Suicide Agreements and No Suicide Assurances: An exploratory study of their nature, utilization and perceived effectiveness*. Dissertation. Perth, Western Australia: Discipline of Social Work and Social Policy, University of Western Australia.

Egan, M. (1997). Contracting for Safety: A Concept Analysis. *Crisis: Journal of Crisis Intervention & Suicide*, 18 (1), 17–23.

Farrow, T. (2003). No Suicide Contracts in Community Crisis Situations: a conceptual analysis. *Journal of Psychiatric and Mental Health Nursing*, 10, 199–202.

Jacobs, D. G. (1992). Evaluating and Treating Suicidal Behavior in the borderline patient. In D. G. Jacobs (Ed.). *Suicide and Clinical Practice*, (pp. 115–131) Washington DC: American Psychiatric Press.

Karasu, T. B. (1996). Ethical issues in psychotherapy practice, In S Bloch (Ed.), *An Introduction to the Psychotherapies*, (pp. 320–349), New York, Oxford Medical Publications.

Maddux, J. E. & Rodgers, R. W. (1983). Protection motivation and self-efficacy: A revised theory of fear appeal and attitude change, *Journal of Experimental Social Psychology*, 19, (5), 469–479.

Mahrer, J. (1993). *The Use of No Suicide Contracts and Agreements with Suicidal Patients.* Dissertation. Palo Alto, California: Pacific Graduate School of Psychology.

Murphy, G. E. (1984). The Prediction of Suicide: Why Is It So Difficult?, *American Journal of Psychotherapy*, 38, (3), 341–349.

Pokorny, A. D. (1993). Suicide Prediction Revisited. *Suicide and Life Threatening Behaviors,* 23, 1–10.

Shaffer, D. A., Garland, M. A., Gould, M., Fisher, P. & Trautman, P. (1988). Preventing Teenage Suicide: A Critical Review. *The American Journal of Child and Adolescent Psychiatry,* 13, (3), 675–687.

Stanford, E., Goetz, R. & Bloom, J. (1994). The No Harm Contract in the Emergency Assessment of Suicidal Risk. *Journal of Clinical Psychiatry*, 55, 344–48.

Stummer, G. (2002). An Update on the Use of Contracting. *Journal of Transactional Analysis*, 32, (3), 121–123.

Tesch, R. (1990). *Qualitative Research: Analysis Types and Software Tools.* New York: The Falmer Press.

CHAPTER 7

Boyatzis, R. E. (1998). *Thematic Analysis and Code Development: Transforming Qualitative Information.* Thousand Oaks: Sage Publications.

Davidson, M., Wagner, W.G. & Range, L. M. (1995). Clinicians' Attitudes Towards No Suicide Agreements. *Suicide & Life-Threatening Behavior*, 25, 410–14.

Davis, S., Williams, I. S. & Hays, L. W. (2002). Psychiatric Inpatients' Perceptions of Written No Suicide Agreements: An Exploratory Study. *Suicide & Life-Threatening Behavior*, 32, (1), 51–61.

Decant, J. & Range, L. M. (1997). No Suicide Agreements: College students' perceptions. *College Student Journal*, 31, (2), 238–43.

Edwards, S. J. & Sachmann, M. D. (2010). No Suicide Contracts, No Suicide Agreements and No Suicide Assurances. A Study of Their Nature, Utilization, Perceived Effectiveness, and Potential to Cause Harm. *Crisis: Journal of Crisis Intervention & Suicide Prevention,* 31, (6), 290–302.

Farrow, T. (2002). Owning Their Expertise: Why Nurses Use "No Suicide Contracts" Rather Than Their Own Assessments. *International Journal of Mental Health Nursing,* 11, 214–219.

Farrow, T. (2003). No suicide contracts in community crisis situations: a conceptual analysis. *Journal of Psychiatric and Mental Health Nursing*, 10, 199–202.

Farrow, T. & O'Brien, A. (2003). No Suicide Contracts' and Informed Consent: An Analysis of Ethical Issues. *Nursing Ethics*, 10, 201–207.

Farrow, T., Simpson, A. & Warren, H. (2002). The Effects of the Use of No Suicide Contracts in Community Crisis Situations: The Experience of Clinicians and Consumers. *Brief Treatment and Crisis Intervention*, 2, (3), 241–246.

Garvey, K., Penn, J., Campbell, A., Esposito-Smythers, C. & Spirito, A. (2009). Contracting for safety with patients: clinical practice and forensic implications, *Journal of the American Academy of Psychiatry and the Law*, 37, 363–70.

Gutheil, T. G. (1992). Suicide and Suit: Liability after Self-Destruction, In D.G. Jacobs (Ed.), *Suicide and Clinical Practice*, (pp. 147–67), Washington DC, American Psychiatric Press.

Hage, G. (2000). On the Ethics of Pedestrian Crossings: Or Why Mutual Obligation Does Not Belong in the Language of Neo-Liberal Economics. *Meanjin*, 4, 27–37.

Hope, A. (16.06.2006). State Coroner of Western Australia; personal correspondence

Jones, R. N. & O'Brien, P. (1990). Unique Observations for Child Inpatient in Psychiatry. *Journal of Psychosocial Nursing and Mental Health Care*, 28, 29–31.

Kroll, J. (2000). Use of No Suicide Contracts by Psychiatrists in Minnesota. *American Journal of Psychiatry*, 157, 1684–86.

Linehan, M. M., Goodstein, J. L., Nielsen, S. L. & Chiles, J. A. (1983). Reasons for staying alive when you are thinking of killing yourself, *Journal of Consulting and Clinical Psychology*, 51(2), 276–286.

Mahrer, J. (1993). *The Use of No Suicide Contracts and Agreements with Suicidal Patients'*, Dissertation, Palo Alto California, Pacific Graduate School of Psychology.

Miller, M., Jacobs, D. G. & Gutheil, T. G. (1998). Talisman or Taboo: The Controversy of the Suicide-Prevention Contract. *Harvard Review of Psychiatry*, 6, 78–87.

Murphy, G. E. (1984). The Prediction of Suicide: Why Is It so Difficult?, *American Journal of Psychotherapy*, 38, (3), 341–349.

Nussbaum, M. C. (2006). *Frontiers of Justice: Disability, Nationality, Species Membership.* Cambridge: The Belknap Press.

Page, S. & King, M. (2008). No Suicide Agreements: Current Practices and Opinions in a Canadian Urban Health Region. *The Canadian Journal of Psychiatry*, 53, (3), 169–76.

Pokorny, A. D. (1993). Suicide Prediction Revisited. *Suicide and Life Threatening Behaviors,* 23, 1–10.

Range, L. M. (2005). No Suicide Contracts, In D Lester & R Yufit (Eds.), *Assessment, Treatment and Prevention of Suicidal Behavior,* pp. 181-203, New York, Wiley & Sons.

Resnick, P. (2011). Suicide Risk Assessment. *Psychiatric Times*, Podcast by Susan Kweskin posted on the 11th February 2011, retrieved 7th March 2011. (http://www.psychiatrictimes.com/suicide/content/article/10168/1796523?GUID=94B2CBBF-0947-4501-81AF-34DB8CCED214&rememberme=1)

Rudd, M. D. (1996). The Role of No Suicide Agreements in the Treatment of Suicidal Ideation and Behavior. *Suicide & Life-Threatening Behavior,* 26, 216–217.

Rudd, M. D., Joiner, T. & Rajab, M. H. (1996). Relationships among suicide ideators, attempters, and multiple attempters in a young-adult sample. *Journal of Abnormal Psychology,* 105, (4), 541–50.

Sanders, S., Ting, L., Power, J. & Jacobson, J. (2006). Social Worker's Views of No Suicide Contracts, *Social Work in Mental Health,* 4, (4), 51–66.

Scott, J., House, R., Yates, M. & Harrington, J. (1997). Individual risk factors for early repetition of deliberate self-harm, *British Journal of Medical Psychology*, 70, 387–393.

Semmler, P. (09.05.2006). St. James Legal Chambers, Sydney; personal correspondence.

Shaffer, D. A., Garland, M. A., Gould, M., Fisher, P. & Trautman, P. (1988). Preventing Teenage Suicide: A Critical Review. *The American Journal of Child and Adolescent Psychiatry*, 13, (3), 675–687.

Shneidman, E. S. (1993). *Suicide as Psychache: A Clinical Approach to Self-Destructive Behavior,* New Jersey, Jason Aronson, Inc.

Simon, R. (1999). The Suicide Prevention Contract: Clinical, Legal, and Risk Management Issues. *Journal of the American Academy of Psychiatry & the Law,* 27, 445–50.

Simon, R. I. & Hales, R. (2006). *Textbook of Suicide Assessment and Management,* Washington, DC: American Psychiatric Publishing, Inc.

Stanford, E. J., Goetz, R. R. & Bloom, J. D. (1994). The No Harm Contract in the Emergency Assessment of Suicidal Risk. *Journal of Clinical Psychiatry,* 55, (8), 344–48.

Stone, M. H. (1980). The Suicidal Patient: Points Concerning Diagnosis and Intensive Treatment. *Psychiatry Quarterly,* 52, 65.

Weiss, A. (2001). The No Suicide Contract: Possibilities and Pitfalls. *American Journal of Psychotherapy,* 55, (3), 414–19.

Data from the SPC study

1. Clinician Questionnaire # 311
2. Clinician Questionnaire # 134
3. Clinician Questionnaire # 78
4. Clinician Questionnaire # 354
5. Clinician Questionnaire # 14
6. Clinician Questionnaire # 433
7. Clinician Questionnaire # 227
8. Clinician Questionnaire # 211
9. Clinician Questionnaire # 410
10. Clinician Questionnaire # 330
11. Clinician Questionnaire # 292
12. Clinician Questionnaire # 36
13. Clinician Questionnaire # 420
14. Clinician Questionnaire # 218
15. Clinician Questionnaire # 400
16. Clinician Questionnaire # 318
17. Clinician Questionnaire # 129
18. Clinician Questionnaire # 72
19. Clinician Questionnaire # 349
20. Clinician Questionnaire # 125

CHAPTER 8

Brent, D. (1997). The After Care of Adolescents with Deliberate Self Harm. *Journal of Child Psychiatry,* 38, 277–286.

Edwards, S. J. & Sachmann, M. D. (2010). No Suicide Contracts, No Suicide Agreements and No Suicide Assurances. A Study of Their Nature, Utilization,

Perceived Effectiveness, and Potential to Cause Harm. *Crisis: Journal of Crisis Intervention & Suicide Prevention,* 31, (6), 290–302.

Goldney, R. D. (2010). *Suicide Prevention.* New York: Oxford University Press.

Mahrer, J. & Bongar, B. (1996). Assessment and Management of Suicide Risk and the Use of the No Suicide Contract. (pp. 277–294), In L. VandeCreek, S. Knapp, and T. L. Jackson (Eds.), *Innovations in Clinical Practice: A Source Book.* Sarasota, FL: Professional Resource Press.

Range, L., Campbell, C., Kovac, S. H., Marion-Jones, M., Aldridge, H., Kogos, S. & Crump, Y. (2002). No Suicide Contracts: An Overview and Recommendations. *Death Studies,* 26, (1), 51–74.

Rudd, M. D. (1996). The Role of No Suicide Agreements in the Treatment of Suicidal Ideation and Behavior. *Suicide & Life-Threatening Behavior,* 26, 216–217.

Shea, C. S. (1999). *The Practical Art of Suicide Assessment.* New York: John Wiley and Sons, Inc.

CHAPTER 9

Brent, D. (1997). The After Care of Adolescents with Deliberate Self Harm. *Journal of Child Psychiatry,* 38, 277–286.

Clark, D. & Kerkhof, Ad. J. F. M. (1993). No Suicide Decisions and Suicide Contracts in Therapy. *Crisis: Journal of Crisis Intervention and Suicide,* 14, (3), 98–99.

Clark, D. & Kerkhof, Ad. J. F. M. (1997). No Suicide Contracts and No Suicide Decisions. *Crisis: Journal of Crisis Intervention and Suicide,* 18, 1–2.

Decant, J. & Range, L. M. (1997). No Suicide Agreements: College students' perceptions. *College Student Journal,* 31, (2), 238–43.

Drye, R. C., Goulding, R. L. & Goulding, M. E. (1973). No Suicide Decisions: Patient Monitoring of Suicidal Risk, *American Journal of Psychiatry,* 130, (2). 171–74.

Edwards, S. J. & Sachmann, M. D. (2010). No Suicide Contracts, No Suicide Agreements and No Suicide Assurances. A Study of Their Nature, Utilization, Perceived Effectiveness, and Potential to Cause Harm. *Crisis: Journal of Crisis Intervention & Suicide Prevention,* 31, (6), 290–302.

Farrow, T. (2002). Owning Their Expertise: Why Nurses Use "No Suicide Contracts" Rather Than Their Own Assessments. *International Journal of Mental Health Nursing,* 11, 214–219.

Jacobs, D. G. (1992). Evaluating and Treating Suicidal Behavior in the borderline patient. In D. G. Jacobs (Ed.). *Suicide and Clinical Practice*, (pp. 115–131), Washington DC: American Psychiatric Press.

Mahrer, J. (1993). *The Use of No Suicide Contracts and Agreements with Suicidal Patients.* Dissertation. Palo Alto, California: Pacific Graduate School of Psychology.

Mahrer, J. & Bongar, B. (1996). Assessment and Management of Suicide Risk and the Use of the No Suicide Contract. (pp. 277–294), In L. VandeCreek, S. Knapp, and T. L. Jackson (Eds.), *Innovations in Clinical Practice: A Source Book.* Sarasota, FL: Professional Resource Press.

Miller, M. (1999). Suicide-Prevention Contracts: Advantages, Disadvantages, and An Alternative Approach. In D. J. Jacobs (Ed.), *The Harvard Medical School Guide to Suicide Assessment and Intervention.* (pp. 463–481), San Francisco: Jossey-Bass Publishers.

Page, S. & King, M. (2008). No Suicide Agreements: Current Practices and Opinions in a Canadian Urban Health Region. *The Canadian Journal of Psychiatry*, 53 (3), 169–76.

Reid, W. H. (2005). Contracting for Safety Redux, *Journal of Practical Psychiatry & Behavior,* 11, (1), 54–57.

Rudd, M. D., Mandrusiak, M. & Joiner, T. E. (2006). The Case Against No Suicide Contracts. The Commitment to Treatment Statement as a Practice Alternative. *Journal of Clinical Psychology*, 62, 243–251.

Simon, R. & Hales, R. (2006). Textbook of Suicide Assessment and Management. Washington, DC: American Psychiatric Publishing, Inc.

Weiss, A. (2001). The No Suicide Contract: Possibilities and Pitfalls, *American Journal of Psychotherapy,* 55, (3), 414–19.

CHAPTER 10

Beautrais, A. L., Joyce, P. R. & Mulder, R. T. (1997). Precipitating Factors and Life Events in Serious Suicide Attempts Among Youths Aged 13 Through 24 Years. Journal of the *American Academy of Child & Adolescent Psychiatry*, 36, (11), 1543–1551.

Beck, U. (1992). *Risk Society: Towards a new modernity.* London: Sage Publications.

Beck, U. (1999). *World Risk Society.* Malden, MA: Blackwell Publishers, Inc.

Beck, U. (2000). *The Brave New World of Work.* Oxford: Blackwell Publishers, Inc.

Brent, D. A. (1989). Suicide and suicidal behavior in children and adolescents. *Pediatrics in Review,* 10, (9), 149.

Brent, D.A. (1997). The After Care of Adolescents with Deliberate Self Harm. *Journal of Child Psychiatry,* 38, 277–286.

Brent, D. A., Poling, K. D. & Goldstein, T. R. (2001). *Treating Depressed and Suicidal Adolescents.* New York: The Guildford Press.

Clark, D. & Kerkhof, Ad. J. F. M. (1997). No Suicide Contracts and No Suicide Decisions. *Crisis: Journal of Crisis Intervention and Suicide,* 18, 1–2.

Davidson, M., Wagner, W. G. & Range, L. M. (1995). Clinicians' Attitudes Toward No-Suicide Agreements. *Suicide & Life-Threatening Behavior,* 25, 410–414.

Davidson, M. & Range, L. M. (2000). Age Appropriate No Suicide Agreements: Professionals rating of appropriateness and effectiveness. *Education & Treatment of Children,* 23, (2), 143–155.

Edwards, S. J. (2000). *The 4Rs: A Youth Suicide Prevention Handbook. A Step-by-Step Guide for Social Workers and Welfare Workers, Youth Workers and Group Workers, Community Support Workers and Accommodation Workers Youth Education Officers and Pastoral Care Workers.* Western Australia: The Little Blue Book Publishing Company.

Edwards, S. J., Gostelow, C., Pfaff, J., Baily, S., Hyde, J., Follett, D. & Leung, P. (1995). *Managing Suicidal Behaviour in General Practice: A Guide for General Practitioners.* Perth: Health Department of Western Australia.

Goldenring, J. M. & Cohen, E. (1988). Getting into adolescent heads. *Contemporary Pediatrics,* 5(7), 75–90.

Goldney, R. D. (2010). *Suicide Prevention.* New York: Oxford University Press.

Hockberger, R. S. & Rothstein, R. J. (1987). Assessment of Suicide Potential by Nonpsychiatrists Using the SAD PERSONS Scale. *The Journal of Emergency Medicine,* 6, 99–103.

Jobes, D. A. (2006). *Managing Suicidal Risk: A collaborative approach.* New York: The Guildford Press.

Jobes, D. A. (2012). The Collaborative Assessment and Management of Suicidality (CAMS): An Evolving Evidence-Based Clinical Approach to Suicide Risk. *Suicide and Life-Threatening Behavior*, 42, (6), 640–653.

Lang, W., Ramsay, B., Tanney, B. & Tierney, R. (1989). Caregiver Attitudes in Suicide Prevention: Help for the Helpers. In R.F.W *Prevention: The Role of Attitude and Imitation.* (pp. 260–75). New York: The World Health. Diekstra, R. Maris, S. Platt, A. Schmidtle, and G. Sonneck (Eds.). *Suicide and its* Organization.

Lee, J. & Bartlett, M. (2005). Suicide Prevention: Critical Elements for Managing Suicidal Clients and Counselor Liability Without the Use of a No Suicide Contract, *Death Studies,* 29, 847–65.

Mahrer, J. & Bongar, B. (1996). Assessment and Management of Suicide Risk and the Use of the No Suicide Contract. (pp. 277–294), In L. VandeCreek, S. Knapp, and T. L. Jackson (Eds.), *Innovations in Clinical Practice: A Source Book.* Sarasota, FL: Professional Resource Press.

Mann, J. J., Apter, A., Bertolote, J., Beautrais, A., Currier, D., Haas, A., Hegerl, U., Lonnqvist, J., Malone, K., Marusic, A., Mehlum, L., Patton, G., Phillips, M., Rutz, W., Rihmer, Z., Schmidtke, A., Shaffer, D., Silverman, M., Takahashi, Y., Varnik, A., Wasserman, D., Yip, P. & Hendin, H. (2005). Suicide Prevention Strategies: A Systematic Review. *The Journal of the American Medical Association*, 294, (16), 2064–2074.

McKelvey, R., Davies, L., Pfaff, J., Acres, J. & Edwards, S. J. (1998). Psychological distress and suicidal ideation among 15-24-year-olds presenting to general practice: a pilot study. *Australian & New Zealand Journal of Psychiatry*, 32(3), 324–34.

Miller, M. C. (1999). Suicide-prevention contracts: Advantages, disadvantages, and an alternative approach. In DJ Jacobs (Ed.), *The Harvard Medical School Guide to Suicide Assessment and Intervention,* pp. 463–81, San Francisco, Jossey-Bass.

Miller, M., Jacobs, D. G. & Gutheil, T. G. (1998). Talisman or Taboo: The Controversy of the Suicide-Prevention Contract', *Harvard Review of Psychiatry,* 6, 78-87.

Pfaff, J., Acres, J. & McKelvey, R. S. (2001). Training general practitioners to recognise and respond to psychological distress and suicidal ideation in young people. *Medical Journal of Australia*, 174, 222–226.

Posner, K., Brown, G. K., Stanley, B., Brent, D. A., Yershova, K. V., Oquendo, M. A., Currier, G. W., Melvin, G. A., Greenhill, L., Shen, S. & Mann, J.J. (2011). The Columbia-Suicide Severity Rating Scale: Initial Validity and Internal Consistency Findings from Three Multisite Studies With Adolescent and Adult. *American Journal of Psychiatry*, 168, (12), 1266–77.

Potter, M. & Dawson, A. (2001). From Safety Contract to Safety Agreement, *Journal of Psychosocial Nursing & Mental Health Services*, 39, (8), 38–46.

Range, L. M. (2002). The Family of Instruments That Assess Suicide Risk. *Journal of Psychopathology and Behavioral Assessment*, 27, (2), 133–40.

Range, L., Campbell, C., Kovac, S. H., Marion-Jones, M., Aldridge, H., Kogos, S. & Crump, Y. (2002). No Suicide Contracts: An Overview and Recommendations. *Death Studies*, 26, (1), 51–74.

Ridsdale, L., Mandalia, S., Evans, A., Jerrett, W. & Osler, K. (1999). Tiredness as a ticket of entry. The role of patients' beliefs and psychological symptoms in explaining frequent attendance. General Practice Fatigue Group. *Scandinavian Journal of Primary Health Care*, 17(2), 72–74

Rudd, M. D. (1996). The Role of No Suicide Agreements in the Treatment of Suicidal Ideation and Behavior. *Suicide & Life-Threatening Behavior*, 26, 216–217.

Rudd, M. D., Joiner, T. & Rajab, M. H. (2001). *Treating Suicide Behavior: An Effective, Time-Limited Approach*. New York: The Guildford Press.

Rudd, M. D., Mandrusiak, M. & Joiner, T. (2006). The Case Against No Suicide Contracts. The Commitment to Treatment Statement as a Practice Alternative. *Journal of Clinical Psychology*, 62, (2), 243–51.

Samra, J. & Bilsker, D. (2007). Coping with Suicidal Thoughts, Consortium for Organizational Mental Health (COMH;www.comh.ca), Faculty of Health Sciences, Simon Fraser University, Vancouver, BC. http://summit.sfu.ca/item/1115, retrieved 29.06.2013.

Shea, C. S. (1999). *The practical art of suicide assessment*. New York: John Wiley and Sons, Inc.

Shneidman, E. S. (1993). *Suicide as Psychache: A Clinical Approach to Self-Destructive Behavior*. New Jersey: Jason Aronson, Inc.

Stanley, B. & Brown, G. K. (2012). Safety Planning Intervention: A Brief Intervention to Mitigate Suicide Risk. *Journal of Cognitive and Behavioral Practice*, 19, (2), 256–264.

CONCLUSION

Kroll, J. (2007). No Suicide Contracts as a Suicide Prevention Strategy. *Psychiatric Times*, 24, (8), 1–2.

FREQUENTLY ASKED QUESTIONS

Clark, D. & Kerkhof, Ad. J. F. M. (1997). No Suicide Contracts and No Suicide Decisions. *Crisis: Journal of Crisis Intervention and Suicide*, 18, 1–2.

Colucci, E., Kelly, C. M., Minas, H., Jorm, A. F. & Chatterjee, S. (2010). Mental health first aid guidelines for helping a suicidal person: A Delphi Consensus Study in India. *International Journal of Mental Health Systems,* 4, (4); DOI: 10.1186/1752-4458-4-4. http://www.ijmhs.com/content/4/1/4: Retrieved 01.06.2012

Colucci, E., Kelly, C. M., Minas, H., Jorm, A. F. & Nadera, D. (2010). Mental health first aid guidelines for helping a suicidal person: A Delphi Consensus Study in the Philippines. *International Journal of Mental Health Systems,* 4, (32); DOI: 10.1186/1752-4458-32. Retrieved 01.06.2012: http://www.ijmhs.com/content/4/1/32

Colucci, E., Kelly, C. M., Minas, H., Jorm, A. F. & Suzuki, Y. (2011). Mental health first aid guidelines for helping a suicidal person: A Delphi Consensus Study in Japan. *International Journal of Mental Health Systems,* 5, (12); DOI: 10.1186/1752-4458-5-12. Retrieved 01.06.2012: http://www.ijmhs.com/content/5/1/12

De Vries, P., Huisman, A., Kerkhof, A. J. & Robben, P. B. (2008). The no suicide contract: a risky ritual. *Tijdschr Psychiatr,* 50, (10), 667–71.

Drye, R. C., Goulding, R. L. & Goulding, M. E. (1973), No suicide Decisions: Patient Monitoring of Suicidal Risk, *American Journal of Psychiatry*, 130, (2), 171–74.

Edwards, S. J. & Sachmann, M. D. (2010). No Suicide Contracts, No Suicide Agreements and No Suicide Assurances. A Study of Their Nature, Utilization, Perceived Effectiveness, and Potential to Cause Harm. *Crisis: Journal of Crisis Intervention & Suicide Prevention,* 31, (6), 290–302.

Farrow, T. (2002). Owning Their Expertise: Why Nurses Use "No Suicide Contracts" Rather Than Their Own Assessments. *International Journal of Mental Health Nursing,* 11, 214–219.

Hiroto, I., Kawano, K., Kawashima, D. & Kawanishi, C. (2008). Responses to patients with

suicidal ideation among different specialties in general hospitals. *General Hospital Psychiatry*, 30, (6), 578–80.

Kroll, J. (2000). Use of No Suicide Contracts by Psychiatrists in Minnesota. *American Journal of Psychiatry,* 157, 1684–86.

Linehan, M. (1993). Skills Training Manual for Treating Borderline Personality Disorder. New York, Guildford Press.

Mishara, B. L. & Daigle, M. S. (1997). Effects of Different Telephone Intervention Styles with Suicidal Callers at Two Suicide Prevention Centers: An Empirical Investigation. *American Journal of Community Psychology*, 25, 861–885.

Page, S. & King, M. (2008). No Suicide Agreements: Current Practices and Opinions in a Canadian Urban Health Region. *The Canadian Journal of Psychiatry*, 53, (3), 169–76.

Frequently Asked Questions

> No suicide contracts resemble the superstition of the soccer player who wears his or her jersey inside-out to every game because they believed it helps their game; because his or her team-mates told them it would. (Clark & Kerkhof, 1997, pp. 1–2)

Question: How are the Western Australian SPC study findings meaningful with only a 31 percent response rate?

Upon submitting the findings for peer review to *Crisis: The Journal of Crisis Intervention and Suicide Prevention*, one of the four anonymous reviewers raised this very point: "A major issue is the response rate. Of a total N = 1347, 445 questionnaires were returned of which 420 were useable. Thus the response rate is only 31 percent." The reviewer added, however: "This does not necessarily mean that the findings are not meaningful."

The study deliberately selected all available practicing mental health clinicians in an Australian State's public mental health service and identified those clinicians (31 percent) who reported using SPC procedures, comparing their responses with findings from studies primarily focused on North American and New Zealand mental health clinicians, and found broad commonalities in most sets of findings. The study concluded that the dimensions of SPC, reasons why SPC is used, clinician opinion towards SPC and therefore the related potential for creating hazardous conditions (the core concepts in the book), are consistent across many Western countries.

Question: How do the Western Australian SPC study findings relate to all clinicians and crisis center volunteers, when some 50 percent of the study was based on nurse practitioner data?

The participants from the study are representative of the spectrum of mental health clinicians in the public mental health services. In reality, use of SPC is probably associated with a clinician's professional discipline (Page & King, 2008; Edwards & Sachmann, 2010). So while some of the opinion findings may not generalize to specific professions, or to specific practice settings, for example, public vs. private practices, or beyond those five professional disciplines who gave us responses, the study was not so concerned with individual discipline-specific profiles. Rather, it sought to explore the inherent potential problems—SPC's potential to compromise treatment—irrespective of clinician demographics.

Question: Do the Western Australian SPC study findings apply when it comes to different ethnicities and cultures?

Peer-reviewed research established the use of SPC in the United States (Kroll, 2000), New Zealand (Farrow, 2002), Australia (Edwards & Sachmann, 2010), Canada (Page & King, 2008), the Netherlands (de Vries, Huisman, Kerkhof & Robben, 2008) and Japan (Hiroto, Kawano, Kawanishi & Kawanishi, 2008). Using Delphi cultural panels of mental health clinicians, Colucci and colleagues have described recommendations for first responders using SPC in India (Colucci, Kelly, Minas, Jorm & Chatterjee, 2010), the Philippines (Colucci, Kelly, Minas, Jorm & Nadera, 2010) and Japan (Colucci, Kelly, Minas, Jorm & Suzuki, 2011). Additional descriptive research is needed to further define and articulate the profile of SPC in these and other non-Western countries.

Caution is needed against generalizing all findings from the SPC study to practice settings and societal cultures vastly different from that of a typical Western industrialized society. Several key findings from the SPC study require further exploration with regards to variables of race, ethnicity or culture, for example: *(i)* Other factors may be present in the origins of SPC in non-Western countries; *(ii)* Race, ethnicity and cultural variables of status and authority can play a central role when communicating with another, influencing the utilization and perceived effectiveness of SPC (*cf.* Miller's Paradox); *(iii)* Some cultural imperatives, perhaps spiritual and religious factors, may dictate the non-use of SPC in certain situations (*cf.* primary and secondary contraindications for SPC); *(iv)* Clinico-legal concerns motivating use of SPC may be overridden by culturally based imperatives (*cf.* Simon's Paradox).

Question: What's the problem in using SPC for only therapeutic reasons with patients I have a long-term and solid therapeutic relationship with?

The best answer is to re-read the sections in chapter 9 describing the primary and secondary contraindications for SPC and Bongar's Rule in chapter 10.

Question: Can having minimal reliance on an SPC procedure whilst using a comprehensive evaluation and management approach remove the dangers of SPC while gaining any benefit they may offer?

Conducting a careful clinical evaluation and standard management response, as described chapter 10, is the preferred approach to all suicidal crises. Yet here there are two basic problems with the inclusion of either NSC or NSAg. First is the nature of the patient's understanding of what SPC is and the clear potential for activating Miller's Paradox resulting in the loss of some of the therapeutic alliance gains already made. Second is the plain fact that *in vivo* learning has long been a significant factor in the ongoing use of SPC. You may well instigate a comprehensive and careful evaluation and standard management response with the inclusion of SPC. Yet others who are aware of your use may learn from you, use SPC *without* such a comprehensive approach—following an Edwin Shneidman maxim: "easy steps for little feet"—and simply perpetuate the injudicious use of SPC. Also, see chapter 8, where I discuss the application of NSAs with patients, and chapter 10, where I discuss the application of NSAs with caregivers of children and adolescents.

Question: I work in an inpatient unit where SPC is used and required, do these *findings apply to me?*

They absolutely apply. And they come in two parts. First, if you have faith in what the book has presented, then discuss the key findings with your inpatient colleagues. Second, see the end piece of chapter 4 and chapter 7, describing the ethical concerns with using SPC.

Question: What is the role of SPC with Deliberate Self Harm (DSH)?

Most clinicians today understand the sometimes subtle differences between DSH behaviors (without suicidal intent) as a possible coping strategy and evaluated suicidal behavior. As our study focused solely upon suicide and its prevention, the findings should not be generalized to DSH until further investigation confirms or rules out the relevance of the core SPC concepts to DSH behaviors.

Question: Can a new style of 'no suicide contracting' reduce the problems of SPC outlined in the book?

If a newly developed SPC procedure that enters clinical practice largely conforms to The Anatomy of SPC (specifically The ABC Stress Defense Model of SPC and The DMS of SPC) described in chapter 6, then the same basic ideas apply.

Question: Is the initial Dialectical Behavior Therapy (DBT) treatment contracting phase with a potential DBT candidate the same as SPC?

Several participants from the SPC study justified use of SPC by likening it to a step taken in DBT treatment. Unclear nomenclature seems like a plausible reason for this point of confusion: Terms such as 'treatment contracting' with a suicidal patient and 'Suicide Prevention Contracting' may be viewed more widely as the same process. DBT is a justifiably well-regarded, evidence-based practice (Linehan, 1993). Despite our best efforts to locate data, it remains unclear if this phase of the DBT process has been singled out for scientific confirmation of its effectiveness. Treatment contracting prior to engaging in a specialized DBT programme is one initial part of a highly programmatic therapeutic process and as such does not conform to or suffer from the same vagaries as the SPC procedures detailed in this book.

Question: Is a promise also a form of SPC?

Re-read the section in chapter 3 where SPC procedures are defined, chapter 8 describing the use of NSAs, and the first part of chapter 10 describing Bongar's Rule.

Question: The Western Australian SPC study focused upon clinicians operating in the public health system, so how do these findings apply to private practice?

Directly! My answer is that fully 95 percent of our findings apply. We can conclude with confidence that the finding that does not fully apply to clinicians in private practice is one aspect of using SPC for clinico-legal protection. Here, the practice of an instructing superior requesting a junior clinician to use SPC (likely for their own perceived self-protection) is largely irrelevant to some private practices.

Question: I am a crisis telephone counselor working in a non-government organization. Do these findings apply to me?

In the 1970s, the developers of the no suicide decision, renowned U.S. mental health clinicians Robert Drye and Mary and Robert Goulding advocated for the additional use of their procedure over the telephone (Drye, Goulding & Goulding 1973, p. 174). As we saw in chapter 2, unfortunately the evidence behind their no suicide decision—the precursor of the contemporary SPC—was flawed. As many such contemporary telephone crisis centers use the securing of a no suicide agreement with a suicidal caller as a marker of a successful call (Mishara & Daigle, 1997), our findings absolutely apply. Especially, re-read the sections in chapters 6 and 7 detailing *The Curse of the False Positive.*

Appendix A

Teaching Tools and Educator Notes & Activities

The following set of teaching tools has been included to provide educators an off-the-shelf resource when teaching SPCs' capacity to compromise treatment and the available alternatives procedures. Teaching Tools are divided into three parts:

1. Summary points outlining the SPC twenty core concepts
2. Reading lists
3. Tutorial activity sheet sample

A QUICK FIND READER'S GUIDE TO THE TWENTY KEY SPC CONCEPTS

Five Features of SPC

1. SPC originated from a confluence of factors—Redecision Therapy, emergence of telephone crisis centers, nursing patient management, behavioral and cognitive approaches to managing suicidality, and clinico-legal concerns—spanning some forty years which ultimately saw it established as a commonly used and—in some circles—a well-regarded intervention, despite there being no evidence of effectiveness (*The Confluence Effect:* see chapter 2).
2. Understanding the component parts of SPC and its mode of operation enables clinicians to evaluate their use/their service's use of SPC, highlighting potential risks to patient and clinician (*The Anatomy of Contemporary SPC*: see chapter 6).

3. Contemporary SPC is characterized more by the tensions of legality, expedience and a perceived duty of care requirement than as a best practice intervention (*Ethics of Expedience*: See part 3 and chapters 7, 11).
4. Clinicians are often driven to use SPC by right-minded objective values in the *hope* it will provide advantage *AND, at the same time*, SPC's potentially negative consequences—manufactured hazards with potential for compromising treatment—make it a misguided intervention in spite of those values (*The Central Values Paradox of SPC*: see chapters 4 and 7).
5. SPC is perfectly positioned to be misinterpreted—maintaining its use in contemporary practice—under the current recovery model approach to mental health care. For example, a potentially frequent circumstance is where this may lead the clinician to decide against admitting a person to hospital instead seeking to increase a patients' self-responsibly by placing them under SPC (*Sixth Wave in the Resurgence of SPC*: see chapter 11).

The Four Fatal Flaws of SPC

1. Clinicians can offer SPC in the complete absence of hard data attesting to its validity, efficacy *AND, at the same time*, can be largely unaware of its potential to compromise treatment when seeking its perceived therapeutic, diagnostic or clinico-legal advantage (*All Things to Some People*: see chapters 7 and 11).
2. Due to the relative rarity in communities of serious suicide attempts and completed suicides, the 'prediction' of future suicidal behavior (the prevention of suicide) is plagued by a significant rate of false positive evaluations. That very rarity provides rich and fertile ground for a false sense of security—to attribute validity and efficacy to an intervention when, seemingly as a result of the intervention, "nothing bad happens" (*The Curse of the False Positive*: see chapters 7 and 11).
3. A surface-level analysis—where SPC is judged to provide patient care *and* clinician self-protection—makes SPC a *liability*, not an asset. Yes, it may add something. Yet a naive faith in and reliance upon SPC merely perpetuates its injudicious use (*The Misguided Duality in the Use of SPC-The Each Way Bet*: see chapters 6, 7 and 11).
4. The quasi-legal status granted to SPC creates a mild sense of self-protection for some clinicians (and some workplaces) via a paper trail leading straight to patient responsibility for any serious attempt or completed suicide (*The Quasi-Legal Status of SPC*: see chapter 7).

Six Core Concepts of SPC

1. The least experienced clinicians appear to use SPC procedures more *AND, at the same time,* more experienced clinicians seem to use SPC procedures less (*Mahrer's Paradox*: see chapters 1, 7 and 11).
2. Clinicians seem to use NSC according to suicide risk severity to increase safety. Yet there is simply no evidence that any SPC procedures offer any evidence of effectiveness according to risk levels, thereby increasing potential to compromise treatment by decreasing safety—placing patients in less secure environments—for increasing risk patients (*McArdle's Paradox*: see chapters 1, 7 and 11).
3. High-risk patients who are more likely to be unable to give informed consent appear more likely to be offered written NSC. Yet those at less risk, being more likely to be able to give informed consent, are possibly less likely to be offered a verbal no suicide agreement or written no suicide contract (*Farrow's Paradox*: see chapters 1, 7 and 11).
4. Clinicians use SPC procedures to communicate their care and concern to a patient. Yet, some patients believe SPC is merely used by clinicians for self protection—likely resulting in a weaker therapeutic alliance and potentially more risk for suicide (*Miller's Paradox-The 3C's*: see chapters 1, 7 and 11).
5. Some clinicians who use SPC perceive that it offers some level of clinico-legal protection. Yet over-reliance on SPC procedures as a replacement or moderator of accepted standards of care can leave clinicians open to legal and professional claims of negligence (*Simon's Paradox*: see chapters 1, 7 and 11).
6. *The One in Four Concept* is an algorithm. What it clarifies is just who is the 'right patient type' to offer SPC. Yet the set of rules behind the algorithm that could be used to evaluate which patients are suitable for SPC remain, for the most part, unknown (*The One in Four Concept*: see chapters 1, 7 and 11).

New SPC Clinical Practice Rules, Contraindications for SPC and Alternative Approaches

1. The SPC study led to the conclusion that clinicians' see multiple clinico-legal benefits in SPC, and not just the reduction of legal liability. To be specific, four dimensions (reasons why clinicians use SPC for perceived self-protection): (i) reduce legal liability, (ii) abide by a superior's request,

(iii) reduce professional recriminations, and (iv) due to reduced access to resources. Yet according to Robert I. Simon, MD: "If a practitioner's over-reliance on SPC results in an inadequate risk assessment, treatment or management response, a standard of care and skill expected from the average practitioner, "it can service as an indictment of his or her clinical judgement, rather than offering protection (Simon, 1999, p. 446)"; a powerful caution to those clinicians (and their workplaces) who choose to use SPC (*Simon's Rule*: see chapter 7).

2. Here is what we finally came to call *Fenner's Rule*: Within a comprehensive and ongoing evaluation and suicide risk management response (medical, psychological and/or social), the routine use of a no suicide assurance aims to gain a subjective level of risk for suicidal behavior (*Fenner's Rule*: see chapter 7). Granted, some clinicians will use NSAs to get information as to whether a patient can control suicidal impulses, while other patients may be asked to assure a clinician that they're able to refrain from suicidal behavior. However NSAs are presented, they appear to represent a brief yes/no verbal exchange, likely used as an adjunct to an evaluation, to establish a subjective measure of self-reported suicide risk. This for us represented the single most important and safe use (when used under *Fenner's Rule*) of any SPC *type* procedure. Whichever way we looked at it, NSAs under *Fenner's Rule* escaped the fate of NSC and NSAg. It did not create a false sense of safety; it did not produce an over-reliance at the expense of critical elements in the management of suicidal behavior.
3. We came to know an alternative to SPC as Bongar's Rule: Within an established therapeutic relationship, as part of a suicide risk assessment and management plan; in the context of an appropriate (e.g., noncrisis setting) clinical environment, a practitioner seeks an assurance from the patient who has been previously assessed to be competent that if he or she feels unable not to act upon suicidal urges, he or she will contact the clinician. Importantly, contingency measures are agreed regarding the limits of the clinician's availability and when the clinician is unavailable to take their call (*Bongar's Rule*: see chapter 10).
4. The SPC study developed the primary contraindications for SPC based upon the four fatal flaws and the six core concepts indicating SPC compromised treatment. The secondary contraindications go to the heart of a

clinical presentation, the nature of a therapeutic alliance, and the elements in a clinical setting which are considered, based upon expert opinion, averse to employing any form of SPC (*Primary and Secondary Contradictions for SPC*: see chapter 9).

5. Having considered the findings in this book, some of you will hopefully by now concur with what I take to be incontrovertibly true: *that the risks of using SPC obviously and overwhelmingly outweigh the benefits, AND, that any benefits lost by not using an SPC procedure can be more than recovered by using alternative interventions that carry substantially less risk for everyone.* These two claims represent, for me, the most highly distilled summary of years of research that I could formulate (*Seven Alternatives to SPC*: see chapter 10).

READING LISTS

The literature on SPC is sparse. The following articles are some essential pieces in the limited SPC literature. It is recommended that tutorial participants become familiar with a least one of the following six articles.

Farrow, T., & O'Brien, A. (2003). No Suicide Contracts and Informed Consent: An Analysis of Ethical Issues. *Nursing Ethics*, 10, 201–207.

Garvey, K., Penn, J., Campbell, A., Esposito-Smythers, C. & Spirito, A. (2009). Contracting for Safety with Patients: Clinical Practice and Forensic Implications, *Journal of the American Academy of Psychiatry and the Law*, 37, 363–70.

Miller, M. (1999). Suicide-Prevention Contracts: Advantages, Disadvantages, and An Alternative Approach. In D. J. Jacobs (Ed.), *The Harvard Medical School Guide to Suicide Assessment and Intervention* (pp. 463–481). San Francisco: Jossey-Bass Publishers.

Miller, M., Jacobs, D. G. & Gutheil, T. G. (1998). Talisman or Taboo: The Controversy of the Suicide-Prevention Contract. *Harvard Review of Psychiatry*, 6, 78–87.

Stanford, E., Goetz, R. & Bloom, J. (1994). The No Harm Contract in the Emergency Assessment of Suicidal Risk. *Journal of Clinical Psychiatry*, 55, 344–348.

Weiss, A. (2001). The No Suicide Contract: Possibilities and Pitfalls. *American Journal of Psychotherapy*, 55, (3), 414–19.

The following readings have been located under the relevant SPC study's key finding:

Origins—No Suicide Decisions

Drye, R. C., Goulding, R. L. & Goulding, M.E. (1973). No Suicide Decisions: Patient Monitoring of Suicidal Risk. *American Journal of Psychiatry*, 130, (2). 171–74.

Goulding, R. L., & Goulding, M. E. (1979). *Changing Lives Through Redecision Therapy.* New York: Brunner/ Mazel.

See chapter 2.

Types of SPC Procedures

Edwards, S. J., & Sachmann, M. D. (2010). No Suicide Contracts, No Suicide Agreements and No Suicide Assurances. A Study of Their Nature, Utilization, Perceived Effectiveness, and Potential to Cause Harm. *Crisis: Journal of Crisis Intervention & Suicide Prevention,* 31, (6), 290–302.

See chapter 2 and 5.

SPC Prevalence Data

Page, S., & King, M. (2008). No Suicide Agreements: Current Practices and Opinions in a Canadian Urban Health Region. *The Canadian Journal of Psychiatry*, 53, (3), 169–76.

Potter, M., & Dawson, A. (2001). From Safety Contract to Safety Agreement. *Journal of Psychosocial Nursing & Mental Health Services,* 39, (8), 38–46.

Weiss, A. (2001). The No Suicide Contract: Possibilities and Pitfalls. *American Journal of Psychotherapy,* 55, (3), 414–19.

Anatomy of SPC

See chapter 6.

Watson, D., (2000). *Scare Tactics: Arguments That Appeal to Fear and Threats.* New York: Springer.

Fatal Flaws of SPC

All Things to Some People

Stanford, E., Goetz, R. & Bloom, J. (1994). The No Harm Contract in the Emergency Assessment of Suicidal Risk. *Journal of Clinical Psychiatry*, 55, 344–48.

The Curse of the False Positive

See chapter 7.

Pokorny, A. D. (1993). Suicide Prediction Revisited. *Suicide and Life Threatening Behaviors,* 23, 1–10.

Shneidman, E. S. (1993). *Suicide as Psychache: A Clinical Approach to Self-Destructive Behavior.* New Jersey: Jason Aronson, Inc.

The Misguided Duality in the Use of SPC (The Each Way Bet)

Simon, R., (1999). The Suicide Prevention Contract: Clinical, Legal, and Risk Management Issues. *Journal of the American Academy of Psychiatry & the Law,* 27, 445–50.

Stanford, E., Goetz, R. & Bloom, J. (1994). The No Harm Contract in the Emergency Assessment of Suicidal Risk. *Journal of Clinical Psychiatry*, 55, 344–48.

Weiss, A. (2001). The No Suicide Contract: Possibilities and Pitfalls. *American Journal of Psychotherapy,* 55, (3), 414–19.

The Quasi-Legal Status of SPC

Garvey, K., Penn, J., Campbell, A., Esposito-Smythers, C. & Spirito, A. (2009). Contracting for Safety with Patients: Clinical Practice and Forensic Implications. *Journal of the American Academy of Psychiatry and the Law*, 37, 363–70.

Simon, R. (1999). The Suicide Prevention Contract: Clinical, Legal, and Risk Management Issues. *Journal of the American Academy of Psychiatry & the Law,* 27, 445–50.

Core Clinical Concepts

Mahrer's Paradox (Use by Experience Curve)

Edwards, S. J., & Sachmann, M. D. (2010). No Suicide Contracts, No Suicide Agreements and No Suicide Assurances. A Study of Their Nature, Utilization, Perceived Effectiveness, and Potential to Cause Harm. *Crisis: Journal of Crisis Intervention & Suicide Prevention,* 31, (6), 290–302.

Kroll, J. (2000). Use of No Suicide Contracts by Psychiatrists in Minnesota. *American Journal of Psychiatry,* 157, 1684–86.

See chapter 7.

McArdle's Paradox (Use by Risk Curve)

Edwards, S. J., & Sachmann, M. D. (2010). No Suicide Contracts, No Suicide Agreements and No Suicide Assurances. A Study of Their Nature, Utilization, Perceived Effectiveness, and Potential to Cause Harm. *Crisis: Journal of Crisis Intervention & Suicide Prevention,* 31, (6), 290–302.

See chapter 7.

Miller's Paradox (The 3 C's)

Miller, M. (1999). Suicide-Prevention Contracts: Advantages, Disadvantages, and An Alternative Approach. In D. J. Jacobs (Ed.), *The Harvard Medical School Guide to Suicide Assessment and Intervention* (pp. 463–481). San Francisco: Jossey-Bass Publishers.

The One in Four Concept

Davis, S., Williams, I. S. & Hays, L. W. (2002). Psychiatric Inpatients' Perceptions of Written No Suicide Agreements: An Exploratory Study. *Suicide & Life-Threatening Behavior*, 32, (1), 51–61.

See chapter 7.

Simon's Paradox

Garvey, K., Penn, J., Campbell, A., Esposito-Smythers, C. & Spirito, A. (2009). Contracting for Safety with Patients: Clinical Practice and Forensic Implications. *Journal of the American Academy of Psychiatry and the Law*, 37, 363–70.

See chapter 7.

Simon, R. (1999). The Suicide Prevention Contract: Clinical, Legal, and Risk Management Issues. *Journal of the American Academy of Psychiatry & the Law,* 27, 44–50.

Farrow's Paradox

Farrow, T., (2003). No Suicide Contracts in Community Crisis Situations: A Conceptual Analysis. *Journal of Psychiatric and Mental Health Nursing,* 10, 199–202.

Farrow, T. (2002). Owning Their Expertise: Why Nurses Use "No Suicide Contracts" Rather Than Their Own Assessments. *International Journal of Mental Health Nursing,* 11, 214–219.

Farrow, T., & O'Brien, A., (2003). No Suicide Contracts' and Informed Consent: An Analysis of Ethical Issues. *Nursing Ethics*, 10, 201–207.

Farrow, T., Simpson, A. & Warren, H. (2002). The Effects of the Use of No Suicide Contracts in Community Crisis Situations: The Experience of Clinicians and Consumers. *Brief Treatment and Crisis Intervention*, 2, (3), 241–246.

Primary and Secondary Contraindications for SPC

Miller, M. (1999). Suicide-Prevention Contracts: Advantages, Disadvantages, and An Alternative Approach. In D. J. Jacobs (Ed.), *The Harvard Medical School Guide to Suicide Assessment and Intervention* (pp. 463–481). San Francisco: Jossey-Bass Publishers.

See chapter 9.

Fenner's Rule

See chapter 8 and 10.

Alternatives to SPC

See chapter 10 Reference List.

ACTIVITY #1: SPC RISKS ANALYSIS

Purpose

To understand how alternatives to SPC provide positive strategies for patients/clinicians, with less risk for compromising treatment associated with using SPC.

Process

- Participants necessarily will have completed a lecture-style session outlining the pitfalls, the perils, and alternatives to SPC prior to participating in this activity.
- Break into small groups, with each group allocated one of the scenario cards.
- Assign each group with one of the three SPC types of deployment categories: clinico-legal protection, diagnostic clarification, therapeutic advantage.
- Distribute and discuss the blank SPC Risk Analysis Sheet.
- Ask each group to discuss their case scenario and to note the principle core concepts (i.e., primary contraindications) activated when using SPC for

each reason for use statement listed in the SPC Risk Analysis Sheet. Next, note at least one alternative to SPC that can offer similar levels of advantage specific from their type of deployment category: clinico-legal protection, diagnostic clarification, and therapeutic advantage.

- Return to the larger group and discuss the strengths and weaknesses of different group responses. The case scenario, blank and completed SPC Risk Analysis Sheet provided are the resources required.

SCENARIO CARD: SPC RISK ANALYSIS

You are a newly appointed substance abuse counselor with five years' experience working at a rehabilitation center. You have been counseling a male patient for four sessions now who is a heavy user of alcohol, and has been showing signs of depression. In the last session, he's made comments that life is not worth living. You are concerned for his welfare; that he may be at risk for suicide. You are anxious about the personal and professional consequences if he seriously attempts or completes suicide under your care. You have heard other colleagues talking about contracting with patients not to suicide, and you're considering using SPC at the next appointment. In fact, if you consulted your supervisor you're sure he would instruct you to do just that. You are of two minds. You think that if you can make a contract the risk for suicide may reduce by strengthening the therapeutic alliance with the patient. However, you're uncertain if he will accept the notion of contracting for living.

Table A.1. SPC Risk Analysis Sheet (student sample)

Reasons for using SPC	Principle core concepts (i.e. primary contraindications) activated when using SPC for each reason are?	Alternative(s) to SPC increasing clinico-legal, diagnostic and therapeutic advantages are?
Clinico-Legal protection ☐ Increase clinician's legal protection ☐ Lack of available resources ☐ Abide by a superior's request ☐ Reduce recriminations from peers		Alternative to SPC increasing clinician *clinico-legal protection* are:
Diagnostic clarification ☐ Aiding in dispersal decision-making ☐ To assess for suicide risk ☐ To assess for precipitating risk factors		Alternatives to SPC increasing *diagnostic clarification* are:
Therapeutic advantage ☐ Increasing a patient's sense of safety ☐ Encouraging patient self-responsibility ☐ Communicating care and concern ☐ Providing alternatives to suicidal behavior ☐ Specifying behaviors to cease ☐ Strengthening a therapeutic relationship		Alternatives to SPC increasing clinician/patient *therapeutic advantage* are:

Table A.2. SPC Risk Analysis Sheet (completed sample)

Reasons for use	Principle core concepts (i.e. primary contraindications) activated when using SPC for each reason	Alternative(s) to SPC
Increasing clinician's legal protection	-*Simon's Paradox* (Over-reliance on SPC moderating accepted standards of care, can leave clinicians open to claims of negligence.	Critical Elements in the Management of Suicidal Behavior (CEMSB)
Due to a lack of available resources (e.g., access to inpatient care)	-*McArdle's Paradox* (Using NSC as a stop gap measure due to a lack of resources implies SPC was used with a relatively high risk patient) -*Simon's Paradox* (see above.)	-CEMSB -Safety Plan
Abiding by a superior's request	-*Simon's Paradox* (see above.)	-CEMSB -Safety Plan
Reducing recriminations from peers	-*Simon's Paradox* (see above.)	-CEMSB -Safety Plan
Aiding in dispersal decision-making	-*The One in Four Concept* (Patients with a multiple suicide attempt history can hold little value in SPC) -*Miller's Paradox* (Patients can have a negative view of SPC, compromising alliance and discussion of ideation)	-CEMSB -Alliance for Safety -Fenner's Rule -Safety agreement (inpatient)
Assisting to assess for suicide risk	-*The One in Four Concept* (see above.) -*Miller's Paradox* (see above.) -*McArdle's Paradox* (Offering NSC as a means to assess risk when patients refuse/accept SPC, may in fact, be tapping into The One in Four Concept, NOT the patient's current risk for suicide.) -*Farrow's Paradox* (Using NSC with high risk patients likely less able to give informed consent is ethically questionable.)	-CEMSB -Alliance for Safety -Fenner's Rule

Assisting to assess for precipitating risk factors	-*The One in Four Concept* (See above.) -*Miller's Paradox* (See above.)	-CEMSB -Alliance for Safety -Fenner's Rule -Safety agreement (inpatient)
Increasing a patient's sense of safety	-*Miller's Paradox* (See above.) -*The One in Four Concept* (see above.)	-CEMSB -Safety Plan -Safety agreement (inpatient) -Commitment to Treatment Statement (CTS) -Bongar's Rule -Alliance for Safety
Encouraging patient self-responsibility	-*Miller's Paradox* -*McArdle's Paradox* -*Simon's Paradox* -*The One in Four Concept* (see above.)	-CEMSB -Safety Plan -Safety agreement (inpatient) - CTS -Bongar's Rule -Alliance for Safety
Communicating care and concern	-*Miller's Paradox* -*The One in Four Concept* (see above.)	-CEMSB -Safety Plan - CTS -Bongar's Rule -Alliance for Safety
Providing alternatives to suicidal behavior	-*McArdle's Paradox* -*The One in Four Concept* (see above.)	-Safety Plan - CTS -Bongar's Rule -Safety agreement (inpatient)
Specifying behaviors to cease	-McArdle's Paradox -Miller's Paradox -Farrow's Paradox -One in Four Concept (see above.)	-Safety Plan - CTS -Bongar's Rule -Alliance for Safety
Strengthening a therapeutic relationship	-Miller's Paradox -Farrow's Paradox -One in Four Concept (see above.)	-CEMSB -Safety Plan - CTS -Bongar's Rule -Alliance for Safety

Note: *Mahrer's Paradox* is when new career clinicians view SPC more favorably than more experienced clinicians and is relevant in each one of the reasons for use.

Date: __________ Time: __________

SAFETY AGREEMENT

Definition: The safety agreement is a tool, which assists the nurse in assessing and obtaining the patient's cooperation and participation in an agreement for safety. The nurse validates with the patient the nurse's perceptions related to the patient's current distress level and actual or potential threats of harm to self or others. Perceptions are anything the nurse hears, sees, tastes, touches, and/or smells (i.e., any observation obtained involving the five senses, as described by Orlando's Nursing Theory).

Frequency of Nurse's Assessment: Every shift, and more often as indicated.

Use of Information: Share information from this assessment with staff on duty and with staff at change of shift. Place written assessment in patient's chart (pending approval of Medical Records Committee).

Circle number that applies and write number in code box at right. Code

1. Nurse's rating of the patient's current level of distress. ❑

   Bockenhauer/Potter Scale of Immediate Distress. Circle the appropriate number.

0	1	2	3	4
No physiological or behavioral (verbal and/or nonverbal) symptoms of distress.	Verbalized requests, complaints, or concerns, or physiological symptoms of distress (e.g., elevated blood pressure, pulse, temperature).	Irritable, marked change in behavior pattern, repeated somatic complaints, trembling, or shaking.	Resistive to limits, threatening with raised voice, teary, pacing, or wringing hands.	Harming property, self, or others; yelling; expressions of hopelessness, panic, or dread; inability to control impulses without external restraint.

2. How would you rate your current harm level? ❑

   This is based on a scale of 1 to 5 (with 5 being the most likely to hurt yourself or another).

   0 Not at all 1 2 3 4 5 Most likely to harm

   Explain: ________________________________

3. Do you have a plan to harm yourself or another? ❑

   0 No 1 Yes

   If yes, explain (include means): ________________________________

4. How impulsive do you feel right now? ❑

   0 Not at all 1 2 3 4 5 Very

5. What kind of observation do you feel your behavior warrants? ❑

   Nurse will explain 30-minute checks, 15-minute checks, constant observation, and 1-to-1 staff-to-patient ratio to the patient.

   0 30-minute checks 1 15-minute checks 2 constant observation 3 1:1 staff-to-patient ratio

6. Nurse's assessment of patient's safety needs ❑

   0 30-minute checks 1 15-minute checks 2 constant observation 3 1:1 staff-to-patient ratio

Safety Agreement sample

7. The nurse should also discuss with the patient whether the nurse agrees with the patient about the level and why. ☐

0	1
No	Yes

Explain: ______________________________

8. Validate with the patient: "How can we manage this together?" Which of the following strategies did the patient select for maintaining safety? (May select more than one.) ☐

0	1	2	3	4	5	6
None	Talk	Music	Journal	Exercise	Request p.r.n. medication	Other or several

Explain: ______________________________

9. Has a safety agreement been made between the nurse and patient that the patient will not harm himself/herself or others for a specified amount of time during this shift? ☐

0	1
No	Yes

10. State how long during this shift the patient feels able to remain safe (e.g., 2 hours). ☐

0	1	2	3	4
None	< 30 minutes	30 minutes to 1 hour	1 to 2 hours	Other

Explain: ______________________________

11. Validation: Does the patient state an understanding of the current safety agreement? ☐

0	1
No	Yes

12. State nurse's intervention (e.g., application of Orlando's Nursing Theory [ONT] with the patient, level recommended, medication administered). (May select more than one.) ☐

0	1	2	3	4
None	Use of ONT	Medication	Level	Other or several

Explain: ______________________________

RN signature: ____________________

Appendix B

Useful Links

Disclaimer: Views expressed in the following websites do not necessarily represent the views of the authors.

ASSESSMENT AND SAFETY PLANNING LINKS

Columbia Suicide Severity Rating Scale (C-SSRS)

The C-SSRS is a questionnaire used for suicide assessment developed by Kelly Posner, PhD, David Brent, MD, Chris Lucas, MD, Madelyn Gould, PhD, MPH, Barbara Stanley, PhD, Greg Brown, PhD, Prudence Fisher, PhD, Jaime Zelazny, NR, MPH, Ainsley Burke, PhD, Maria Oquendo, MD, and J. John Mann, MD.
www.cssrs.columbia.edu

Safety Planning

This site contains information about the safety planning intervention developed by Barbara Stanley, PhD, and Gregory K. Brown, PhD.
www.suicidesafetyplan.com

LINKS BY LOCATION

Australia

Australian Institute for Suicide Research and Prevention
www.griffith.edu.au/health/australian-institute-suicide-research-prevention

Brazil

BRAZIL - 141 - CVV is a crisis center.
http://www.cvv.org.br/

Canada

Centre for Suicide Prevention
www.siec.ca
Canadian Association for Suicide Prevention
www.suicideprevention.ca/

China

Lifeline Shanghai
www.lifelineshanghai.com

Hong Kong

Centre for Suicide Research and Prevention (CSRP), the Faculty of Social Sciences of the University of Hong Kong
http://csrp.hku.hk/WEB/eng/index.asp

India

Maithri is a crisis center operating in the south-west of India.
www.maithrikochi.org/
National Institute of Mental Health and Neuro Sciences (NIMHANS): WHO Collaborating Centre for Injury Prevention and Safety Promotion
www.nimhans.kar.nic.in/epidemiology/epidem_who4.htm

International

International Association for Suicide Prevention
www.iasp.info
World Health Organization
www.who.int/topics/suicide/en/

Ireland
Irish Association of Suicidology
www.ias.ie

Japan
Japan Suicide Prevention Association
www.jspa.jp

Korea
Korean Association for Suicide Prevention
www.suicideprevention.or.kr

New Zealand
Suicide Prevention Information New Zealand
www.spinz.org.nz

Norway
Kirkens SOS
http://www.kirkens-sos.no/

Singapore
Samaritans of Singapore
www.samaritans.org.sg/suicide.htm

South Africa
Careline SA is a crisis center operating across South Africa.
http://www.carelinecrisis.org/

Sweden
Swedish National Prevention of Suicide and Mental Ill-Health (NASP) at Karolinska Institute, Stockholm, Sweden
www.ki.se/ki/jsp/polopoly.jsp?d=13243&l=en

Taiwan
Taiwan Suicide Prevention Center
www.tspc.doh.gov.tw

United States

American Foundation for Suicide Prevention (AFSP)
www.afsp.org
Suicide Prevention Resource Center (SPRC)
http://www.sprc.org

Index

About the Authors

Dr. Stephen Edwards, BSW, PhD is a research (honorary) fellow at the University of Western Australia, and a senior clinical social worker with Child and Adolescent Mental Health Services in Western Australia.

Christopher Goj, MA, (University of Auckland) (philosophy) is the former staff writer and programme manager of Suicide Prevention Education with Lifeline Aotearoa (New Zealand). He is a freelance editor and writer, has been trained in transactional analysis, and has served as a volunteer telephone counselor. He lives in Auckland, New Zealand.

www.ingramcontent.com/pod-product-compliance
Ingram Content Group UK Ltd.
Pitfield, Milton Keynes, MK11 3LW, UK
UKHW012038150926
475560UK00001B/75

9 780765 709967